A THIRST for THE SEA

of Erskine Childers

A THIRST for THE SEA
The Sailing Adventures of Erskine Childers

Introduced & Edited by Hugh & Robin Popham

STANFORD MARITIME LONDON

Stanford Maritime Limited
Member Company of the George Philip Group
12–14 Long Acre London WC2E 9LP
Editor Phoebe Mason

First published in Great Britain 1979
Copyright © Hugh Popham and Robin Popham 1979

Set in 11/13 Baskerville 169

Set and printed in Great Britain by
Ebenezer Baylis and Son Limited
The Trinity Press, Worcester, and London

ISBN 0 540 07197 8

British Library Cataloguing in Publication Data
Childers, Erskine
  A thirst for the sea.
  1. Voyages and travels
  2. Yachts and yachting
  I. Title II. Popham, Hugh
  III. Popham, Robin
  980'.45   G540
  ISBN 0–540–07197–8

Contents

Acknowledgements

As always with a book of this kind, one has many people to thank. First and foremost, Bobby and Christabel Childers for help and encouragement of the most practical kind, as well as the warm and tranquil hospitality of Glendalough House. Andrew Boyle, with his recent comprehensive experience of the Childers papers, gave the idea his blessing from the start, as well as much helpful advice. Burke Wilkinson, author of another biography of Erskine Childers, added some criticism to heartening enthusiasm. William O'Sullivan and Bernard Meehan of Trinity College Library supplied that patient and knowledgeable assistance without which books of this kind would never get written at all. Peggy McGregor, who had once hoped to make a film of *The Riddle of the Sands*, came up with the photographs of the Frisian Islands and West Friesland; and Viscount Runciman was kind enough to go through his family photograph albums in search of pictures of Childers' yachts, several of which appear here. Finally, and when the book was in proof, Mrs J. T. Christie, a niece of Childers' old sailing companion W. R. Le Fanu, came up with her uncle's photograph album, containing unique pictures of *Vixen* under sail, as well as several others which are linked precisely to entries in the logs. The book would have been the poorer without them.

H.P.   R.F.P.

Foreword by Robert A. Childers

In 1931 my mother wrote a preface to the latest edition of *The Riddle of the Sands*. It ended thus:

> the book remains the cherished companion of those who love the sea and who put forth in great or small sailing ships in search of adventure and the magical contentment to be won by strenuous endeavour. To such ardent adventurers, and to the younger generation who hope to follow them, this book is offered anew by a little company of sea lovers who hold it in trust for the known and unknown friends of Erskine Childers.

Every reader of *A Thirst for the Sea* will recognise its authors as two of those unknown friends.

When they first suggested that the logs might form the basis of a book, I was concerned because they are but arid records of each day's progress, or lack of it, winds, tides, and so forth. I need not have worried, for their researches have unearthed a store of my father's original writings about his sailing which clothe the logs with life and humour.

Some of the logs are, unfortunately, missing; and for the years between 1906 and 1913 there are no records of their cruises. I am certain that my father and mother sailed virtually every year during this period, and feel sure that it would not have been mere weekend trips in the Solent. I can clearly remember my mother talking about a cruise which they made to the north of the Gulf of Bothnia, but I have no idea when it took place nor are there any letters or logbooks to confirm it.

FOREWORD

For me, an unlooked-for bonus of this book is the brief biography which forms the first chapter. This, together with what follows, brings to the reader a wonderfully clear picture of Erskine Childers' character, of his urge not to stand back from life. It was this urge which drove him throughout his career to seek adventure, usually sailing in small boats, but also to service in three wars, on land, in the air, and finally, during 1917, on the sea which he loved so deeply and about which he wrote so well.

I

Erskine Childers 1870-1922

'All this year I have had the sea-thirst on me'
—Erskine Childers to Walter Runciman, 1898

I

In May 1903 the London publishing firm of Smith, Elder & Co. issued, with some misgivings, a novel called *The Riddle of the Sands* and subtitled *A Record of Secret Service Recently Achieved*, 'Edited by Erskine Childers'. The anxieties of Reginald Smith, who had insisted on considerable changes to the manuscript, proved unnecessary. The book was received with mainly favourable, if slightly puzzled, notices, achieved immediate success with the reading public, and has rarely if ever been out of print since.

Recently interest in the book and its author has increased, with several editions from various publishers available simultaneously and, after many abortive attempts in the past, a film actually on release. Ever since its publication *The Riddle of the Sands* has been one of those books which draw to themselves a special kind of devotion, rather as, from readers of slightly different tastes, do the works of Jane Austen or certain tales by Kipling.

The puzzlement of the original reviewers stemmed mainly from the two distinct strands of the tale: on the one hand, the vividness of the sailing; on the other, the detailed and very plausible plan for a German invasion of England. Germany was beginning to

I

emerge as the future challenger to Britain's imperial might, and although the book was obviously fiction, was it as far-fetched as it seemed at first sight? The critics had never come across anything quite like *The Riddle of the Sands* before, and they were not sure what to make of it. Nevertheless, on the whole they approved, and their approval was swiftly endorsed by its sales. Only the *Times Literary Supplement* affected a lofty and flippant scorn: 'A recent novelist . . . observes that the indispensable quality of dullness can be obtained by the use of a map. This work has two maps and two charts, which we do not undertake to criticise.' And went on to dismiss it as 'not a novel, but a sketch in naval geography, with adventures incomprehensible to the landsman, thrown in'. The *TLS* critic was particularly hard on the 'love interest' which *The Spectator*, in contrast, found 'convincingly real in its comparative insignificance'.

What intrigued and delighted readers less landlubberly than the *TLS*'s reviewer, and has continued to intrigue and delight readers ever since, was the authenticity of the descriptions of navigating a small yacht in and out of the tricky channels behind the Frisian Islands, and the beautifully balanced relationship between the no-nonsense Davies and the exquisite Carruthers, with its perfectly credible development and the mutual dependence, one upon the other, as the tale unfolds. How did the author come by his precise knowledge of that largely unknown stretch of coast, his unmistakable love of the strong, salt sea?

II

Very few people knew the answers to those two questions then: not many realise even now what a fine sailor Erskine Childers was. At the time of the publication of *The Riddle* he was thirty-two, and had written, almost by accident, one other book, *In the Ranks of the C.I.V.* This vivid personal record of service as a trooper in the City Imperial Volunteers in the South African War had, ironically enough, been edited into a book without his knowledge by a Mrs Thompson, a daughter of W. H. Smith, from the long letters which he had written home to his sisters, and with their connivance. Rarely can any author's first book have cost him so little pain! It went quickly through several editions and brought him some modest preliminary fame: it did nothing to explain how he had come to write *The Riddle of the Sands*.

After his return from South Africa at the end of 1900, Childers had gone back to his old job of Clerk in the House of Commons; gone back, also, to his old and constant love, the sea. His family, friends and a few of his colleagues knew that he owned a boat and was given to 'yachting', though their idea of 'yachting' and his might not have had much in common.

Yachting then as now embraced a multitude of boats, activities and incomes. At one extreme there were the large and luxurious – and increasingly popular – steam yachts, and the great racing cutters and schooners whose names are legends, *Thistle*, *Britannia*, *Meteor*, *Valkyrie*, *Shamrock* and the rest, with their windjammer sail areas and big crews. For the less well-heeled, yacht clubs were being formed at virtually every port of note round the British Isles as well as throughout the Empire and Commonwealth, with regular racing and a steady increase in 'one-design' classes. At the opposite extreme from the wealth and fashion of Cowes, a new kind of amateur sailor altogether was appearing: the man – or woman – who used their boats for cruising.

Inspired by men such as Frank 'Jack-all-alone' Cowper, who cruised singlehanded and wrote a series of pilot books (which he called 'Sailing Tours') for English, Irish and French harbours, Richard McMullen, E. F. Knight of *Falcon* fame, and the great pioneer circumnavigators Joshua Slocum and John Voss of the *Tilikum*, these enthusiasts were setting out with increasing boldness in their sturdy, heavily-sparred gaff cutters to explore the Channel ports, the creeks and harbours of Brittany, and via the newly-opened Kiel Canal the islands and fiords of the Baltic.

This growing interest in offshore cruising had been reflected in the formation in 1880 of the Cruising Club (granted a Royal Warrant in 1902), which Childers joined in 1895 and on the Committee of which he served from 1899 to 1901. Within three years the club was publishing its own small charts for its members, and an annual journal of cruises. These, to which Childers contributed several accounts of his own voyages between 1895 and 1913, give one a clear idea of the scope and variety of the cruising which was being undertaken. One interesting, but unexpected, fact which they reveal is the number of women who cruised, usually with brother or husband. The enthusiasm with which Erskine's wife Molly took to the life was by no means unique.

Childers bought his first boat in 1893, his second in 1895; his third, the famous but unprepossessing *Vixen*, the model for *Dulcibella* of *The Riddle*, in 1897; the 15 ton, thirty-three-year-old yawl *Sunbeam* in 1901 or '02; and was given his last boat, the Colin Archer designed *Asgard*, as a wedding present by his father-in-law in 1905. He owned her until his death, and she remained in the Childerses' possession until 1928 when Molly finally sold her.

Thus by 1902, when he was writing *The Riddle of the Sands*, Childers had already had nearly ten years' experience of small boat cruising; and although he never wrote another novel, nor as far as can be discovered ever considered doing so, he did write quite a lot about his cruises, and a certain amount about sailing in general. Apart from his contributions to the Cruising Club *Journal*, in the years between 1909 and 1913, when he was busy on his book *Framework of Home Rule*, had given up his job, and was dependent on his pen for a living, he wrote a series of articles on various aspects of sailing and cruising for *The Times*. In contrast to the raw material from which they were shaped, his drily factual fair logs, these pieces reveal his deep and abiding love for the sea, that 'sea-thirst' of which he wrote to Walter Runciman, and which he described again in these articles.

'For many a trim little cruiser from the Crouch to Falmouth or the Clyde the winter's sleep is at an end, and her owner's pent-up longings for fresh adventure are soon to be satisfied. His is no ordinary thirst. Most of us "hunt in dreams", but there is no imaginative restlessness so acute and constant as that of the cruising yachtsman during the long night of inaction when his little vessel lies in her mud-berth and he himself, only a degree less inactive to his own ardent thinking, tramps the mud of the drab city or tastes the insipid recreations of the land folk. This is partly because he carries everywhere with him, even when the immediate use of it has lapsed, the habit of studying the skies and winds and all the baffling phenomena of what people call the "weather", and of adapting his outlook to their unending caprices and vicissitudes. Thus every breeze and shower, every calm and storm and fog, has its peculiar train of intimate associations, past and prospective.'

In another, entitled *The First Cruise*, he evokes the very essence of small-ship cruising when he writes of 'persons of regular habits and settled tastes, prudent, fastidious and punctual' who 'embark on voyages in small, half-decked sailing craft, where they are starved and drenched by day and racked by night, where they undertake labour of the most novel and irritating kind, and approach problems for which the accumulated experience of their lives is valueless . . . The squalors and rigours of early days affect them, perhaps, in different ways . . . but deep within their souls there burns an immortal spark of courage and hope, so that when the *Stürm und Drang* are past, and out of the shock of the seas and the smart of the spray they glide before the weakening evening breeze into some quiet haven or cove, to drop the anchor close to trees which never looked so green or cottages which never looked so snug and homely, their spirit rebounds with a leap; painful memories become sanctified, ennobled, glorious, the mystery of pain has been solved, the riddle of happiness guessed. Something has been conquered not only by power, but by love; the world has grown to double its old dimensions, and is seen for the first time in harmony. New values have established themselves upon the wreckage of old standards of utility and gratification.'

There was in Erskine Childers always a sense of the eternal. He inhabited a human context more spacious than the run of mortals, and to such responsive souls the sea is both adversary and solace, both challenge and delight.

III

'One feels so safe and secure with him,' Molly Childers wrote of her husband on one of their cruises together; 'he is a great sailor. He has instinct.' Where that instinct, that seaman's sixth sense, originally came from was a mystery even to himself.

'At twenty-one or twenty-two,' he wrote in one of his *Times* articles, 'he [the writer] and a brother [Henry], educated in different places and for different professions, with no special aptitude or propensity for the sea, but rather with a well-grounded physical aversion to it, with no stimulus from friends, and in the face of solemn warnings of relations, felt themselves impelled simultaneously, in the manner of demented chickens, to take to the water.'

The two boys and their three younger sisters had had an odd

and in some ways tragic childhood. Their father, Robert Caesar Childers, an oriental scholar of unusual distinction, died of tuberculosis when Erskine was six; their mother Anna, from whom they had been compulsorily separated for fear of infection soon afterwards, eight years later in 1884. For the last two of those eight years, and thereafter, their home was at Glendalough in the heart of the Wicklow mountains, under the care of their mother's brother, Uncle Charles Barton, and his wife Agnes, who was their father's sister. If the five children were for all practical purposes orphans, their bereavement was mitigated not only by becoming part of a family with which they already had close ties and by their own close affection towards one another, but by the place itself. Glendalough House, a long low building of grey stone, with a stable wing at right angles to it and a machicolated Victorian gothic extension tacked rather incongruously on to its southern end, lies in a bowl of the hills twenty miles south of Dublin. That part of Wicklow is sheep and cattle country, peat and heather on the tops, lush meadows in the valleys, a land of streams and lakes, of deep woods of spruce and oak on the lower slopes; it combines a gentle grandeur with the snugness of sheltered human habitation, a winter bleakness with a summer luxuriance. It is splendid boys' country. The house itself, with dormer windows and three gables, one with a clock and bell, has a well-loved, well-lived-in feeling: for Erskine, throughout his life, it was in a special sense home.

Arrived at school age, the two brothers separated, Henry via one prep school to Harrow, Erskine via another to Haileybury where he gradually began to develop the particular characteristics and tastes which were to remain constant throughout his life: intense powers of concentration and a love of English and the Classics, with a less conventional passion for long solitary cross-country runs and, according to one of his contemporaries, 'for sailing strange craft on the Lea'.* The running and rugby were out when, at the age of nineteen, after a day-long soaking in the Connemara hills he contracted sciatica which left him slightly lame for life; but he remained an enthusiastic walker and never lost his love of boats and sailing.

One would like to know more of those 'strange craft' which he found to sail while he was still at school. There is no mention of

---

* Quoted by Andrew Boyle in *The Riddle of Erskine Childers* (Hutchinson, 1977), p. 45.

them in his letters to his sisters, and one can only guess: a Rob Roy canoe, perhaps, of the type Mr John MacGregor had sailed and paddled all through Europe twenty years before, or a sailing punt. Whatever they were, these strange craft seem to have provided Erskine with his initiation into sail.

In these descriptions of him as a boy in his middle and late teens, though, one begins to detect the emergence of the particular type of Englishman he was to become. Anglo-Irish he was, Irish he was later to claim to be; yet, in many ways, he was English to the bone. He had in full measure the personal reticence of men of his class and time; that total modesty which, when allied with courage, integrity and unassailable conviction, created many of the sung and unsung heroes of the age before the Great War shattered all the moulds of greatness. One finds it in many of the outstanding soldiers and administrators of the heyday of Empire, men whose dedicated lives rarely betray the existence of other loves and talents, for music or painting or writing or scholarship. That reticence, part shyness, part an intrinsic distaste for the show of emotion, acted as a shield for private qualities of sensitivity and passion which could only be revealed to the closest and most intimate of friends, or obliquely through the mouths of fictional characters such as Davies in *The Riddle of the Sands*.

That outlet was still many years ahead. From Haileybury Erskine went up to Trinity College, Cambridge, in 1890 as an exhibitioner, and for the next three years read his way through Parts I and II of the Law Tripos to take a First in his finals. He then sat the Civil Service exam, passed third, and was appointed a Clerk in the House of Commons. Unable to play rugby at Cambridge because of his limp, he rowed instead – 'rather dull . . . machine-like work' he described it to his sister Dulcibella – and got some sailing on the Broads.

It must have been immediately after his finals that he and his brother Henry decided to take to the water 'like demented chickens', for in June 1893 he was writing to a friend, Walter Runciman: 'I and brother have a nice little 8-tonner which we are going for a cruise in. We start Saturday next and Herbert Jones is with us, from Fort William.' The cruise itself proved an initiation into seagoing in more ways than one: his description of it, written sixteen years later with the fond irony of later experience, will be found in the first chapter.

IV

Wherever it came from, whether from some unremembered Barton ancestor, or, as he suggested himself, 'some hereditary predisposition to the sea' peculiar to Englishmen, there was no doubt that Erskine Childers had 'the sea-thirst' on him; and from the time he joined the House of Commons staff he was rarely without a boat of some sort. The sea was the medium through which he was best able to express his strong and enduring spirit of adventure, just as, later, the cause of Irish independence fulfilled his equally strong and enduring idealism. With almost uncanny precision, his last great exploit under sail – the arms-smuggling run in *Asgard* in July 1914 – brought these two powerful forces in his life into complete accord; just as, in *The Riddle*, Davies' seamanship and patriotism find their fulfilment in the battle of wits with Dollmann and the unravelling of the secret of the seven *siels*.

This is a suitable place in which to dispose of two often-repeated statements about Childers' sailing exploits. One is that he carried out most of his cruising singlehanded; the other, that he wrote *The Riddle* only after a number of cruises to the Frisian Islands. His logbooks and letters contradict both these notions. He sailed alone on many occasions, particularly in the early days when he kept *Marguerite* at Greenhithe and spent his weekends pottering about the Thames estuary. He took her across to Boulogne on one occasion on his own, and coastwise to Poole; and during the middle of the *Vixen* cruise in 1897, he spent three weeks exploring the southwestern corner of the Baltic while waiting for Henry to rejoin him. Most of his extended cruises, however, were made with one or more companions, either his brother or with friends whose names recur year after year, notably Ivor Lloyd-Jones and William Le Fanu, and of course during the *Asgard* years with Molly and various friends such as Gordon Shephard, who was both a pilot in the RFC and a dashing yachtsman in his own right.

Basil Williams, who was one of Childers' closest friends throughout his life and wrote an affectionate memoir* of him after his death, but who was obviously no sailor, gave this vignette of him at sea, 'in his element' as he put it.

---

* Privately printed, 1925.

'Aboard the *Sunbeam* there were no fits of brown study, no undue modesty in the skipper. He was undoubted despot there and we landlubbers had to do what we were told and to look sharp about it without any back-talk, whether it were hauling at a rope, or taking a hand at the helm, or doing something mysterious with a marling spike and the lee-scuppers, or swabbing the decks, or cleaning the brasswork, or stoking the Primus stove, or going ashore to lay in fresh provisions. Of course he was entirely responsible for the navigation ... though his powers were not put to any very severe test on this occasion; but one saw enough to feel one would be perfectly ready to trust oneself to him in any gale or sudden squall off the most treacherous coast. He was also chief cook and, with the most unpromising materials and the help of his pet Primus, he fed us well. I was glad to have had this glimpse of him on his own element, for it afterwards made it easier to understand how he came to write, chiefly from his own experiences, *The Riddle of the Sands.*'

That said, Childers had done enough singlehanded work to know both its strains and its compensations, and to write revealingly, about it and himself, in one of his *Times* articles:

'At bottom, of course, the explanation of its charm for the few lies in the very circumstances which condemn it for the many: in the stark loneliness of the conflict with a formidable element, in the voluntary abnegation of all human aid, moral or physical, and in the submission of a man's own faculties to a merciless ordeal, self-imposed, self-contemplated. Nobody is looking on; if there is no ridicule for blunders, there is no applause for triumphs. Without a rival to vanquish or a tribunal to satisfy, save that of a man's own soul, the competitive and spectacular elements inherent in most sports are totally absent. Absent, too, except for rare and brief intervals, is the sense of recreation pure and simple. Body and brain are continually at high tension. Emergency succeeds emergency, and you are exceedingly lucky if one can be dealt with before the next is on you. Often they accumulate until they produce a situation so complex that there seems to be no solution. But the rude schooling of necessity ripens capacity and sharpens the senses amazingly.'

Characteristically, after this Emersonian reflection ('Trust thyself: every heart vibrates to that iron string' was one of his favourite quotations, from Emerson's *Self-Reliance*) he goes on to describe the difficulties of making tea, eating a boiled egg and steering at the same time! Here lies, one feels, a key to his complex, sometimes rather daunting, but ardent personality: high seriousness never lapsed into solemnity; a detached and ironic sense of humour softened the edges of a character stoic in its obduracy.

It is not too far-fetched to say that if there had been a shift of wind in the English Channel in September 1897, while Childers was waiting for Henry to join him in *Vixen* in Boulogne, there might never have been a *Riddle of the Sands*. From Sonderberg, he wrote to Walter Runciman in October: 'my plan was to make Bordeaux, canal through France and then spend the winter in the Mediterranean: that is the dream of my heart. But fate willed otherwise: the weather broke directly I was ready and a long spell of west winds, low glass and an odd storm set in. I crossed the Channel alone to Boulogne, gave up waiting, and when Henry and Lloyd-Jones joined me turned Hollandwards one gusty dreary day.'

The cruise that followed, 'along the whole line of a strange collection of exaggerated sand heaps called the Frisian Isles', into the Baltic, and back again to lay up for the winter at Terschelling, was the sole source of the book; he did not return to that part of the world until after it was published, when he covered some of the same ground in *Sunbeam*. Moreover, four years elapsed before he even started to write it, for early in 1901 he wrote to great-aunt Flora, his confidante in many of his dreams, 'I have not begun that book yet. I forgot before coming away to get the diary of that cruise from the flat. An idea has struck me that a story, of which I have the germ, might be worked into it as a setting.'

And, as the extracts from his log, quoted below, demonstrate with engaging clarity, he used the events of that cruise for all they were worth. Incident after incident is transferred from logbook to novel with the greatest fidelity, and readers of the book will enjoy identifying them and observing how Childers fitted them into the story. It is like writing a book backwards as one traces the fiction back to the incidents upon which it was based. Nowhere, however, in the log or in his letters, is there so much as a hint that he had the story in mind while they were there; and the tantalising idea that he and Henry were anticipating the exploits, thirteen years later, of Captain Trench and Lieutenant Brandon (see Chapter IV) and doing a spot of unofficial (or officially unrecognised) espionage on behalf of the Admiralty, unfortunately has no facts to support it. Only the vivid background material for the story lay ready in the drab ledger which was *Vixen*'s logbook, and in Childers' memory, waiting for the story in which it would be put to such good use.

V

The following spring, in 1898, Childers and a paid hand, Alfred Rice, went across to Terschelling to bring *Vixen* back to England. In June of that year, partly singlehanded, partly with Le Fanu, he brought *Vixen* round to Bursledon on the Hamble River: from then on this was to be his base. For the remainder of that season and in 1899 his cruising was restricted to the South Coast, his anchorages familiar to everyone who sails from Chichester Harbour or the Solent: Bembridge, Wootton, Cowes, Newtown, the Beaulieu River, and west as far as Poole.

In between, during the winter of 1898, he visited the West Indies. Whether this too was 'a dream of the heart' one does not know: certainly a few years before he had thrown at Walter Runciman the rhetorical question 'Wouldn't it be splendid to sail to the West Indies?' But one feels it was the sailing there, as much as the destination, which inspired the remark. When he did finally go, it was more prosaically, by steamer – a small and ancient vessel which rolled horribly and occasionally broke down. The ship's library consisted of one book, called *Great Disasters and Horrors of the World's History*, but the Purser had read all the works of Marie Corelli, and the Captain, 'a wiry little Welshman' who 'had a little brig of his own once and sailed her up and down the world with every sort of adventure', enjoyed being read aloud to from Kipling's sea poetry. 'He was appreciative and found no errors', Childers remarks drily in his diary of the voyage, after *The Ballad of the Bolivar*.

The holiday, for such it was, would hardly earn a place in this book but for one fact. After visiting Barbados the ship went on to Trinidad, where Childers left her to proceed up the chain of the Windward Islands by other means. His entry for November 13 tells its own story, but only the beginning of it: 'Found out a sloop of 22 tons sailing to Grenada on Wednesday. Bargained with skipper for a passage with use of "doghouse", whatever that may be – kennel, I suppose.'

His account of the somewhat haphazard seamanship practised on the inter-island sailing vessels – quite unchanged fifty years later – will be found in Chapter V. Although he never used the experience, the detailed diary which he kept illuminates with a clear and engaging light facets of his personality which often tend to become obscured by the more serious, and even sombre, events of his life. There cannot have been, for instance, all that many young Englishmen at that time who arrived at one or other of the islands with an introduction to Government House having spent the previous thirty-six hours at the helm of one of those battered old sloops. This was the Erskine who as an undergraduate had adjured his sister Constance to read Tennyson's *Ulysses*; and who on the voyage out to the West Indies had mesmerised the Master of the SS *West Indian* with Kipling's *Anchor Song*.

Ulysses, that marvellous evocation of the perennial romantic, fits the mood of the West Indian interlude to the letter. He had read and loved and quoted it from the urbane seclusion of Trinity, Cambridge; now, under the moon and stars, with the great rough tiller of white cedar wood vibrating under his hand, the patched mainsail bulging with the trade wind, and the phosphorescence glittering away astern, it sprang off the page to become part of experience –

> 'the arch wherethro'
> gleams that untravelled world, whose margin fades
> For ever and for ever when I move.
> How dull it is to pause, to make an end,
> To rust unburnish'd, not to shine in use!

'There', indeed, 'gloomed the dark broad seas,

> The lights begin to twinkle from the rocks:
> The long day wanes: the slow moon climbs: the deep
> Moans round with many voices. Come, my friends,
> 'Tis not too late to seek a newer world.'

Poetry and the sea interact to produce a magic which draws something from each, and for Erskine Childers both touched a nerve close to the centre of his being. Oddly, if he ever wrote poetry himself – and it is hard to believe that he did not – none of it has survived, and he never mentions it.

Two years later he and Basil Williams were at sea together under very different circumstances, 'crowded like rats in a hamper' in a troopship, the SS *Montfort*, with a great many horses (for thirty of which he and his mate were responsible) as a driver in the City Imperial Volunteers Battery, HAC, on their way to South Africa. This six month episode has been described in detail, not only in Childers' own book, but by his biographers, and requires mention here only because there shines through it a gleam of that same romanticism which like Ulysses he was never to lose entirely – though 'romanticism' is too weak a word. It was that fire of the imagination which was never to be quenched; the quickness to respond to standards other than those 'of utility and gratification'. There was nothing weak or dilettante in it, for the mind which that imagination spurred on 'to strive, to seek, to find, and not to yield' was too clear and strong to tolerate half-truths and half-measures. If Erskine Childers was a romantic, he was a disciplined romantic, and that is the hardest avocation of all.

VI

Back to boats. *Vixen* was sold and disappears without trace or reference, to reappear in 1933, when a Mr C. Hapgood of Ryde found her mouldering away in Bursledon and towed her across to Wootton with the intention of restoring her, an intention which he never fulfilled. Later she was taken to Lymington; and in 1939 a fund was even set up to try and preserve her, but the moment was hardly auspicious. During the war she suffered a near-miss from a bomb, and was finally broken up. (As an example of the grip of *The Riddle of the Sands* over its devotees, from the time she was rediscovered she was so completely identified with the book that she is frequently referred to as the *Dulcibella*, never as the *Vixen*.) She has since enjoyed a reincarnation for the film.

In the Ranks of the C.I.V., thanks to the efforts of Mrs Thompson, appeared in 1900, almost as soon as the battery landed in England, and that same winter Childers started 'the yachting story' which was to become, during the subsequent eighteen months, *The Riddle*. During this period, in partnership with William Le Fanu and A. H. Dennis, he bought *Sunbeam*, in which in the summer of 1902 he and two friends had a fortnight's cruise along the South Coast, getting no further than Weymouth, but which, the following year, with the book safely published, he took for a rather tempestuous six weeks to the Baltic, covering over 1,800 miles. But even on this occasion, their only contact with the Frisian Islands was a night in Terschelling on the outward voyage.

That autumn Childers accompanied the HAC on a ceremonial visit to Boston, and from there wrote in November to Basil Williams, 'I am engaged to be married to Miss Mary Osgood of this city.' The attraction had been immediate and mutual, and the love which grew out of it continued for the whole of both their lives.

'Little Molly', as Childers often referred to her, was in all respects a remarkable young woman. She had looks, breeding, intelligence, and a character that had been tempered by a childhood of pain. An accident in her early years had damaged both her hips, and up to the age of ten she had been unable to walk at all. She then managed with crutches, and later with sticks, but she was lame all her life. In the circumstances it may seem enlightened, if somewhat risky, of her father, who was a doctor, to offer the couple a yacht for a wedding present, but she had done some sailing in American waters and enjoyed it.

Back in London, married and busy setting up house, Childers wrote to Dr Osgood, 'We have decided to take a fourth share in the *Sunbeam*, our old yacht . . . it is only experimental, as I am not at all sure that Molly will find it quite comfortable.'

In the event, all went well, and by May Erskine was writing to Dr Osgood again: 'Molly is tremendously keen on making a long cruise in the *Sunbeam* at the end of the session. I am doubtful about the comfort of it, and we hold lengthy arguments on the subject.' Out of solicitude, he was underestimating the sheer stubborn determination of this young wife of his. Many wives, it is true, accompany their husbands to sea in small boats: comparatively few actually enjoy it. In Molly's case her relish was immediate and genuine, as her letters from their cruises, some of which are quoted below, amply show. Only in an occasional brief aside does one catch a glimpse of how hampered she really was, for she cooked and took her watch at the helm with the best, and her sight was acute.

They sailed west as far as Fowey later that summer, and before the end of the year had decided exactly the shape that Dr Osgood's wedding present was to take. They went to the Scottish–Norwegian designer Colin Archer; the lines were drawn by December 1904 and the yacht was delivered in August of the following year. They christened her *Asgard*.

By then Molly was five months pregnant, but that didn't stop them getting as far west as the Helford River during a four week cruise the following month. Erskine junior was born in December, but *that* did not prevent them undertaking the first of their two great Baltic cruises during August and September of 1906. At the end of it they laid the boat up for the winter at Svendborg, near Copenhagen, with the clear intention of returning the following year and making for Finland. Whether they actually did so is uncertain, for from September 23, 1906 until June 25, 1913 there are no logbooks, no letters, no accounts of cruises in the RCC *Journal*: no indications of their having used their beloved *Asgard* at all. Robert Childers believes that they carried out the planned cruise to the Gulf of Bothnia in 1907, yet there is nothing in the 1913 log to suggest that they were coursing over familiar ground. We simply do not know.

We do know that it was a busy time for both of them. In addition to his job at the House of Commons, Erskine produced four books during those years: the fifth volume of *The Times History of the War in South Africa*, two works of military analysis and criticism of the role of cavalry in war, and his monumental *The Framework of Home Rule*, the book that confirmed his conversion from the Tory Unionist convictions of his upbringing and early manhood to the cause of a self-governing Ireland with Dominion status. He was also, briefly, Liberal parliamentary candidate for Devonport. Meanwhile Molly, after one miscarriage, produced a second son, Robert, in 1911. With a book always on the stocks, a growing family, a busy social life, and an ever-deepening involvement in the fate of Ireland, it would not be surprising if they found little time for sailing. Certainly they lent *Asgard* to their friends, William Le Fanu, for one, and Gordon Shephard, whom they had first met in 1909, for another.

VII

In reading these accounts of Erskine Childers' cruises, it is worth remembering, first of all, that none of his boats had engines. There is a scornful note by Molly in 1961, at the time when the Irish Government was in the process of buying *Asgard*, both for sentimental reasons and in order to use her as a training ship for the

Irish Navy: 'You will remember that *Asgard* has had many owners and that a recent one had installed motor engines – to me a degrading action. Those who love sailing ships would share my disapproval.'

The small *reliable* petrol or diesel engine has done more to take the hard work and anxiety out of cruising than any other single technical advance: more than the Bermudan sloop rig, or echo-sounders or radio direction-finding, or the CQR anchor, or synthetic-fibre sails and ropes. Without one you had to sail your way in and out of tight places; and when you could not sail you either anchored and waited for a shift of wind or for the tide to turn, or laboriously towed with the dinghy, or hauled yourself along by laying out a kedge anchor, or by rowing with long sweeps.

Erskine Childers, like other cruising men of his time and the masters of barges and trawlers and many other small coastal craft, went everywhere under sail. Only those who have done it can fully appreciate the skill it takes: the nicety of judgement, the understanding of wind and tide, and the knowledge of one's boat and her limitations. (It probably helps to explain the number of notes in the logs about 'touching up paintwork' and 'repainting' during a cruise!) In many ways, cruising with an engine and cruising without one are two different kinds of activity: in the former, you can to some extent outface the elements, beating a foul tide or a headwind by the brute force of your Perkins or Penta; in the latter, you can only use what the gods send and your own skill and cunning, conquering, as Childers himself said, 'not only by power but by love'. To the true sailing man there is something rather depressing (or 'degrading') about watching sailing boats, most of them probably handier and quicker in stays than those old gaff cutters and ketches, invariably anchoring or slipping their moorings under power, plodding along on their engines and letting a fair wind run to waste – or, the really heinous crime, calling out the lifeboat because their engine won't start.

Since Childers' day sailing has been transformed from being simply the livelihood of shoreside communities and the sport of a minority of enthusiasts into the weekend and summer occupation of countless thousands, on fresh water and salt; ocean-crossing has become a commonplace, and the new breed of circum-navigators has transformed the achievements of men like Slocum and Conor O Brien into a regular occurrence, not beyond the reach or the imagination of anyone with the courage and determination to set off. In the same way more modest cruises to Holland or Brittany or the Channel Islands are now within the summer holiday programme of hundreds of boat owners, while any weekend you can navigate across the Channel to Cherbourg and back by following the empty beer cans.

Of those in particular who find themselves for two or three weeks in the summer in Alderney or Peter Port, St Malo or Lézardrieux, L'Aber Wrach or Benodet, who sail to Southern Ireland or the Baltic or the West Coast of Scotland, Erskine Childers was one of the pioneers. And among all the thousands of people who carry out their regular, well planned, moderately uneventful and seamanlike summer cruises, even today there are probably not all that many who set out from Weymouth in an 18 foot half-decked boat and, on the spur of the moment, turn right and set off across the English Channel. That, as much as the spontaneous decision by Erskine and Henry when weather-bound in Calais in *Vixen* to head northeast for the Frisian Islands, puts the author of *The Riddle of the Sands* firmly in the company of all those who, like him, 'all year have the sea-thirst' on them.

VIII

At the end of June 1913 Erskine and Molly got away on their longest cruise. Over a period of two months, with one paid hand and a variety of crews several of them complete novices, they covered 2,500 miles with Helsinki as their furthest port of call. At the end of it they left the boat at Christiania; whence, during a particularly windy October, Gordon Shephard, with a crew of three, brought her back to Holyhead via Bergen and the north of Scotland, a 'delivery trip' for which he was awarded the RCC Challenge Cup. Shephard was one of the first RFC pilots, became in 1917 at the age of thirty-two the youngest Brigadier-General in the British Army, and was killed in a crash in January 1918. 'He was one of my heroes,' Erskine Childers wrote to Shephard's mother, 'and will always be so.'

Gordon Shephard was also to take part in the Childerses' last, and most remarkable, voyage in *Asgard*. Childers himself wrote only one very brief account of it, as part of what, among all his papers, is perhaps the grimmest and the saddest: the pencilled fragment of autobiography which he scribbled down on the pages of an exercise book during the last days of his life. 'In May 1914 [I] joined a small group of people formed for the purpose of buying and importing arms for the Volunteers.' So it begins; and it is difficult even now, when the shadows of that dark time have been lifted, and the story of the gun-running has been told, as he suggested it deserved to be, at length,* to appreciate fully its impudence and daring. It was a deadly serious operation, with deadly serious consequences; yet, like a stage set, it all seems to take place behind a gauze of such high-hearted innocence, such amateurish cloak-and-dagger precautions, such impromptu ruses and last-minute revisions and improvisations, that the seriousness tends to dissolve in sheer comedy.

It is the intention of this book to avoid the political barbed wire which catches and bids fair to enmesh anyone who writes about Erskine Childers. Our concern is with him as a yachtsman and sailor, and from that point of view the arms run was a masterly feat of seamanship. But it was also the occasion – the only occasion – on which his sailing and his commitment to the cause of Irish self-rule coincided; and to appreciate the full savour of the event, its ironies and triumph, it will be necessary to supply, in all brevity, the context, to be found in Chapter IX. As for Childers himself, from about the age of thirty-five he steadily moved away from the conventional, conservative, Unionist creed of his Anglo-Irish background towards the conviction – which eventually became an article of faith – that Ireland must be granted at least a measure of self-determination. His reading of history, his first-hand experience of both the Boers and the Irish themselves, equally persuaded him that England's ham-fisted treatment of Ireland over four centuries of misrule could no longer be tolerated. The imminence of Home Rule in 1913, with its corollary, increasingly belligerent opposition to it from the Protestants in the North, provided the levers which pushed him from passive support to active participation. When the Ulster Volunteers, the militant expression of that hostility to Home Rule, started to receive substantial shipments of arms – illegally, but with the connivance of the British Government and the armed forces – those levers exerted a critical pressure: Childers

---

* *The Howth Gun-Running*, F. X. Martin (Dublin, Brown & Nolan, 1964).

offered *Asgard*, and himself, to carry out a similar operation for the rival Irish Volunteers in the South.

That voyage and its outcome have become part of the legendary history of the foundation on the Republic of Ireland: as far as this book is concerned, it was the apotheosis of all those other voyages, both in *Asgard* and in other less well-found vessels, over a period of more than twenty years. And unlike them, it was, in Conor O Brien's phrase, a voyage with an object.

As Erskine and Molly and their crew thrashed out of Conway Bay, 'one equal temper of heroic hearts', that last July before the outbreak of the Great War, other lines from *Ulysses* that seem to sum up both the man and that particular side of his life come to mind:

> . . . all times I have enjoy'd
> Greatly, have suffered greatly, both with those
> That loved me, and alone; on shore, and when
> Thro' scudding drifts the rainy Hyades
> Vext the dim sea: I am become a name
> For always roaming with a hungry heart.

And not only that side of his life.

IX

There is a postscript to the story, for after the gun-running trip Childers was by no means finished with the sea. Within a week of his landing the arms Great Britain declared war on Germany, and he was summoned to the Admiralty. There he was set to working out a detailed plan for the occupation of the German Frisian islands of Borkum and Juist preparatory to a full-scale invasion of the mainland: the plot of *The Riddle of the Sands* in reverse and, like it, destined never to be put to the trial.

After that academic exercise he was posted as a Lieutenant RNVR to the seaplane carrier HMS *Engadine*, in which his duties included those of intelligence officer and instructor in navigation to the aircrews. *Engadine* was part of Admiral Tyrwhitt's Harwich Force, whose sphere of operations lay off that stretch of German coast with which Childers was uniquely familiar; the role of the seaplanes was reconnaissance, and to attack the Zeppelin sheds and other targets in the vicinity of Cuxhaven and Kiel. For such work Childers' precise local knowledge was a godsend. He wrote that 'My idea is to show very clearly every sea-mark that can be sighted and identified by the seaplanes en route to their objective'; knowing the inadequacy of Admiralty charts of this locality from his own experience in *Vixen*, he worked from German ones and produced a version of his own specially for aircrew. And, being Erskine Childers, of course he was soon airborne.

He acted as Observer in the leading plane in the first-ever naval air operation, the attack on Cuxhaven on Christmas Day 1914, for which he was Mentioned in Despatches, and commended by Commodore Roger Keyes; and he served in the seaplane carrier *Ben-my-Chree* at the Dardanelles and elsewhere in the Eastern Mediterranean, and was awarded the DSC. At the end of 1916 he was promoted Lieutenant-Commander, but by then he was out of flying and serving as navigator and intelligence officer in a Coastal Motor Boat flotilla.

Eager as ever for action – 'it has always been best for me' he had once written – he took part in more sorties than anyone else in the flotilla, and grabbed every opportunity to get airborne. 'I believe I must be the only person who has been to Zeebrugge twice in one day, both by air and water,' he wrote in his diary on April 26, 1917, having visited it first in the back seat of a De Havilland 4 in the afternoon, and then gone roaring across the Channel again that night on a CMB patrol.

Of the two modes of transport he preferred the former, and he had succeeded in wangling his return to flying when, in July 1917, he was appointed to HMS *President* and then seconded to the Irish Convention, which was sitting in Dublin and through whose deliberations Lloyd George intended that 'Ireland should try her hand at hammering out an instrument of government for her own people.' During the eight months which it took to achieve total deadlock, Childers occasionally escaped 'to his yacht, in which he went sailing whenever practicable on the Shannon'.*

The Convention failed, and the situation in Ireland deteriorated. With the British Government still officially in control of Irish destinies, Sinn Fein set up its own rival institutions, including its own parliament, the Dail, while the Irish Republican Army lost patience and declared war on the occupying British

---

* According to Edward MacLysaght, quoted in Boyle, op. cit. p. 233. If the yacht in question was *Asgard*, this is the only indication we have that she had been shifted from Bangor to the west coast of Ireland, or indeed that he ever sailed her after the arms run.

troops and their disreputable reinforcements, the Black and Tans.

For Childers, identifying increasingly with Ireland, that country's agony demanded more than sympathy: as in the arms run half a dozen years and a long war before, it demanded action, and he and Molly – by no means in total harmony on this issue – left England permanently and settled in Dublin.

Misunderstood in London, mistrusted there, Childers' unflinching dedication to the ideal of Irish freedom drove him inexorably to a position beyond the politically possible. As Secretary to the Irish delegation which, with infinite misgivings, reached agreement with Lloyd George's Government at the end of 1921, he bitterly opposed the compromise Irish Free State which resulted. 'The Irish', in Burke Wilkinson's words*, 'had settled for half a loaf of the good bread of freedom'; and when civil war followed Childers joined the anti-Treaty forces, the IRA Irregulars, dedicated to the replacement of the half-loaf of the Free State by the better bread of a full Republic.

For five months, from June to November 1922, constantly on the move – and a sick man – he produced, virtually singlehanded, a weekly propaganda sheet *An Phoblacht*. In late October he was sent for to meet Eamon de Valera, who was in hiding outside Dublin, and on the way stopped at Glendalough. There, someone betrayed him. Free State soldiers surrounded the house; others went in and arrested him.

He was tried by military court, and because he had a small automatic on him; most of all, perhaps, because the deeply troubled Irish Free State Government were after his blood, he was condemned to death. All pleas for leniency ignored, the great voyage in *Asgard* which, in part, had helped to bring all this about, forgotten, he was executed by firing-squad on November 24, 1922.

It was to be many years before Ireland was ready to admit that in executing Erskine Childers the Free State Government had destroyed not a traitor but an outstandingly gentle, brave and honourable man whose only mistake – and one that he would never have made at sea – had been to try and hasten the making tide of history.

---

* *The Zeal of the Convert* (Henry P. Luce & Co. and Colin Smythe, 1976) p. 199.

II

Initiation 1893

'Our starting-point was this: that we must cruise at once, visit distant places, not merely sail in one prescribed area as a matter of daily sport. It was a sound aspiration, for the essence of the cruising spirit is travel; and it is far better to familiarise the mind at once with the idea of detachment from the land than to rely too long on the same nightly refuge. So there followed logically the need for as stout and seaworthy a yacht as the exigencies of a slender purse permitted. But it is an interesting fact that the nascent impulse for the sea, however healthy at bottom, is susceptible of curious aberrations. I remember that there was a moment when we conceived the calamitous idea of buying, very cheap, an old steam-launch, on the theory, I suppose, that what we lost in weatherly qualities we gained in speed and certainty. This madness was short-lived; we returned to the seaworthy sailing yacht, and having very vague notions of the constituents of seaworthiness, pitched on an ex-racing 8-tonner whose absurdly disproportionate draught (for cruising, that is) of eight feet and a half struck us as ensuring the requisite qualities. So in a sense it did, but at a needless sacrifice of other ends. She was safe and strong, but very "wet"; fast, but over-canvassed; and so deep as to have access to but few ports, comparatively.'

Thus Erskine Childers, describing, many years afterwards,*

---

* *The Times*, May 11, 1909.

how he and his brother Henry bought their first boat, the cutter *Shulah*. They were both in their early twenties, and, considering their inexperience, seem to have been lucky. *Shulah* did not drown them or cost them a fortune; and, because of her draught ensured that they quickly learned that 'detachment from the land' which Childers recommended.

No photograph of her survives, but it is not difficult to picture her: 33 feet long with a beam of 8 feet, low freeboard, long counter, even longer bowsprit, and the huge gaff-mainsail of which they were in permanent awe. She had been built in Southampton in 1890 and they bought her in Kingstown, now Dun Laoghaire, and with only Erskine's experience of those 'strange craft on the Lea' behind them, they had to learn to sail her. The tale continues:

'Determined to become thoroughly grounded in the technique of yachting, we had to procure a yacht-hand. One meant two; for the magnitude of our main-boom, and a swift intuition from our speech that we were inveterate landsmen, evoked from our first choice an immediate demand for a mate. It was a check, because we instinctively predicted a combination against us, in which the "Captain", as he styled himself, would, as in all committees of four, hold a casting as well as a deliberative voice. Financially, too, the wrench was severe.

'However, we started, the main-boom reverently draped and lashed firmly amidships, the trysail set over it; for even with two able and two miserable seamen the mainsail was pronounced to be too formidable to manage. The whole atmosphere of the enterprise was serious. We were barely under way and threading the crowd of yachts which lay in Kingstown Harbour when we were warned to don our oilskins, as there would be a "sea outside". Clambering stiffly back to the deck clad in vivid orange, we winced under the feeling that we, like our main-boom, were the objects of amused criticism. For there was no sea outside, at any rate for some miles; only a fresh offshore wind crisping the smooth waters of Dublin Bay and driving the city murk towards the cliffs of Howth. But the weather signs were held to be adverse: we found they always were – trouble might begin at any moment. So we maintained our strange armour, though it hampered our movements grievously, and by its repulsive texture and odour hastened the inevitable approach of physical distress. To this

B

phase we had been long resigned, though we had always consoled ourselves with the belief that where there was so much active work to be done the distress would be little felt. Pathetic miscalculation! Our services were not needed, even for chartwork, in which academic study had already made us fairly proficient. I cannot adequately express the strange mixture of relief and mortification which this discovery entailed. Happily pride won the day; and in spite of attempts to humour and shield us like lost children, insisted on a pretence of co-operation in the work going forward, all the time nursing a deep resolve to end this abject dependency as soon as possible. One point, however, we gained: the accomplishment of a fresh stage northward up the coast every day, from Howth to Ardglass and Donaghadee; for it was a first result of our imposing draught that we were easily induced to pass by the lovely Carlingford and Strangford Loughs, both having somewhat intricate entrance channels. The omission at the time cost us no regrets, our draught having become a point of sailorly pride, placing us among the lordly ocean-going craft which shun shallow water, keep to orthodox tracks, and regard running aground as an indelible disgrace.

'I smile to think of the subsequent history in ourselves of this lofty creed. At Donaghadee our men discovered that certain structural alterations were necessary to their comfort, and we consented under protest to get the work done in Belfast. The voyage thither was an epoch. Where the Lough narrows for the approach to the city there is a deep-water channel clearly marked by buoys, and up this channel we were beating against a head-wind. With no excuse but the desire, I suppose, to show off before doctrinaire amateurs, our skipper began to tack outside the buoys and eventually ran us hard aground on a falling tide, so that a few hours later we were poised giddily on our wedge-shaped keel and shored up, to avert a fatal collapse, by a scaffolding of spare spars – a horror and an offence to gods and men. Abnormally sensitive in those days, we boiled at this criminal blunder, boiled the more in that the function allotted to us while the scaffolding was being erected was the degrading one of signifying to passing steamers by frantic cries and gestures our prayers that they should slow down and mitigate the wash which threatened our stability. Yet all the while, I well remember, we greedily scrutinised with one eye every detail of the work of stripping and lashing spars, carrying out an anchor from the masthead, and so forth; and later, anger giving way to reflection while we were being towed – another indignity – into a dock at high tide, we were conscious of having gained substantial moral, practical advantages. Our rulers were not infallible, and we had learnt a useful, if dismal, branch of the maritime art.

'We forthwith announced our intention, hitherto kept secret, of cruising to the west coast of Scotland. The plan was coldly received. Three days later, just as our repairs were approaching completion, our crew resigned, leaving us improved sailors but still hopelessly dependent on expert help.'

After a short discourse on the difficulties of finding the right kind of paid hands – advice more useful to novices of 1890 than of the 1970s – Childers goes on with the story.

'We were now engaged by – I can scarcely say we engaged – a breezy, masterful, fascinating ex-racing skipper, who read us through and through, and whom we diagnosed too late as a battered soldier of fortune, brought low by intemperance and anxious for purposes of his own to obtain a passage at our expense to Oban. In his train came a none too clean merchant seaman, over whom our glorious skipper seemed to have some mysterious hold. We were wonderfully happy in the first few days. We revelled in our first night sail from Larne to the Mull of Kintyre, working out our own course and keeping thankfully a lion's share of the night watches. We saw with enchanted eyes the purple mountains and wine-dark seas of Scotland, and on the last stage to Oban obtained leave to replace the *mesquin* little trysail by the mainsail, and so wake our gallant little vessel to full and vigorous life. But Oban was our hero's goal. He brought discredit on us in port, purposely ran us aground in leaving the bay, alleged damage to the keel and the need for docking, and when, in a flame of rage, we gave him instant notice to quit, demanded a sum so large as to suggest blackmail, insinuating our guilty intent to "pile up" our damaged boat with an eye to the insurance. Imagine the effect of this loathsome innuendo upon us, who then would rather have perished of starvation than admit incompetence even to an impersonal corporation! We parted with this gentleman, horribly disillusioned, in a solicitor's office. But again, we noted exultantly that, thanks to his complaisance at sea, we had grown much in wisdom and skill.

'Were we ready to sail alone? Alas! not yet: but from what source to obtain help. In our depression fortune sent our way a young Scotch fisherman, rather slovenly, ignorant of yachts, but infinitely good-natured, and only too delighted to let us go where we pleased and commit all the *gaucheries* we liked, so long as he had nominal control of a spruce little cutter. He asked for no mate and, best point of all, knew nothing of charts, so that we at once became the responsible navigators, only relying on him for practical seamanship. We became fast friends and had a time of pure delight in the only perfect cruising ground which the British Isles afford; one, too, in which our deep draught presented a *minimum* of inconvenience.'

They laid *Shulah* up for the winter at Gourock, to resume their exploration of the west coast the following season. But this time, in place of their carefree young fisherman they took on as hand and mentor an old man from the yard; as Childers explains in the second of his *Times* articles, it was a brief partnership. And he goes on to describe precisely the restlessness which afflicts all cruising yachtsmen.

'In those days scenery and smooth waters gave us little satisfaction. Getting there was the thing; once there, a restless craving to go somewhere quite different poisoned our enjoyment of the fairest scenes. If this point of view seems a little quixotic to us now, it is no wonder that it was incomprehensible to our sailorman, who was elderly and without illusions. Symptoms whose import we knew of old began to appear. Finally, as we lay one evening on the placid bosom of Loch Linnhe, indifferent to the sunset glow on the great shoulders of Ben Nevis, weaving dimly ambitious schemes, whether of a north-about voyage or of the circumnavigation of Ireland, or of Norway or Brest, or what not, and regarding discontentedly the while the oval of enfolding hills and the lap of the petty wavelets, the crisis came. Something – perhaps the proximity of the Caledonian Canal, with its fatally easy access to the bleak North Sea – aroused sudden and black suspicions; and he was gone.

'In an abruptly chastened mood, and with a strange mutual shyness, we were contemplating the new order, measuring our vessel by a new standard, setting ourselves hypothetical problems of strength and ingenuity to solve unaided. Subtle contrasts of character emerged: in my brother a child-like optimism, in myself a temper tinged with philosophic doubt, but ready enough to follow a decisive lead. The truth was that he, with equal moral enthusiasm, had greater physical aptitude – could splice wire rope and conceive appropriate knots as it were by intuition. In both of us apparently inveterate landsmen the buried seed of the maritime instinct had burst and blossomed, but somewhere in our ancestry there must have been a Viking steward as well as a Viking skipper, and by some freak of atavism I took after the former and he after the latter. At any rate, I came to be the cook,* while he wielded the serving-mallet and spike. Outside these functions there was in the nature of things small question of any division of labour.

'Memorable was the first morning after our deliverance, when we set the sails, weighed the anchor and glided down the loch, uncriticised, unaided, masters of our fate. With what a punctilious nicety we adjusted halyards, trimmed sheets, and tuned up our little ship to her utmost turn of speed! How large our ideas were – not without reason, in view of 8 ft. 6 in. of draught – on the class of water fit for 8 ton yachts! Before leaving Scotland we had to revisit Gourock, our last winter's base in the Clyde, for certain alterations and repairs, but the Crinan Canal, that convenient short-cut and means of evading the dreaded Mull of Kintyre, was rejected in favour of the Atlantic route, tempered only by a run through the Sound of Islay; and even the glories of that noble waterway were somewhat obscured by the doubt as to whether its southern outlet were not too rocky to be respectable. Providence smiles on those who tempt her in our impertinent fashion. Mild breezes carried us past the formidable Mull where certain queer eddyings and ripplings aroused our negligent curiosity without calling up any picture of the savage tumult which would riot round the headland in a hard wind on the weather-going tide. It was not until we actually entered Gourock Bay late on a dark blowy evening that we became thoroughly alive to some of the difficulties of short-handed sailing. Too long accustomed to solitude and sea-room, we came storming with magnificent nonchalance into an anchorage thickly dotted with anchor lights swaying above hulls invisible in the darkness and balefully warning us off from every discernible resting-place. "Two's enough to

---

* Members of his crews in later years, including Basil Williams quoted earlier, testify to Erskine's culinary skill.

manage her" had been one of our smug commonplaces latterly; but six seemed scarcely enough now, with the tiller, the anchor, the lead, the sheets, the halyards, and the arrangements for a lookout all crying for attention from two harassed mariners inaudible to one another in the whistle of wind and rattle of canvas. Our executive system dissolved in anarchy; we blundered miserably about, missing stays, gybing cataclysmically, shaving a bowsprit here and a jigger there, until more by accident than design we brought up in an apparently free space, sullenly deaf to the cries of a dim figure in pyjamas on board a neighbouring craft. We turned in with a presentiment of evil, to find in the morning that our anchor was irrevocably foul of some moorings whose owner presently swept up in a spruce racer and gave us his views on our seamanship. The sequel was both ignominious and expensive. For us the sharpest sting in the episode was that it was incidental not to blue-water hazards but to harbour work, a secondary and inglorious side of the maritime career. We had yet to learn that this kind of work, honourable or not, was in the long run the most troublesome and difficult part of sailing short-handed or singlehanded.'

This was not the only occasion on which Gourock gave them problems. They were joined by Walter Runciman, son of a rich shipping magnate and a keen yachtsman, who would later own a series of boats a great deal more splendid than anything Childers ever aspired to – and draw some gentle mockery from him as a result! – and cruised up the Western Isles. After Runciman had left them, Childers wrote to him: 'I must tell you about our adventures after. We left Rothesay that afternoon with a reef down and were becalmed for hours. We got to Gourock at 11 p.m. Drawing near, we had a great dispute as to which was Gourock Bay, complicated by opposite statements about lights in the chart and Directions. We ultimately cast anchor by a steam yacht in a place which Henry swore to be Gourock, and woke up to find it wasn't, next day! However it was the next bay to it and a good anchorage.'

His *Times* account goes on:

'It was a relief, two days later, to regain the peace and privacy of the open sea, there, as we vowed, to vindicate ourselves in our own eyes by some enterprise of real moment. A run from the

Clyde direct to Dublin Bay would obliterate many evil memories, and a pleasant northerly wind carrying us slowly past the Cumbraes confirmed us in this purpose. Night fell, fine and clear – our first complete night at sea since our emancipation. Who can describe the emotions of that first night, with the rapture of freedom in adventure, and the strangely paradoxical sense of added loneliness and at the same time, of wider companionship? It is true that the low hiss of the foam under the lee bow takes a mysterious, almost a sinister note, unlike the vivacious melody which it plays in the sparkling sunlight, and the vessel, with her slender upper rigging fretting against the stars, seems very small and isolated. On the other hand, the flashing of distant light-houses – flashing for you, and far easier to identify than the outline of a foreshortened headland – speaks of a great watchful organisation for mutual help; and even the passing steamers, rather formidable juggernauts by day, especially in confined waters, conform, provided your lights are bright (and they cannot, within the limits of reason, be too big, bright, and high in the rigging), to the code of sea law which was made for you in common with all sea travellers. In short, you are conscious of full membership in a great masonic brotherhood with all its rights, privileges and obligations. But these are high thoughts, and there remain a great number of prosaic, practical matters, connected with the log, the binnacle lamp, the chart, the stowage of movables below, and above all the accessibility and tidiness of ropes on deck, which in fine weather seem easy and sometimes superfluous, but which in rough weather are apt to assume over-whelming importance. The only safe rule, though a counsel of perfection for beginners, is systematically to provide in such like matters for a gale of wind. Though we were tolerably conscientious, I know that the gentle wind and the undimmed stars lulled us into a certain indifference as to the course of things under less favourable conditions.

'The breeze died away towards morning, and left us becalmed, and still, I think, just in sight of Ailsa Craig. There were several hours of tantalizingly variable airs, and then a steady breeze from the northeast, bringing up a rapid succession of compact white clouds. We held on our way rejoicing, even wishing, in our folly, that our mainsail, already too big, were bigger. These feelings underwent a change as the wind grew stiffer and squallier and the sea began to rise. We held on too long, as beginners are always inclined to do, and only under pressure of the last necessity hove-to to reef. Then indeed we were face to face with realities. When reefing in sheltered water, with a hand to help, we had never estimated the numbing and blinding effect of violent motion and driven spray; the difficulty of doing the simplest thing with the fingers, the impossibility of exerting continuous force on the reef-tackle, with the slippery deck bucking and heeling beneath one's clumsy seaboots. Inch by painful inch, with many pauses for breath and balance, we brought the tackle home, lashed the pennant to the boom, and laboriously tied each reef-point round the intractable folds of wet canvas.

'Then we looked at one another and at the empty cringle of the second reef, mocking us far out of arm's reach. What fools we had been not to sail with the second pennant ready rove! But there was no use looking at the job. "Reeve it or take the consequences" shrieked the voice of a passing squall, and I can feel now the sinking sensation as my brother climbed out astride the leaping boom, suspended over the foam, and clutching the leech for dear life, worked the rope through the cringle and down to the sheave on the boom. There, swollen with wet, it stuck for an agonising minute or two while, crouching beneath, all the romance knocked out of me, I saw behind the sport we followed with such ardour and gaiety the solemn issues of life and death. Spent but triumphant, he came back out of the very valley of the shadow, it seemed, and we slowly completed our second reef. The third would not have come amiss, but we were tired out and resolved to make shift, should occasion arise, with tricing up the tack or dropping the peak.

'So we bore up for the run down the Irish Channel. And what a run it was! There was no real vice in the weather; only one of those hard, persistent northeasters which in summer sometimes attain, but never exceed, the force of a moderate gale. Hour after hour, as we gripped the quivering tiller by turns, the good-natured greybacks shouldered up on the quarter, hove us on their broad backs, and swept majestically ahead. Yet it was certainly a grim enough prospect when evening came on, with the wind still holding shrill and hard, and the sea growing grey and menacing to the view. Already cold, wet, and tired, we must face the manifold ordeals of the second night, so dramatically different from the first. It was hard enough on deck, and more daunting still below, in the reeling, rocking little cabin, where divers unsecured impedimenta drifted about – here a broken glass, there a sodden cushion – and where everything was wet (for that rare luxury in small yachts, a completely watertight skylight, was not ours), where the lamp, tossing in its gimbals, smoked and flared, and where a permanent odour of paraffin, coupled with an infernal jingle from the forecastle, spoke of a stove or oil-can overturned. In this unnerving environment one must pencil courses and bearings, laboriously humour the parallel rulers over a chart clammy with spray, and scrutinize the small print of Brown's *Nautical Almanac* for the details of lights and currents. In the midst comes a despairing cry from the helmsman that the binnacle lamp – that eternal bane of the small yachtsman – has blown or flickered out, and that means a disgusting but infinitely delicate task of manipulation and adjustment. It is wonderful how the smell of oil pervades all one's most strenuous memories of cruising; and naturally, for these rather sordid functions below decks are often more trying to the spirit than the stirring, driving life above, whatever its hardships and perils.

'In the longest and hardest passage, however, there comes a moment when you begin to feel definitely that all is well, when humour banishes care and fatigue, and the thought of arrival in port inspires a splendid exultation. Rockabill light was far astern, Howth light as we approached succumbed to the strengthening dawn, and at last, blear-eyed, worn out, but unspeakably proud and happy, we swung round the pierhead of Kingstown Harbour, picked our way smoothly and warily – though, alas! with no one to applaud – among the still sleeping yachts, dropped our anchor, stowed our sails, and slept.'

This account was written fifteen years later. Childers' letter to Walter Runciman, written soon after their arrival, is much more matter-of-fact. A couple of details which do not appear in the above are worth inclusion. 'We had two gybes to negotiate,' he wrote, 'and by Jove I shan't forget getting in that mainsheet. Most of the time we had the sail scandalized a good deal, but the pace was splendid. We came the last hundred miles in eleven hours.' Which is good going by any standard.

Henry and Erskine made one more cruise that season. It was their most ambitious, and, it seems, their last in *Shulah*. Erskine described it vividly in a letter to Walter Runciman from Glendalough.

'We had a great ambition to sail direct to Land's End so on Sept. 22 (I think) we left Kingstown in a strong NW breeze and had only the trysail as a precaution for a long passage, but by dint of the balloon foresail we got to Wicklow very quick; then the wind shifted right round to S by W and left us swearing! We beat all night round the line of lightships down there, but she goes to windward horribly slowly under trysail and we were only off Wexford at dawn, so we got a pilot in. Next day we vowed we would chance it, bustled the trysail down below and set the mainsail; the same thing happened; we beat all night and put in at Waterford, a lovely harbour ending in a long piece of river sailing till you reach the town. We had burst our jib halyard and smashed a light-board so we decided to wait there for repairs and a fair wind. Two days later it was a glorious morning with a fair wind about W by N, so away we went, under whole mainsail. We reached open sea about 12 midday and steered due S; there was a steady beam wind, just enough and not too much for the canvas; it lasted all night and at dawn we were in sight of the north coast of Cornwall. Then Land's End and the Longships came in sight; when just off the Longships we were becalmed in a heavy tumbling sea chiefly due to a tiderip. It was misery and involved starvation! The wind was very light all that day and spoilt our time into Penzance which we crept into at 5 o'clock threading through scores of luggers. Next morning there was a fine breeze from the W and we left about 1 with two reefs down. We had a grand run to the Lizard, but then it came on thick and rainy and the wind increased, dead aft though. Altogether we were very glad to sight the Breakwater light at Plymouth about 9. We had been in sight of the Eddystone for some time but it kept mysteriously disappearing for long intervals in the most uncanny way – rain, I suppose. There is a breakwater a mile long across the mouth of Plymouth Bay and we anchored behind this. I was pretty tired as Henry had had a bad headache and I had been steering the whole time. Next day we woke up to find ourselves in a simply glorious harbour; we jogged down under foresail only and annexed moorings near the Promenade pier. At Plymouth we stuck, though we wanted to get to Southampton, but the blow we had the night before proved to be the forerunner of hard equinoctials. So we found a yard at Plymouth, made terms and laid her up there and then and went home.

'A jolly little wooden punt is a new acquisition since you were with us: it goes on deck beautifully and weighs nothing and tows marvellously. We had her towing behind that evening going to Plymouth; like fools we were too lazy to get her on board. The sea was heavyish after the Lizard, but she never shipped a drop: once only she bore bang down on the stern of the yacht and gave her a peck, which frightened Henry out of his wits down below!'

And that is the last we hear of *Shulah*; they sold her in 1895 to a Plymouth man. Childers, though a prolific letter writer, did not keep a diary, except on special occasions, nor any regular record of his boats beyond the fair logs describing his cruises. For information on when he bought or sold a particular boat we have to rely on *Lloyd's Register of Yachts*, an occasional mention in one of his letters to Runciman, or a laconic note at the start of a logbook, where these have survived. *Shulah*'s has not, nor is she mentioned after that autumn of 1893. In any case, a new phase of his life was about to start. Cambridge and the Law Tripos were behind him, and the next year he took up his appointment as a Clerk in the House of Commons. Much of his spare time was spent at Glendalough and in 1894 he was writing to Runciman 'I have bought a Kingstown "Waterwag", i.e. a local type of open sailing boat shaped so [a rough sketch suggested something vaguely pear-shaped] with a centreboard, carted it up to the lake. . . .' Lough Dan, in fact, close to the house, on which he and Henry used to take friends for a sail.*

Sailing was very much in his mind, and it was in October of that same year that he suggested in another letter to Runciman 'Wouldn't it be splendid to sail to the West Indies?' Six months later, he wrote, 'Now for some sailing shop! Just before Easter [1895] I bought an 18 foot half-decked centreboard boat, lug and jib, and lodged her at Greenhithe . . . she is not beautiful but very workmanlike and I was quite satisfied with her.' This was *Marguerite*, to be nicknamed *Mad Agnes*. In her, Childers considerably extended his experience both of sailing and cruising.

---

* See Edith Picton Turbervill's contribution to *Myself When Young*, edited by the Countess of Oxford and Asquith, for she was one of them.

III

Mad Agnes 1895-7

The purchase of *Marguerite* marked the second stage in Erskine Childers' cruising education. After the monstrous *Shulah* she might seem a surprising choice, for she was no more than a dayboat; but in fact there was sound logic in the move. For most of the waters round the British Isles a draught of 30 inches is a lot more practical than one of 8 feet 6 inches; more important still, she was perfectly manageable singlehanded.

Childers gave a detailed, fondly detached description of her in *The Cruise of the Marguerite*, published in the Cruising Club *Journal*.

'The *Marguerite* is a small half-decked sailing boat, 18 feet in length overall and 6 feet beam. Her draught, without plate, is 2 feet 6 inches aft and 2 feet 1 inch forward. The centreplate is 5 feet 6 inches long, and, when down increases the draught to 4 feet 6 inches. The boat is clinker-built and varnished, and her canvas consists of a balance lug and jib. As to deck, she has a foredeck from stem to mast and 18 inch waterways, with a 3 inch coaming all round.

'She has one 20 pound anchor, with 20 fathoms of chain, a pair of sweeps, one of Norie & Wilson's spirit compasses (50s.) in one of their most convenient guinea binnacles.

'As for sleeping accommodation, I have a specially designed bell-tent of oiled canvas, laced (when in use) round the coaming, and bent to a halyard or runner by an eyebolt at the apex and hauled taut. The bedroom under apex is 4 feet 6 inches. Our couches consist of two reindeer hair mattresses, which make most efficient life-preserving gear.

'Comfort was not, naturally, at the highest pitch; its chief foe was bad weather, of which I had relatively little, for rain complicated everything. However, management and practice did much. The tent was waterproof, and my kit could be kept perfectly dry. I spread waterproof sheets on the floor after a wet day, and I may say I never slept better on a big yacht, or even on shore. For cooking I used two simple spirit stoves. In disregard of ancient precedent I have excluded meals from my log altogether as of less than no interest to anybody but the consumer at the moment of consumption; but I may say in general that it was easy to provide oneself with all the usual amenities of cruising life. Nevertheless, I must admit that in practice, lack of space and the absence of a permanent roof tended to make one content with great simplicity.'

Characteristically, within a week of his first sail in her he launched out by himself on a ten-day Easter cruise, arranging to pick up two friends, Ivor Lloyd-Jones and Richards, at Folkestone. All his accounts of sailing from the Thames are charged with detail of a world that has quite vanished, and the log of this trip is a fair sample.

'*11 April*. Wind NW light, very fine . . . started at 2 p.m. on first of the ebb, feeling pleasantly experimental. Went down with fleet of barges, beautiful to see and valuable to observe: no need of charts. Lovely afternoon. Worked the south shore to Broadness, then close in to the north shore to the Ovens buoy, past Northfleet, Gravesend and Tilbury. Well inside the Ovens on this tide. Then the south shore again for the rest of the day, round all the Blyth buoys. A little nervous about the Swatchway but with barges to follow found it easy. Getting dark at the Grain Spit buoy. Had intended to spend night at Sheerness but breeze and fine weather induced change of mind, so held on. Lit lantern, hauled up centreplate, and with certainty of plenty of water steered SE by E, all barges having disappeared up the Medway. Just caught glimpse of the Middle Cant buoy in the dark. Passed south of the 4 fm channel, wind very light. At 10 p.m. anchored

2½ miles off Herne Bay. First night at sea. Rather restless but quite warm.'

He spent the next night in Ramsgate Harbour, and reached Folkestone at 5 p.m. on the 15th. Next day he and his friends set off on their first-ever Channel crossing.

'*16 April.* Ivor, Richards and self. Started for Boulogne at midday. Wind E moderate. Very sunny. Started double-reefed, deceived by lightness inshore into shaking one out: soon blew much fresher, biggish sea. Richards, weather side amidships, wet but patient. Steered S to allow for E-going tide. Very little traffic; passed under stern of Varne lightvessel; fired two condensed questions about tide and the Colbart Bank, sailor bawled answers and spontaneous rider which none of us could catch: uneasiness on board! Thick haze hid all trace of Gris Nez but calming of sea told us we were under its lee – wind lighter. Sighted Napoleon's monument above Boulogne and then cathedral and town. At 4 wind very light, later dead calm. Then small breeze. Came slowly between piers; ransack of brains and books for French sea phrases. '*Ou faut-il jeter l'ancre?*' almost launched. Abandoned from suggestiveness of habits of polypus. Observant crowd on pier. '*Ou faut-il mouiller?*' Yells from shore. '*Voulez-vous venir à bord.*' Prolonged yelling. Shipped a youth who promised to take her to a good berth for night. Ashore ourselves – to Post Office and piers to find out steamer for Richards who must return same night. (N.B. his first visit abroad!) 9 p.m. before we dined, at hotel next to station. Cigars at a *café-chantant*. Saw Richards off at midnight. I. and self back to hotel – dead tired.

'*17 April.* Breakfast at 9 and stroll round harbour. Watched morning drill on a French revenue cutter. All the weight of officialdom couldn't hoist a pennant correctly. Slovenly show. On board at 12 and rowed out: talk about tides, etc to youth – said tide adverse till 2, but we started hoping for wind. Dead calm. Drifted S for 2 hours then light SW air. Tide turned, made slow way N. Heavy showers at 6. From 6 till 12 dead calm – light airs from every quarter – heavy showers. In the clear intervals South Foreland and Gris Nez lights marvellously brilliant. Passed E of Varne light 4 miles to allow for W-going tide on the English shore, but so long getting over that that tide ended and new one

set in. Off Dover got into a thick stream of traffic. Ivor worked
lantern. A crisis once: lantern went out – all matches wet – all
lights obscured by rain – compass invisible and a steamer bearing
down on us from astern. Found a dry match!'

They got to Folkestone at 4.45 a.m., slept all day and spent
most of the next night at a fancy-dress ball, but the log does not
explain or comment on this laconic and surprising entry.
Afterwards they sailed back to Greenhithe by easy stages, and the
cruise ended with a race against a barge called *Black Duck* as
they beat back to their mooring.

That summer Erskine and Ivor Lloyd-Jones or another friend,
William Le Fanu, began to explore the creeks and inlets and
rivers of the Essex coast – complicated work which he would
later draw upon for a *Times* article and which was useful training
for cruising among the Frisian Islands two years later. At night
they slept on the bottomboards under a sail or tent rigged over
the boom; they cooked on a Primus; and the log is alive with
the high spirits of young men thoroughly enjoying their adventures. 'New awning for night unluckily left behind (so had to use
mop-uplifted sail every night). Le Fanu had old cricket bag –
good idea – fits into bows. Pressed beef staple food. Other extreme
Green Chartreuse' is one entry that suggests the mood; the
following, some idea of the ditch-crawling in which they became
involved.

'It was now dusk but we determined to push right through
Swale and knowing there must be very little water thought best
to use the flood we had. Charts were silent and we had no local
knowledge. There ensued a most interesting piece of sailing in
which, with much difficulty, we picked up what channel there
was by sounding in the dark, often running ashore. Unhappily,
owing to the dark, it is impossible to give an idea of the true
channel as we hammered it out. All that can be said is that for
most of the way it followed the north shore. We were much
confused by a barge which seemed to be sailing on dry land on our
port hand (south shore): we concluded it was going behind
Fowley Island, though the chart gives less water there than anywhere. I should have given it up and gone back to deep water, but
Ivor was indomitable and showed inspired appreciation of the
faintest surface appearances. Having the wind dead foul made it

all the more difficult.* It was midnight before the water got permanently deeper. A yacht which followed us up from Warden Point at about 10 p.m. ran on a shoal on which we had been sitting for ten minutes. She promptly submitted to fortune and made ready for the night. We anchored at 12.30 in a narrow reach (between Elmley Chapel and Saltbox?) opposite a huge factory, in 15 ft. (high water) with a comfortable sense of difficulties overcome.'

Sounding, like supporting the sail at night, and other functions, was achieved with the invaluable mop. Later, they crossed the Medway – the heat was 'awful' and there was no wind – and anchored off the Isle of Grain to wait for the tide to take them back to Greenhithe. It was a 'lovely evening with a gorgeous western sky. Breeze from the Essex shore was loaded with perfumes, hay, clover and flowers, rudely varied by the Mucking lighthouse which gave us a powerful gust of paraffin! A wonderful night for smells.'

There could be no sharper contrast than between this kind of sailing and that which he and Henry had been doing in *Shulah*; indeed, Childers reversed the normal order of things by starting with the Irish Sea and the west coast of Scotland, and then pottering among the shoals and mudbanks of the East Coast. But unlike many cruising men, he showed an equal partiality for both blue water and tortuous inshore navigation – the more tortuous the better. The latter, demanding accurate chartwork and close concentration, and involving very often a continuous series of emergencies, some humorous, some uncomfortable, and a few downright alarming, presented a challenge which he loved.

One or two notes from his logs of those early cruises are worth quoting. On one occasion, anchored in the River Colne above Brightlingsea, they were asked the way by a passing barge. 'Said we were strangers in these parts: barge ran aground!' Nearing Harwich the next day, 'sighted *Britannia* and *Ailsa* in last round of race, also the Twenties and Forties and host of miscellaneous yachts. Cruised in the bay, watching.' But Harwich itself they found 'dirty, mean and blatant.'

Later that same year Childers decided on something very much more ambitious. He was now a member of the Cruising Club,

---

* 'This part of the channel, known as the Grounds, is very intricate and difficult. . . . As the East Swale is unlit, its navigation is not advised after dark.' *Pilot Guide to the Thames Estuary.*

and the cruise which he undertook, in three separate stages from early July to the beginning of October, won him the Admiral de Horsey Silver Cup for the best cruise of 1895. The first two parts took him, singlehanded, from the Thames round to Bembridge on the Isle of Wight, and from there on to Poole, where he 'spent the next few days sailing about the sheltered waters, generally three-reefed in very stormy weather, with limited cargoes of small South London boys, a camp of whom had been organised by some friends of mine at Ower Farm, on the south side of the harbour. It is interesting work (even with shifting boy-ballast) exploring the labyrinths of creeks and islands. The channels, though narrow, are excellently boomed, but it is the very multiplicity of marks which bewilders the eye and causes confusion. Deviate a yard and you are embedded in mud of unique tenacity. But after all deviation was the only sure road to knowledge, and the more tenacious the mud, the better one remembered the error.'

This from his published account in the Cruising Club *Journal*. His log gives a rather more lively picture of what was entailed. '*3 August*. Took five boys for a sail. They behaved well though wildly excited and formed valuable shifting ballast. Unhappily we grounded on the ebb and remained stuck for three hours, "alone in the woide woide sea" as Tommy Atkins said. Boys demolished every ounce of food on board and then like a litter of puppies simultaneously dropped down and slept. In an hour all woke up simultaneously and were very rowdy. Another boatful passing finally towed us off.' On another occasion the tiller broke, and, once more, the versatile mop was brought into service.

Despite the weather and the mud, one feels the lads regarded the whole thing as a mad adventure: Childers himself seems to have been less sure. In a letter to Walter Runciman, he says, 'I was rather a failure having got not an altogether correct idea of what I was meant for there. However, we will pass over that.'

In between the two stages he had left *Marguerite* at Bembridge and joined Runciman for a trip in his very different vessel, the *Edith*. In apologising for not writing subsequently, Childers said, 'I can only plead the contrast between the luxurious facilities of *Edith* [a 30 foot cutter, of 12 tons TM] and the somewhat ignoble limitations of *Marguerite* – especially for writing purposes.' He enjoyed pulling 'Runcy's' leg about his very superior yachts. The following year he was writing to him about *Waterwitch*, his 'brand new line of battleship. I will go and smell round your boat at Lymington at Easter perhaps and it will be interesting. A bathroom, ye Gods what debauched luxury! A ladies' cabin! Shades of our Viking forefathers!!'

When several years later Childers was to create the character of Carruthers in *The Riddle*, he had, thanks to Runciman, the background at his fingertips. 'Cowes, with a pleasant party and hotels handy, was all very well. An August cruise on a steam yacht in French waters or the Highlands was all very well, but what kind of a yacht was this?' (*Riddle*, Chapter I, p. 19. Chapter II, p. 28.) In the account of the present cruise there occurs also the authentic voice of Davies. Forced, on passage from the Thames, to lie alongside the Admiralty Pier in Dover, he wrote, 'I may say that I always made a point of keeping in open anchorage at night in preference to the inside of a tidal harbour whenever and wherever this was possible. I have the strongest antipathy to the dirt, odours, publicity and general discomfort of a quayside berth in a crowded basin.' 'No dues, no stinks, no traffic, no worries of any sort,' Davies remarks contentedly, as he anchors *Dulcibella* in the lee of the Hohenhorn, among the Frisian sandbanks. 'It's better than a Baltic cove even, less beastly civilisation about.' (*Riddle*, Chapter XII, p. 110.)

Back in the Solent with Ivor Lloyd-Jones as crew, Cowes during the Regatta Week was 'a bewildering, brilliant spectacle. Every yard of anchorage occupied with every size and sort of steam and sailing yacht. The whole edged with English and German battleships, the *Hohenzollern* conspicuous, a marvellous compound of destructive force and graceful luxury.'

Those German battleships were not yet regarded as presenting a threat to British naval supremacy: Russia and France, with their ability to challenge, from the Dardanelles to Toulon, Britain's hold over the Mediterranean and the Suez Canal, and therefore her lines of communication with the Far East, seemed far more dangerous; while in the Far East itself Japan was suddenly emerging as a naval power to be reckoned with. Gradually, however, and in ways which in 1895 were still only dimly visible, the complacent nineteenth century was melting and reforming into the turbulent and dangerous twentieth.

That evening Childers and Lloyd-Jones watched the German Emperor land at the Royal Yacht Squadron steps. Cowes was packed, and after dark there was a fireworks display which they watched from the comparative seclusion of *Marguerite*.

'It was five weeks', Childers wrote in the Cruising Club *Journal*, 'before I could join my boat again for another short cruise, this time with my brother. We had no definite plan before us, but made up our minds to sail west for a little, with a vague intention of returning to the Thames before long, as it was now late in the season for cruising. Circumstances, as will be seen, altered our views.'

Apart from falling foul of the tiderace off Peveril Point at the southern arm of Swanage Bay, and breaking the tiller for the *third* time, they had a calm and fairly uneventful sail as far as Weymouth. Then, on September 25, comes the log entry:

'Under way at 7. Wind E, fresh to light. Started to go E, but at 9 decided to cross Channel. Set course SE by E for Cherbourg. Good breeze all day, at first two reefs, then whole sail. In the evening dead calm – lovely night – moonlight.

'*26 Sept.* Had kept sailing all night with faint air from the E; just before broad dawn picked up Cap Barfleur light, electric flashing. At sunrise, so only sighted land at 10 – breeze still very slight. Identified Caps Barfleur and Levi and steered for the latter against a strong tide but with a better breeze. Sailing Directions gave terrifying account of race off Cap Levi but this day it was nothing. Arrived at Cherbourg at 2 p.m. and moored in the Avant Port by a revenue lugger. Declined services of a ruffianly-looking sailor who warned us against robbers, accepting assurance of honest looking ferryman that boat would be all right.' In their 18 foot open boat, with only light airs to joggle them along, they had covered the 60 miles in 29 hours: not a fast passage, perhaps, but by far *Mad Agnes*'s longest in open water. Considering the lateness of the season, they had been lucky – but their adventures were to come.

'Ashore to Hotel du Louvre,' the log continues, 'where we dined and H. slept. Coffee and billiards afterwards in a *café* – then a *café chantant*, one degree lower in the scale than Calais, but amusing in a way. Town mean, dirty and uninteresting. Dinner very disappointing.'

So much for Cherbourg! Next morning the two brothers set sail once more, for Le Havre. That night, in brilliant moonlight and drifting across the Baie de la Seine in light airs, Erskine notes:

'About 1 a.m. I was steering – Henry sleeping – when I noticed she was going very dead and presently discovered that the wire rope raising centreboard had broken short at the plate and left plate hanging plumb down, giving us a draught of 7 feet 6 inches with no possible means of lessening it or raising the plate. She refused to go properly to windward, so we bore up to the south to make the land. Wind very light. 1 p.m. before we sighted land very close in the haze. Couldn't identify it at first: ran in to anchor but took ground. Decided to beach her and signalled to shore for assistance. At 4.30 a boat and three men came out. The place turned out to be Ver. But for the haze, easily recognisable by lighthouse on hill. Beach of sand shoals out very gradually for half a mile.* After discussion decided to go on to Courseulles, 2 miles, taking two men to pilot us. During the turn to windward had most entertaining talk to the men, one red and round, the other tall and black, both vivacious amusing fellows and eaten up with curiosity. Made Courseulles at dusk. The usual French harbour – narrow channel between rocks, then between two long piers where you get becalmed. Then the Avant Port, almost dry at low water, then wet dock. Sleepy do-nothing place little frequented by ships, but a good dock. After lengthy search for the *pontier*, gates were opened and we moored in the wet dock. Paid our men and parted on the best of terms. I went ashore and supped in the Café au Parc des Huîtres.

'At 7 I went ashore and searched for the *Constructeur de bateaux*. Explained accident and he promised to help. Lowered mast and rowed her over to a large brig (almost our sole companion in the *bassin*) whose crew rigged a tackle to a yard, passed the rope under our bows, and hoisted the forepart out of the water in order to get at the plate. Rope broke so we emptied her of ballast and succeeded in getting at the after end of the plate and attaching a rope and raising it. Took her out of *bassin* at once and beached her on a hard in the Avant Port for remaining work.

'Courseulles is commercially dead, its only life being that of a watering-place in a small way. This means some rows of chalets and fantastic *café-restaurants* on the seaside, but the old town is

---

* Which was one of the reasons why that stretch of coast was chosen for the Normandy landings forty-nine years later.

pretty and interesting. We saw some beautiful old gateways fast going to rot. The people we found in every way delightful. We had all our meals at the same *café* (des Huîtres) and very good they were, especially the wine. The sailors who helped us were very good fellows. We talked to a lot of them and got on very well. We found they could talk amusingly on almost any subject whether within or beyond their intelligence. The one subject that irritated them was Germany. There was no wire rope to be got so we had to get a bit of our chain filed off and shackled onto the plate.

'This and other things caused delays but the work was at length finished in the evening. By the light of the moon we replaced the ballast and rigged the boat again. When all was ready we collected in a little knot on the bridge and asked what we should pay. They were five men altogether. They had a long whispered confabulation, and then the *Constructeur* as senior came forward and asked an absurdly small sum. Adjournment to a café where we paid it and something over. Men were delighted and stood us coffee, vermouth and cognac. Spent a most amusing half-hour with them. At 8 p.m. we went to get dinner, after which they met us again and "assisted" us to get under way. They all got on board, all talked at once, and all hauled at the same rope, generally the wrong one. We at last got out of the harbour and they left us on the bar in a scene of enthusiasm bordering on frenzy.

'It was 25 miles to Havre across the Bay of the Seine, but the electric flash-light on Cap de la Héve was brilliant on the horizon (it is said to be sometimes visible 50 miles). We left with a faint S air, but it so happened we had just started with the first of the bad weather, which lasted three weeks. Rain came on and we were soon two-reefed in a stiff breeze and rising sea. About 2 sighted the town lights of Havre, but had great difficulty in picking up the harbour lights. Had to run off course to windward to avoid a heavy beam sea, and hove-to (and three-reefed) for about an hour (it being low water) and fearing to approach the bar in the dark. Finally bore up to run for the harbour. No sooner done so than some violent rain squalls came obscuring all lights, even the electric at intervals, and making steering very difficult.

'*1 Oct.* In the first dawn we were approaching the land, but the mist prevented our seeing the position of the piers. Suddenly sighted a large fishing boat just ahead, apparently running for the harbour too. Thought it safe to follow her, and did so. Suddenly the wind changed instantaneously from SE to NW, causing us to gybe all standing (no damage) and set the topping-lift adrift, also setting up a confused cross-sea in which the boat behaved admirably. Blowing a hard gale. Suddenly made out both piers at distance of 200 yards, now right to windward owing to the change of wind. When quite near realised that we couldn't make the entrance. The question was, would she stay in the heavy sea there was? The fishing boat failed to do so and was driven on the rocks (or rather wall of the inner dock) and wrecked.

'We put her about, and she stayed beautifully. We tacked out about ¼ mile, shipping one nasty sea, came in again, and found we had gained nothing owing to strong adverse tide. Tacked out again but no better. Bore up and ran before the sea, following the coast south along miles of sheer brick wall forming the Havre docks and building yards. At length came to a beach and shallow water. Identified the tower on the Pointe du Hoe, and rounded the point in very shoal water, though it was nearly high tide. Anchored in calm water: went on to a little land-locked creek onto the mud, where we dried almost immediately. Secured boat fore and aft and walked into Havre, leaving boat rather recklessly in a completely dreary waste of marsh and mud with only one or two fishermen visible in the distance. Put up at Hôtel de l'Angleterre – good, but not for meals.'

That they escaped without foundering or sharing the fate of *Espoir en Marie*, dashed to pieces against the harbour wall, speaks well both for Erskine's coolness and seamanship and for *Marguerite*'s qualities as a sea-boat. A cutting from the local paper tucked into the logbook and headed '*Naufrage d'un bateau de pêche*' amply supports Childers' description: in fact, it sounds even more perilous in French:

'Dans la nuit de mardi à mercredi une violente brise du sud-ouest soufflant en tempête forçait les bateaux de pêche à rentrer au port. Une plâte de peche, l'*Espoir en Marie*, s'étant présentée vers six heures, hier matin, a l'ouverture du port a été drossée par le courant sur le front de la Floride où elle vint se briser. La plâte coula à pic. A ce moment les lames deferlaient avec fracas et balayaient les jetées.'

The vessel was a total loss, but the crew of four '*après bien des efforts'* were rescued. The gale continued for the next three days, and it was not until October 4 that they were able to reach the boat and strip her out, preparatory to shipping her back to England by steamer. On the 5th:

'Less wind so went to the Hoe to sail boat to Havre. In the nick of time to see her being towed bodily away by piratical fishermen to a distant shore. Hastily chartered a boat and gave chase. Pirates, seeing us, anchored the *Marguerite*. We came up and a fire of questions and answers began. Some cock-and-bull story ready about the chain having broken. Boarded and found a terrible mess: chain gone, two locked lockers burst open and contents (whisky and wine) gone. It was high water and they had taken her to a place where she would have dried in another half-hour. As she was anchored (on a lee shore) by the jib halliards (!) we found it rather difficult to get under way. Managed it and sailed away chainless, grateful that it was no worse.'

They decided not to try to sail home, and the last two log entries complete the story.

'*7 Oct.* Brought her under the crane by the steamer, emptied ballast and had her hoisted on board. Very well and quickly done.
'*8 Oct.* Southampton at 6.30. Went ashore to breakfast and on return found her in the water with ballast in and all spars and gear on board. The job was admirably and rapidly done by the Company's men. Paid £2 11s 9d inclusive of every expense. Most satisfactory.'

Erskine Childers not only wrote the cruise up for the Cruising Club *Journal* but also for *The Field*, in which it appeared in December of the following year. Of the three versions, the last is the most consciously – even self-consciously – literary, and the second the most matter-of-fact. The log, itself obviously expanded from rough notes made under way, retains best the freshness and spontaneity of the adventure. But he was rapidly developing a clear concise style of his own, and one which, by the time he came to write *The Riddle*, could compass humour, dramatic action and, if less surely, character and dialogue.

In Chapter I we quoted from the article 'Single-handed

Cruising' which Childers wrote, anonymously of course, for *The Times* in 1909. The inclusion of the rest of it here is apposite, not merely as an example of how his writing had matured in the intervening nine years, and for the light it shines on his character, nor merely for its intrinsic interest, but because much of it is based on his memories of this first year in *Marguerite*. With the invulnerability of retrospection he is able to reveal more of his motives and feelings than he allows to appear in the casual bravado of the accounts written immediately after the events. The piece begins:

'Any one who has begun cruising in the truly independent spirit, who has gained nerve and practical skill by relying on his own wits and muscles and those of his amateur friend or friends, is sure to experience sooner or later a craving to pursue the sport, if only for a short time, single-handed. It is not easy to explain and justify this craving to those unacquainted with the life of the sea and accustomed to regard all sport as a social affair. Of all forms of solitude, solitude on the sea seems to most people the most unnatural and repellent.' There follows the passage quoted (on page 9), ending: 'It becomes a more and more fascinating exercise to see how far you can disprove the old copybook axiom that it is impossible to pay proper attention to two things at once.' And he goes on:

'Two! Let us suppose a comparatively simple case: breakfast between the North and South Foreland, a fair wind, a fair tide, and fair weather. There is no question of anchoring. Such conditions have to be accepted thankfully and used to the full, whatever the time of day or night, if you really mean to get anywhere. First and foremost there is the tiller, with its ceaseless claim for a hand which can only occasionally be spared. Back, thigh, shoulders, neck, any part of the body which happens to be most convenient, must be used in turn to apply the necessary pressure. Two spirit lamps, one for the tea, one for the eggs, however cunningly jammed into place, require vigilant watching and manipulation from eyes and fingers which have many other functions. A close lookout must be kept for the fairway buoys and passing ships, for this is one of the world's most crowded waterways. The chart, the binoculars, the compass are in frequent requisition. Here is a sheet to be trimmed, there a runner to be slackened; and just at the culinary climax there is sure to come an extra puff of wind which taxes all your sleight of hand and presence of mind – converts you into a veritable conjuror for the maintenance of the delicately balanced scheme of arrangements upon which your nourishment, and for that matter the safety of yourself and your vessel, depend. The strain lasts until the last spoon is washed up and stowed away. There has never been a moment at which you have not been distracted with little cares and apprehensions: and yet in retrospect, with the pipe going and leisure to appreciate the sun, breeze and swift motion, this seems to be the only way of really enjoying a meal.

'But – there are always many buts – you have probably bought this morning's amusement dearly. It seems to be a stern law of the sport that one gets nothing for nothing; generally, indeed, the charge is exorbitant for the most modest return in ease and relaxation. For the writer, who has been narrating from memory, the price of this breakfast idyll had already been paid in advance in the shape of a night of terrors in the Thames estuary. It was my first essay at a single-handed cruise, and from Greenhithe to Hole Haven and thence almost to the Nore there had been nothing to mar the exultant sense of freedom and power. A west wind and a sluicing ebb had whirled me down Sea Reach in company with a whole fleet of Thames barges, and it was not until I was abreast of Sheerness that I realised how much of my careless fortitude was due to the companionship of these homely, motherly craft. The sun was setting in a sombre haze, the estuary broadening into vast and dim proportions, and just at this solemn moment one after the other of my dusky friends hauled their wind for the Medway and, like heavy-winged moths, faded into gloom. It was a fearful temptation to turn and follow them, but defeat at this crisis would have been irretrievable. That thought braced my nerves for the lonely night to come.

'Off the East Swale I lost the ebb tide, and off Whitstable all but a faint draught of my westerly wind. There was nothing for it but to anchor in the open. It was a black night, with a mist just opaque enough to shroud all lights; the barometer was inclined to fall, and a swell beginning to roll in from the east was at once a presage of headwind to come and a source of much physical discomfort; for this was my first day of the season in open water. Supperless, spiritless (save for that last residuum of will which in the face of all reason insisted that this martyrdom was worth while), I trimmed and hoisted my anchor light and tried to sleep.

The mast whined with every roll; with every roll there were flickings and slappings of ill-tautened ropes which I had neither the energy to pacify nor the philosophy to ignore. Fevered dreams came at last, culminating in a hallucination that, like Shelley's doomed mariner "longing with divided will, yet no power to seek or shun", I was drifting in fatal impotence over a stormy sea. In point of fact, a brisk northeast wind, blowing athwart the flood, had awakened my little vessel into very lively motion. In daylight this would have seemed a very simple and welcome phenomenon; alone and in the chill depressing hour before dawn, when vitality is at its lowest, with shoals on either hand and all guides to navigation obliterated, I shivered miserably at the prospect. Now, as always, however, salvation came from the cogent need of immediately doing something definite, under capital penalties. Merely to light the binnacle lamp was to find a companion, benevolent, imperturbable, indicating the direction of the wind and the lie of the land and shoals. Enlightenment on these vital points heartens one for the wrestle with the anchor and sails, and when once the vessel has become a thing of life and action half the battle is over. At the worst one can heave-to and wait; at the best, groping with lead and compass, one can make progress in a light-draught boat even through such a restricted channel as the "overland passage" abreast of the Kent coast. And now dawn is breaking, grey and ghostly enough but not so misty as you thought, a buoy is sighted and safely identified, blurred traces of the coast appear, marks multiply, and at length the sun, dispelling the last vapours, dispels with them all that remains of mystery and doubt. Once more the ebb is under you. With an occasional northward tack you can lie your course fairly well for Margate Roads and the glistening Foreland cliffs beyond. One final board to clear the Longmore buoy, and the mainsheet sings through the sheaves – delicious music – as you bear up for Ramsgate and the Gulf Stream. Short as a child's is the recollection of those evil night hours, keen as a child's the zest for this reward, rightfully yours by conquest. And now for breakfast!

'Practice soon accustoms the spirit to severer tests than that of a misty night in "London River". On a coasting voyage one must always be prepared to be "caught" by bad weather at an exposed point, whether in the open or at anchor. The essential thing is to decide quickly and definitively which of two policies to pursue, that of blue water or shelter. It is nearly always a nicely balanced choice of evils, but the choice must be made and maintained without vacillation. Otherwise you court unnecessary risks, from which only good luck can save you, such as embayment on a lee shore or a prohibitive surf on a harbour bar which you have reached too late. Working down Channel, for example, along that inhospitable sixty miles of coast between Dover and Newhaven, you are assailed by a sou'wester between Hastings and Eastbourne. To go on or go back? Make your resolve and stick to it. If you harden your heart for a stiff thrash round Beachy Head, reef down and tackle the job with dash and tenacity. But the current round the Head may be adverse or the race too formidable. If you must turn, turn at once. Short of the Downs and Ramsgate the coast offers few alternatives: Rye, on the angle of a bay, approachable only at high water and highly perilous even then; Dungeness East Road, an open anchorage, exposed to any shift of wind south of sou'west; Folkestone, the last place for a small yacht; and Dover, a perfect refuge once gained, but in heavy weather presenting a most dangerous entrance to small craft, owing to the violent currents and backwash. You cannot afford to hesitate over these alternatives. Rye is a question of minutes, an error in which may leave you stranded or embayed, and Dungeness is eighteen miles – say, nearly three hours – from Dover, time enough to make the difference in the practicability of the latter harbour. Another and wholly different plan, more stimulating morally, more exhausting physically, easier in many ways for the boat, but involving substantial risks of its own, is to stretch out on the starboard tack for an offing, heave-to or lie to a sea anchor, and see the trouble through. What seems a heroic measure may in reality be the safest.

'A fair daylight run from port to port is to be regarded as a lucky windfall. Plans must be laid on the contrary assumption, and, as a rule, the main governing factors are sleep and the currents. A golden rule is to study and learn by heart in moments of leisure the run of the tides, the hours of high water, the buoys, lights and shoals on the coast ahead of you. It is waste of energy to beat to windward against a foul current. Those are the hours for rest and recuperation, if by hook or crook any resting-place not too precarious can be found. I am speaking, of course, of more or less exposed coasts. A cruising ground like the Highlands or the Danish fiords once gained, night problems are rarely serious.'

Childers goes on to describe the qualities to look for in a boat, and ends up with a portrait of *Marguerite* – 'stout and workmanlike, with no concessions to coquetry'. He also issues a measured warning against newfangledness in rig and gear: his advice throughout is that of experienced and well-tried common sense.

The final paragraph of the article seems puzzling unless one remembers that the entire soliloquy reflects his own experience, including the down-rating from the 8 ton *Shulah* to the 18 foot *Marguerite*, and up again, via *Vixen* and *Sunbeam*, to the near-Runcimanesque splendours of *Asgard*.

'There is only one drawback to single-handed cruising. By what seems at first an inexplicable contradiction, the very exercise which elicits self-reliance in solitude is liable to sap confidence in that wider range of adventure which companions and a larger vessel permit. The very smallness of your vessel opens your eyes to dangers which before you ignored. To meet these you instinctively take the line of least resistance, resort to creeks and tidal harbours hitherto undreamt-of, and cultivate a taste for short-cuts across banks and inshore channels behind tide-rips. In a word, you are apt to learn too much, and when you return to the larger life you may find you have lost something of the *élan* and unreserved enthusiasm which inspired long, bold passages and scorned shoal water.' And he ends with a characteristic Childers admonition: 'The only cure is stern self-arraignment at the bar of logic and common sense. If that checks the ailment, you may be sure that your strenuous solitary hours have not been spent in vain.'

Erskine Childers kept *Mad Agnes* throughout 1896 and for part of 1897. The logbook ends in April 1897: in August he bought *Vixen*. If he did any sailing during the intervening summer months, there is no record of it. His log for 1896 begins with the note that *Marguerite* had been fitted with new teak lockers – to replace those burst open by the 'piratical fishermen', presumably – new running rigging, and with the shrouds doubled to take light-boards: she was fitted out and in the water by the end of March.

All that season, either alone, with Henry, or with one or more of his old and well-tried friends, he coursed up and down the Solent, reached Poole again, sailed round the Isle of Wight, and weekend after weekend thrashed in and out of Lymington, Cowes,

Beaulieu River, the Hamble, and so on. These pleasant but on the whole unexacting trips are not worth reprinting in full, but one or two incidents give the flavour of them and will, without doubt, remind a good many sailing men of the joys and terrors of their 'prentice days.

Not, perhaps, the nightingales in the woods above Buckler's Hard, up the Beaulieu River; nor the following, all-too-familiar contretemps: 'Off Hurst lost tiller overboard and had to heave-to and convert the mop handle, now alas a familiar process, though this was a hitherto virgin mop handle.' Later, and none too soon, he replaced this wooden tiller with an iron one.

In May he had a rendezvous with Runciman in his new 'line of battle ship' *Waterwitch*, 24 tons, at Cowes. Childers' log reads: '*23 May.* R.E.C. alone ... found them moored in an awkward berth a good way up. Went across and anchored myself on the other side and foolishly left the boat in order to dine and sleep on the *Waterwitch*. It blew very hard in the night and I went off in the dinghy once as I thought *Marguerite* was dragging but she seemed all right – there was a heavy swell rolling in. Cowes is a brute of a place in NE winds.

'*24 May.* In the morning came on deck to see *Marguerite* going gaily upriver at her own sweet will. Chased her with Walter in the dinghy, boarded and found three turns of the chain round the fluke. Made sail two-reefed and beat down again. Suddenly dinghy got adrift and we had to chase it. Got up to it and Walter jumped in, but trying to jump over our rail on board again with the painter, upset the dinghy and got a ducking. Climbing back, however, successful. Tried to tow the dinghy bottom up, but it was like being anchored, so we had to cast her adrift to be rescued by a waterman. Beat down and anchored opposite Ratseys in a most unquiet berth, and then went back to *Waterwitch* for breakfast, I previously having also gone overboard while getting in the jib.'

Thereafter they sailed more or less in company as far as Poole and back. On the last day, 'Both bore up and ran for Southampton, I being much the fastest. Walter photoed me several times, and then boarded me and photoed *Waterwitch* while still running on our course.'

At this time he was keeping *Marguerite* at Picketts yard at West Quay, Southampton; with his later boats he made Bursledon on the Hamble his base. With a good train service to London, he could return on Sunday evening, sleep on board, have breakfast ashore, and be in his office in the House of Commons by 11 o'clock on Monday morning.

If, with the internal combustion engine still in its infancy, it was still perfectly possible to live in London and sail on the South Coast at weekends, there were occasions when to have had an engine in one's boat might have saved a certain amount of embarrassment: '*4 July* . . . At 4.30 tacked up Lymington channel to the town and anchored about ¼ mile from the railway pier. At 5.45 W.R.L. [William Le Fanu] arrived in train, but being no boat I had to get under way and go over to him. Got into a horrible mess on mud banks: it was the top of high water. Got him on board, but ran aground twice afterwards. Ultimately I had to swim off to the pier with a line and haul her off. Luckily the Yarmouth steamer had just left the pier and a grave scandal was averted!'

But 'short as a child's is the recollection of those evil [night] hours'; and laughter and sheer zest, for life, for sun and wind and salt water, for companionship and the pure delight of scudding along under sail, soon erase the memory of awkward moments like these. The next day after a glorious reach back across the Solent from Wootton they 'crept slowly against the ebb up to Southampton, dining in the light of the lantern at 8.30 and rowing to our moorings about 1.30 a.m. It was a lovely warm night and very pleasant. Just caught the 8.48 in the morning by dint of dressing in the dinghy up to the last moment.'

The Solent, then as now, was crowded in the summer. On one occasion Childers notes, 'Hoped to see the start of the big race (RSYC) but just arrived to see the finish at Calshot about 2.30, getting grand view of *Meteor* and *Britannia* and the rest: hundreds of yachts there.' And on another: 'Fine run with spinnaker back to Cowes, passing a dozen destroyers anchored at Spithead or steaming up to anchor; Nelson's *Foudroyant* was anchored there too. Saw the *Britannia* etc at Cowes.'

And so it went on right through into the autumn. From the pages of the logbook a number of vivid vignettes emerge. In Gosport in September, 'anchored and sent a note to Capt. Barrow of the *Majestic*. Reply inviting us aboard. Dressed our smartest. L. [Ivor Lloyd-Jones] winced under our waterman's tactful criticism of his yachting cap and bought new one . . . inspected ship with curiosity and amazement and subsided with whiskies and sodas with the captain.'

The following evening found them in Bursledon. 'Ashore and had a jolly walk. Lovely evening. Aboard at 7 to an elaborate table d'hôte of three courses. [In an open boat with two spirit lamps! – Ed.] Read Daudet till a late hour. Fearful night. Storms of wind and deluges of rain. At 2 a.m. tent leaking so that we got up, lit cigars and read *Pickwick* – "The Postman's Soirée" – for an hour and then to bed again.' The next day they gave up and went home, at that time, for Childers, a flat in the Temple, and back to the frowsty Clerks' Office in the House of Commons where, according to Basil Williams, 'Few realized that the unobtrusive little man with the glasses and the sciatic limp was leading a double life. He let none of us know until the information tumbled out one day, quite by chance that his weekends were spent in the Thames estuary, sailing singlehanded a scrubby little yacht.'

That October, singlehanded again, he took his 'scrubby little yacht' over a series of weekends back to Greenhithe. The weather was blustery and wet: there is a telling note for the 29th when, after struggling round the South Foreland, he crept into Ramsgate at five in the morning and tied up – 'Coffee in a shop near, very consoling!' – and he smashed the bowsprit on the pier of the railway bridge at Kingsferry, having 'disdained a tow'. Bowspritless but otherwise intact, *Marguerite* was back in the care of Bob Eales, to be laid up for the winter, on November 1.

So ended a long and active season's sailing with plenty of variety, if lacking the dramas of the previous year's hop across the Channel. With every trip he was gaining experience, knowledge and confidence – and thoroughly enjoying himself into the bargain. He never mentions specifically the difficulties of navigating in an open boat, but particularly in dirty weather they would have been formidable: only matched, possibly, by navigating in an aircraft with an open cockpit, which he was to undertake many years later. Unquestionably, with his meticulous mind and intense powers of concentration, teamed with a delight in taking calculated risks, he had the temperament for the work and a great relish for it. Little wonder that every detail in *The Riddle* rings true.

Before the cruise that was to supply him with the setting for that novel, however, he still had one more short cruise ahead in *Mad Agnes*, in the spring of 1897. With a new bowsprit, a new tent, and her bottom painted light green, she was in commission by the end of March. Three of them had a stormy Sunday roaring down the Thames and back; and then, early in April, he and Le Fanu went out for the day with 'the first ladies to patronise the *M.A.* – Dulcie and Constance.* Wind N. strong, three-reefed. Cold. Started about 2 and had a fine reach up to Purfleet and back to Northfleet and beat home. The ladies enjoyed themselves greatly, showing the utmost coolness and fortitude when we shipped a green sea from a steamer's wash, and proved themselves very good sailors. Tea at inn. Back by 7.' Despite the success of the expedition, however, it never seems to have been repeated.

A few days later Erskine, Henry, Le Fanu and G. Garland set off for their Easter cruise in half a gale and with three reefs down. Henry left them at Queenborough; the other three headed down-river through the West Swin to the River Crouch. They were stormbound in Burnham for thirty-six hours, then got away for the double mouth of the Blackwater and the Colne. They were safely across Bachelors Spit and reaching across for Mersea when 'Bewildered by a forest of booms and ran straight on the Long Spit at about half-ebb. Soon dried and found ourselves stranded on a dreary mudflat with half a gale blowing, till 9.30. Took out an anchor and waited philosophically. Dined at an angle of 45° about 8 with tent up, and then made all ready – three-reefed and double-reefed jib – and floated off after some bumping from the sea rolling in, and in a few minutes were safely anchored in Mersea Creek.' A couple of days later, after thrashing round in the estuaries, Le Fanu and Garland departed, and Childers decided, after some hesitation, to explore Havengore Creek, which opens onto the Maplin Sand in the approaches to the Thames estuary. This turned out to be a very bad idea.

'Turned back for the creek and tried to beat in against foul wind and tide. Tacked too far over on the east shore and grounded fast and was soon dry on the highest part of the bank, just at the entrance, on sandy mud at 2.30 p.m. Awkward position, as very near high water of the best tide for some time to come. The local idiot soon came up and blinked mistily at me, with an occasional drip of gloomy comment on the situation. Hailed Coastguard on opposite shore and got rowed across, as I saw a village in the distance and wanted to wire to L. [Ivor Lloyd-Jones, who was to join him next day]. Coastguard a nice

---

* Two of Erskine's three sisters.

fellow but very pessimistic; said I might get off at 3 a.m. that night, but must on no account attempt to work up the creeks in the dark but wait for the next afternoon tide. Directed me to Wakering where I walked and wired L. to meet me at Burnham. By the time I got back the creek was dry and I walked across to the boat, bent the anchor to the warp and carried it to the centre of the creek. Lovely evening, and I took a longish walk on the Maplin Sand outside – hard, firm stuff, seeming to stretch a vast distance, with steamers throbbing down the Swin in the distance and carts rattling over what is called the Broom Road across the Sand from Havengore to Foulness. Noted the depths in the creek and the channel outside. Returned and dined, after setting tent, and after careful selection found the one comfortable site for a bed at that angle. Read and slept till 2.30 a.m.

'Woke to find the water lapping round, and a cloudy night with a light W wind. The latter circumstance (being a beam wind) decided me to disregard the Coastguard's warning and thread the creeks in the dark, rejecting both alternatives of going round the Whittaker [at the mouth of the Crouch] or of anchoring in deeper water to wait for the next day's tide, which meant that I should be late for L., and the prospect of nearly a whole day more on the Maplins was not enticing.

'Water rose to a depth of 1 foot 6 inches and then I began to haul on the anchor madly. Time went by, and the water seemed to stop rising; but after tremendous hauling I got her head round and swung her off safely. I am sure I should never have floated off. The anchor never dragged a hair's breadth. I was soon under way, but found a foul tide and made slow way, so I anchored and made Bovril, knowing the current would turn soon and ebb right out to the Crouch. When it turned I went on groping through the maze of creeks cautiously, and twice laboriously working up a turning only to find it a cul-de-sac. It was a relief when I was in deeper water and could disregard the falling tide a little. At dawn I was at the turn to the Broomhill River, and thence had a simple run out through the River Roach to the Crouch, where I anchored about 6, and set tent and slept.'

The weather continued vile, with hard nor'easterly winds and rain. With Ivor Lloyd-Jones, and a couple of days later William Le Fanu as well, Childers charged about the Crouch and the Roach. On their last day they 'ran right up to the New England

creek to within a mile of Havengore outlet, and began a pande-
moniacal anchoring, looking for a deep spot, and lowering and
weighing, setting and lowering sails, sticking, floating, rowing,
poling and sounding, and all talking at once, till we finally rested
in 9 feet at two hours ebb in the exact centre of a driblet of a
channel about 20 feet broad, just by the sea end of Potton
Island.'

The next day the weather suddenly faired and they had a
pleasant peaceful run back to Greenhithe, meeting on the way
'a prodigious fleet of barges which, we supposed, had been
accumulating weather-bound upriver.'

'A pleasant, but very cold and stormy, cruise,' Childers sums
it up in the last entry in the log of *Marguerite*. But he did not get
rid of her for almost twelve months, when he sold her to two of his
friends, Lawes and Hurst. She had served him well, and had
surely been made to live up to her soubriquet of *Mad Agnes*. She
also supplied him with a great deal of the material for a two-part
article entitled *The Londoner's Cruising Ground* which appeared in
The Times in July and September 1908. The extracts which
follow reflect both the similarities and the differences between the
familiar cruising grounds of today and of three-quarters of a
century ago.

'A Londoner who wishes to temper town life with cruising and
whose duties forbid him to wander out of easy reach of the
metropolis has a choice of two, and only two, cruising grounds –
the Essex coast and the region round and about the Isle of Wight.
Both are rich in natural beauty and in opportunities for sport,
but there the resemblance ends. The spirit of melancholy reigns
over the greater part of the Essex coasts. The charm is the charm
of a low and lonely country where the view is bounded by a
delicate fringe of trees, by a few red farm buildings, or a distant
church spire; where vast and desolate flats, screamed over by
wildfowl, are slowly laid bare as the tide falls and the ribbons of
navigable water shrink into smaller and smaller dimensions. . . .

'In the southern cruising ground, centring round the Isle of
Wight, the *genius loci* is a gayer spirit and the scenery far more
varied. Cliffs, hills or rolling downs generally provide a background, more or less distant, to every view. There are rocky coves
and sandy beaches, as well as secluded tidal creeks and great
natural harbours. There is one veritable forest, besides a quantity

of rich woodland. The sun glances on blue, if not on translucently blue, water, and on livelier land colours; navigation is far more varied and interesting, and havens far more numerous.

'In the matter of accessibility by railway, Essex possesses, in pretty and popular Burnham-on-Crouch, a yachting base nearer than any on the South Coast. On the other hand the express services to Southampton are, relatively, so much superior that the difference of distance is of very little account; and, if it is a question of weekend sailing only it must be borne in mind that any expedition from Burnham involves a preliminary sail of some six miles down a none too wide river with a strong tidal current, a formidable consideration if the tides happen to be inconvenient. . . . Down south it is otherwise. Besides Southampton, which is the best centre, Portsmouth, Bosham, Emsworth, Fareham, Hamble, Bursledon, Lymington, Poole, to say nothing of the less convenient island ports, all constitute halting-places within three hours of London. . . . Short as the distances are and sheltered as much of the water is, there are difficulties and contingent risks enough to afford that exercise of wits and nerve which the true cruising spirit always demands. There may very well be a need for hints of this sort; for the neighbourhood of the Isle of Wight is so closely associated on the one hand with great racing regattas, and on the other with the gorgeous idleness of more fashionable yachting, that the humble devotee of cruising proper may be inclined to look askance on the whole district.

'At the outset it is necessary to postulate a vessel drawing, at the outside, not more than 7 feet. Below that limit, and consistently with being a thoroughly good sea boat, the smaller she is the better. The proviso is important, for under certain conditions of wind and tide even the sheltered water behind the Island is liable to be a severer test of seaworthy qualities than the open sea outside. Secondly, in planning his expedition the traveller must never fail to study and work his tidal currents, which are strong, and his tidal rise and fall, factors rarely coincident and often widely divergent. It is generally a waste of time and patience to work in opposition to the currents, and if it is a question of railway communication, the tidal chart and the train table should be studied in close conjunction overnight.

'Let us start, then, from Southampton. . . . Fawley Creek and Ashlett Creek, if crept into with great wariness, offer peaceful anchorages, though only for small craft. Our 7 foot draft vessel will probably make for Hamble River on the opposite shore, where for some three miles she will have a profusion of berths to choose from, all amid beautiful surroundings. At Hamble itself and at Bursledon, both very popular yachting resorts, she may find herself uncomfortably crowded. Should there be a day to spare for boat work, or even an afternoon, the dinghy should be rowed upriver to Botley – five delicious miles through woods and opulent pastures and by many a little sandy strand suitable for a picnic. But if for your first evening out you want the perfection of beauty and solitude ... steer west for the Beaulieu River. ... You may drop anchor almost anywhere short of Buckler's Hard, and after supper either listen (in the early summer) to the nightingales, on deck, or, should you lie near Exbury Hard, walk up through the woods to the village and order milk for the morrow.

'... we shall touch next at Lymington, approached by two miles of narrow channel winding between vast reedy flats. So crowded and confined is the space near the town that it is best to lie downstream within half a mile of Jack-in-the-Basket, the outer mark for the entrance, not forgetting if it is humanly possible to carry a line to a post, for the holding ground is not perfect. Not far west of Lymington is Hurst Castle, and behind the castle and closely skirting the bare spit which connects it with the mainland runs the little creek of Keyhaven, leading to the charmingly sleepy old village of that name. The deep-draught yacht must anchor in Hurst Roads, and even her smaller sister will find it a puzzle to hit off the very tricky entrance of this creek; but it is well worth the trouble, and once over the bar there are no further difficulties. We now quit the Hampshire shore, cross the fierce tidal turmoil of Hurst Narrows, and find in Totland Bay and Alum Bay quiet and secure anchorages in ordinary fair weather, but to be shunned in strong northwesterly or northerly winds. Thence, leaving the ominous golden humps of the great Shingles Bank to starboard and the Needles Rocks to port, we stretch away for a thirteen mile spin over open sea to the outermost of the long line of buoys which trace the course of the navigable channel to Poole. ... It is an excellent alternative to turn into Studland Bay for the night, climb the thickly-wooded bluffs and visit the ancient church of one of the prettiest villages in Dorset. As to Poole Harbour, it is a miniature cruising ground in itself, to whose many labyrinthine creeks and wild scenery it would be impossible to do justice in this short paper.

'. . . one of the havens best beloved by those who travel these waters in small craft [is] Newtown Creek, with its access to prim old Newtown village, full of proud memories, political and war-like. The navigation requires great care. Getting in is easy enough, but getting out in a headwind is a very delicate operation. Newtown left behind, we shall (it is to be hoped) hasten past the gay and crowded roads of Cowes and Ryde, stopping only at Wootton Creek . . . a very charming little haven, though awkward for a vessel of any size owing to the extreme narrowness of the entrance and a very sharp turn to starboard. . . . Bembridge, a safe enough little natural harbour but as a very popular resort is liable to be overcrowded, and redolent of civilisation. The sea-ward channel, moreover, is perilously narrow. Still, either the harbour itself or, a pleasanter alternative, the roadstead outside, is a convenient point of departure for the next expedition, namely, to Chichester Harbour, once more on the mainland.

'There is a spice of unusual excitement in making this harbour – or rather, inland sea – for it is comparable only to Poole in the variety and complexity of its creeks, an excitement due to the vast expanse of outlying shoals, on which in bad weather the sea breaks viciously, and to the ever-shifting sandbar which blocks the actual entrance. In a strong onshore wind the harbour should not be attempted by a stranger; but in fair summer weather and at half-flood it presents little difficulty. Beyond a stringent warning against a short-cut inshore, detailed directions are useless. Very easy canvas, constant sounding, and if possible a man aloft to look out, are the best precautions. Once over the bar the tide whirls the vessel past a naked, desolate bank of shingle, and suddenly the whole expanse of the inland sea is revealed. . . . An easterly ramification, ending in a short length of canal, will carry the yacht to Chichester, should the thought of the cathedral conquer a wholesome aversion to large towns. My own advice is to steer – warily, too, for the bends are sudden and the perches none too obvious – for peaceful little Bosham, the true Mecca of pilgrims in these waters, reached by a waterway of the daintiest beauty, stealing past woods on the one hand and far-flung stretches of watery sedge on the other, narrowing gradually till mingled copse and marsh flank it on both sides, broadening once more as it approaches the red and white village, finally squander-ing its current northward over a great shallow mere.

'. . . the tale of pleasant places is not yet complete. Langston

Harbour . . . so bleak and desolate as to discourage all but the most passionate lovers of solitude. Last comes Portsmouth Harbour – the very name sinister in sound to the shy amateur skipper who dreads manoeuvring, on a strong and treacherous tide, through a throng of vessels of all sizes, from the anchored battleship to the bustling ferryboat. But . . . he will penetrate to scenes as quiet . . . as his heart can desire: Fareham Creek . . . and Porchester Creek, dominated by the gaunt shell of the old castle, whence at sunset, and especially at one of those wild sunsets which close a stormy day, there is a prospect of haggard splendour not to be forgotten. . . .

'I hope I have said enough to persuade doubters that the cruising ground is neither hackneyed nor monotonously limited. I have said nothing of trips round the Island or of drenching beats on the weather-going tide from Cowes Point to Hurst against one of the most vicious short seas to be met with anywhere in our sheltered sounds. Yet these are joys which count and add salt to the gentler attractions of cruising round and about the Island.'

In the second article Childers turned to the East Coast of England. Predictably, for a man who succumbed to the barren charms of the Frisian shores and islands, he responds to the particular flavour of the Essex creeks and estuaries, and beyond them the Suffolk rivers.

'We weigh from Burnham on the last drain of the ebb, pick our way through the mingled throng of pleasure craft and oyster boats, sail eastward down the Crouch for a couple of miles, and then turn south on the young flood into the Roach. This is the little river which, with its many sinuous crooks and shallow lagoons, connects the Crouch with the estuary of the Thames and makes an island of Foulness. That broad expanse of low dyked country, Frisian in aspect, stretches far to the east. Foulness – the very name seems to embody the wild melancholy which is the dominant characteristic of the Essex lowlands. The cruiser must have something in his temperament which responds sympathetically to this sad appeal; and if you wish to put to a supreme test your capacity to love Essex as she deserves to be loved, you cannot do better than explore the Roach and its branches on a grey day when a searching wind from the east moans over the flats, when colours are all toned down to the neutral and a sense of infinite desolation lays hold of the senses. If, instead of discouragement and depression, you feel your spirit animated and thrilled, you may feel safe once and for all, whatever the weather and wherever you go. You will not find yourself dreaming regretfully of cliffs and blue water, but will accept with an open heart all that is antithetic to that dream: weed-grown dykes, sedgy margins, vast prospects over scenery almost featureless save for a farm or two crouching behind stunted trees; tracts of marsh and saltings, enormous mud-flats and sand-flats alternately veiled and visible as the tide rises and falls. Once you have fairly caught the charm, weather will make no difference. Indeed, for its most faithful lovers this region is at its best when southern cruising grounds are at their worst. On the other hand, the recollection of wild, grey days quickens appreciation for those bright and sunny times when even the most forlorn scenes reveal unsuspected beauties, some of them so subtle and delicate that they will be missed by an unsympathetic eye.'

After a dissertation on the Thames estuary, he turns to the Blackwater.

'Let us regain our original cruising ground, not by Havengor Creek but by the longer route down Swin and round the Whittaker buoy. Our next destination is the Blackwater: to gain it we must skirt the great Buxey bank and take the restricted Ray Sand channel lying between it and the Dengie Flats. Then there are three or four miles of shoal water before we cut into the broad, swift and deep channel of the Blackwater – well named since its waters, even in bright weather, have a peculiarly sombre hue, an effect thoroughly in keeping with the surrounding scenery. For here we are in the heart of things, and it seems impossible to realize that only a dozen miles away, by the route we have just followed, flows the world's most crowded waterway, bearing a vast and varied commerce to the greatest of all capitals. The sense of solitude is profound, and the remote little hints of man's presence seem only to accentuate the loneliness. Far away to the north there is a hay-barge, coming slowly down some invisible creek for all the world as though the golden stack itself, surmounted by the square of rich brown sail, were moving by some magic over the dry land. She is coming out of the strange maze of islands and creeks known as Mersea Quarters, equal to the Roach for purposes of exploration and richer far in historical associations. . . .

'The Orwell should be regarded, perhaps, as the limit towards the northeast of the cruising ground with which we are dealing. If we like, however, we can extend it to the Deben, whose bar, always difficult and in bad weather dangerous, lies some four miles northeast of Landguard Point, the promontory facing Harwich. It is one of those contrasts which make the joy of cruising to rush over the turmoil of the bar, borne by one of the swiftest currents of any on this coast, and suddenly to find oneself safe in peaceful Woodbridge Haven, whence a pleasant river sail will lead to the town of Woodbridge (two and a half hours from London). That, probably, will be our most northerly point.'

For a man so methodical, so legalistic, so meticulous over details, Erskine Childers had also a surprisingly impulsive side to his character. It reflected, and was a reflection of, his love of adventure and his recurrent need for action; but it was invariably tempered by sound knowledge and a cool assessment of the risks involved. If this will stand as a definition of courage, perhaps its highest definition, then it will stand as a judgement of his character as a whole. In the sea and sailing, even though they occupied only a corner of his life, this romantic Ulyssean aspect of his nature found its fulfilment: they provided him with the equivalent of the knightly 'ordeal', in which a man's character is put to the test. If the ordeal is self-imposed it has an added validity, for the first ordeal is choosing to undergo it.

In a purplish passage (one of the few) in *The Riddle of the Sands*, Childers allows Carruthers to express it exactly:

'Close in the train of Humour came Romance, veiling her face, but I knew it was the rustle of her robes that I heard in the foam beneath me; I knew that it was she who handed me the cup of sparkling wine and bade me drink and be merry. Strange to me though it was, I knew the taste when it touched my lips. . . . It was the purest of her pure vintages, instilling the ancient inspiration which, under many guises, quickens thousands of better brains than mine, but whose essence is always the same: *the gay pursuit of a perilous quest.*'

Discomfort, danger, even death itself, he seems to be saying prophetically, are of no importance so long as they are faced with steady purpose and a high heart.

The impulse is normally subconscious, especially when one is twenty-seven; the motives are only analysed and put into words in retrospect. *Mad Agnes*, the English coast from Orfordness to Portland Bill, the Baie de la Seine, had served their purpose. Suddenly in that summer of 1897 Erskine Childers felt the need for wider horizons, and the confidence to go in search of them.

IV

Vixen - and Immortality 1897

'But did I ever tell you', Erskine Childers wrote to Walter Runciman from *Vixen* in Sonderburg, North Germany at the end of October 1897, apropos *Marguerite*, 'I had got another one. I expect not as the whim seized me and the whole thing was over and done in the first days of August and I was off I scarcely knew where.' A laconic note at the beginning of the new logbook is hardly more informative: 'The *Vixen* bought in Dover Aug. 1 and fitted out for cruising in the Granville Dock'. Ten days later he left single-handed for Boulogne, intending when he had picked up Henry, who was in Austria and was to join him, to 'make Bordeaux, canal it through France and then spend the winter in the Mediterranean. But fate willed otherwise,' his letter to Runciman continues; 'the weather broke directly I was ready, and a long spell of west winds, low glass and an odd storm set in. I crossed the Channel alone to Boulogne, gave up waiting, and when Henry and Lloyd-Jones joined me turned Holland-wards one gusty, dreary day.'

So inauspiciously, and through the perversity of the weather, began the cruise which would eventually provide the basis for *The Riddle of the Sands*, give *Vixen* a surrogate immortality, and ensure for Erskine Childers a secure, alternative niche in the hall of fame.

As usual, Childers wrote up the cruise in a number of different versions: for the Cruising Club *Journal*, for *The Yachting Monthly*

Magazine and for *The Times*. The account that follows is drawn from all of these, but mainly from his log. Passages in parenthesis are from the novel, the page references being those in the Mariners Library edition though the chapter numbers are common to all editions. These are included purely for the diversion of the book's devotees, who may like to compare the fact and the fiction.

The opening paragraphs of his *Yachting Monthly Magazine* article 'How We Drifted to the Baltic in a Seven-tonner', published in 1898, describe the boat in affectionately disparaging terms – very much those, in fact, without the affection, in which Carruthers describes *Dulcibella*.

'I never began a cruise', Childers opens his piece, 'under (seemingly) less propitious conditions. To start with, no one could call the *Vixen* beautiful. We grew to love her in the end but never to admire her. At first I did not even love her for she was a *pis aller*, bought in a hurry in default of a better, and a week spent in fitting her for cruising – a new era for her – had somehow not cemented our affections. Nor could the most sympathetic friend, tactfully ignoring the aesthetic point of view, dwell on her weatherly and workmanlike appearance. A low freeboard, a high coach-house cabin roof, and a certain over-sparred appearance aloft, would un-nerve the most honied tongue. Comfort below might be the flatterer's last resource, but there again the words of compliment would die on his lips. In the "saloon" he would find but just enough headroom to allow him to *sit* upright; and before he could well help himself the observation would escape him that the centreplate was an inconveniently large piece of furniture. Confronted with the forecastle, candour and humanity would wring from him a sigh of pity for the crew; but here he could be comforted, for there were to be no paid hands. I had been trying to change her name, but a growing conviction of its obvious fitness had paralysed my ideas. . . .

'Nothing could make the *Vixen* a beauty, but she proved to be admirably suited for the work we gave her (which, as it turned out, was very different from that which we intended her for). She is a cutter, 30 feet overall by 7, drawing 4 feet, or 6 feet 6 inches with the centreplate lowered. Her ballast is 3 tons of lead, carried inside in small pigs. Three comfortable berths are available, and plenty of accommodation for stores and sails. A couple of small bilge keels make her set nearly upright when on the ground, a feature which we found most valuable in North Germany. As to headroom below, we very soon decided that it did not matter in the least. For heating and cooking we found a large oil stove admirable. I had the main-boom and mainsail reduced in size before starting, and then found her handily and adequately canvassed. We were in the habit of speaking contemptuously of her seagoing qualities, but she never, as a matter of fact, justified our strictures.'

Childers goes on to recommend their route to the Baltic by way of the Frisian Islands as being 'novel and amusing' and practicable in any sort of weather. 'We extended our cruise into an unusually late season, but we found that with a warm cabin, sound decks, and plenty of books, discomfort and tedium were very rare visitors.'

Her owner's reluctant and somewhat apologetic affection for *Vixen* is exactly matched by the responses of Davies and Carruthers to *Dulcibella* in *The Riddle*; for, as others have noted, those two heroes express not two separate identifiable people, nor precisely the opposing sides of their creator's own character, but certainly a number of aspects of it: objective and subjective, intellectual and emotional, detached and committed. Virtually all first novels contain a measure of disguised autobiography: where this one is remarkable is in its lack of intrusiveness. By creating two such different characters, even though the difference becomes less and less as the story proceeds, Childers achieved a humour and a lightness of touch which account in great measure for its unfading popularity.

Tyros at sailing sympathise with Carruthers, all thumbs, disgust and funk; old hands share Davies' love of the sea, and understand his quiet pride in his scruffy old converted lifeboat. Without doubt the two of them were derived partly from Childers' friends and sailing companions: this does not alter the fact that the two protagonists between them express a great many of their author's feelings.

But that is neither here nor there. The main thing about them is that they are merrily alive; and their vigour, like their adventures, springs from Childers' own experiences, his own enthusiasms and dreams and ideals. Burke Wilkinson* puts it well: 'the book

---

* *The Zeal of the Convert*, op. cit. p. 69.

seems forever young in spirit. It has the exuberance of youth, the innocence that precedes first love, and that sense of adventure that knows that the race is to the bold.' This is not entirely surprising. Although Childers was thirty-two when he wrote it, he was drawing not only on his cruise with Henry in *Vixen* but also on all those jaunts in *Mad Agnes*, blundering about the rivers and creeks of the East Coast in every sort of weather, sleeping under a tent slung over the boom, cooking on a Primus while crouched beside the centreboard case, reading *Pickwick* or Thackeray by lamplight with the wind piping in the rigging and the rain sluicing down. What is remarkable is the vividness with which he caught the mood, and how professionally he set it all down.

The Riddle of the Sands, announced a leader in the *Westminster Gazette* in January 1904 nine months after it first appeared, 'was widely noticed at the time of its publication last year as a literary accomplishment of much force and originality. It was manifestly, however, intended to be something more than that, and it has, we learn, attracted much attention among students of naval and military questions abroad as the serious statement of a state of facts either now existing or likely soon to exist which has an important bearing on British naval and military policy.' It was a book, the writer continued, 'with a purpose, clearly stated and strongly enforced. It is meant to secure our national safety, and to increase the prospects of peace by making greater the risks to be faced by any nation which may contemplate the invasion of these islands.'

This is a considerable accolade for an adventure story, even if it was then into its third printing, and it illustrates the unique position the book occupies in its genre. The writer of the article, a 'High Naval Authority', does not go so far as to suggest that such a plan as that postulated in the book actually existed: what he does say is, 'It is not unreasonable to assume that in the official "pigeon-holes" of that department [the German General Staff] may be found more or less elaborated schemes for an invasion.' It was not unreasonable, and he was quite right.

Such a plan had been in existence for over six years; indeed, by coincidence, marked 'VERY SECRET: HAND TO HAND ONLY', it was being considered by the Commanding Admiral of the Imperial German Navy, Admiral Wilhelm von Knorr, during the very time that Erskine and Henry were exploring the channels inshore of the Frisian Islands. But between these two events there was no historical connection whatever. 'As a fact,' Childers wrote to Basil Williams, 'I invented the whole thing, building it, though, on careful observations of my own on the German coast. . . .'

It may be as well to remind the reader at this point of the date of the cruise, 1897, and the time when the book was written, 1902–3, for a great deal had happened in the international scene in those five or six years. At the former time Queen Victoria was still alive (it was the year of her Diamond Jubilee) and on the surface relations between Great Britain and Germany were reasonably cordial. If the British Government were afraid of anyone invading our shores, it was France. By 1902, however, matters were rather different. Partly as a result of Germany's support for the Boers during the South African War, partly because of the overt challenge to British naval supremacy launched by Admiral Tirpitz by means of the two German Navy Laws of 1898 and 1900, with their huge building programme, partly because of the Kaiser's undisguised belligerence and his country's increasingly aggressive thrust for a colonial empire, Germany was more and more clearly recognised as the power to watch.

'By the autumn of 1902, therefore,' writes Arthur J. Marder,* 'public opinion, the government and the Admiralty were as one in viewing the German fleet as a potential menace', and again: 'During the winter of 1902–3 the German menace hardened into an *idée fixe*'. Two years before this, even, the possibility of a German invasion of England was being widely discussed in Germany and commented on in British newspapers and periodicals, and the *Morning Post* was calling for the establishment of a naval base on the East Coast. In 1902 it was known that docks were being hastily built at Emden capable of embarking 300,000 men; and in March 1903 the British Prime Minister, Arthur Balfour, announced that a new naval base was to be created in the Firth of Forth – a measure duly noted in the postscript to *The Riddle*.

The novel, therefore, reached the bookshops at exactly the right moment, for the German naval building programme was periodically giving Britain the jitters. What is odd is that it had

---

* A. J. Marder, *The Anatomy of British Sea Power* (Frank Cass, 1964).

taken so long to do so. In his detailed study of German naval policy* Jonathan Steinberg writes that Germany's determination to challenge Britain's exclusive hegemony over the world's oceans originated in 1895. 'It was not a response to the failure of Anglo-German relations to improve after 1899 which led to the formulation of the "risk theory" in the preamble to the Second Navy Law of 1900. That theory was fully developed by June 1897'. And in that same month, 'The Kaiser also discussed his ideas about a plan for the invasion of England'.

The preliminaries for that plan were worked out by one Corvette Captain Schröder, and submitted in November.† Entitled 'An Operation against Antwerp', it proposed an amphibious attack on Antwerp, Walcheren and South Beveland, with an almost simultaneous surprise assault overland by two Army Corps into Belgium and Holland. 'Once the Scheldt estuary and Antwerp were firmly held, the invasion of England could be mounted.' Belgium's neutrality, like Holland's sovereignty, were to be ignored – as they were in 1914 – for, as the memorandum goes on, 'The value which possession of the Dutch and Belgian coastal bases would have for us, if an invasion of England is involved . . . is clear from the mere fact of the distances. . . . From Wilhelmshaven to the coast of Norfolk at Great Yarmouth, the distance is approximately 270 sea miles . . . the distance from Vlissingen to Dover or to Sheerness is approximately 80–85 sea miles.' And the summary concludes: 'The above represents a first stage in a larger operation against England.'

The possibility of invading England, the fear of invasion, were therefore very much present in both German and British minds at the turn of the century; but whether detailed plans for 'the larger operation' were ever worked out, and what form they took if they were, is unknown. The German Army records of the period were destroyed during the Second World War, and it has not been possible to trace any such plans in the surviving naval archives. Childers' tantalising remark to Basil Williams that 'I have since had most remarkable confirmation of the ideas in it [*The Riddle*]. Source confidential of course and details too, but I think there is no doubt that my method of invasion – in general

---

* Jonathan Steinberg, *Yesterday's Deterrent: Tirpitz and the Birth of the German Battle Fleet* (MacDonald, 1965).

† Jonathan Steinberg, 'A German Plan for the Invasion of Holland and Belgium, 1897' in *The Historical Journal* (Cambridge, 1963). Vol. 6, no. 1.

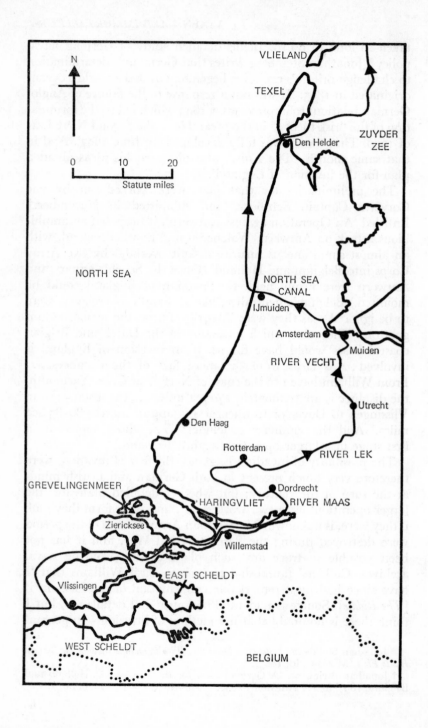

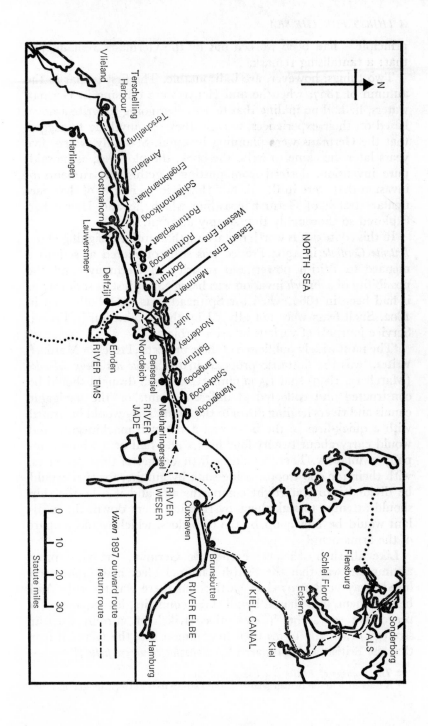

NORTH SEA

North
N

Vlieland
Terschelling
Harbour
Harlingen
Terschelling
Ameland
Engelsmanplaat
Schiermonnikoog
Oostmahorn
Rottumerplaat
Western Ems
Rottumeroog
Lauwersmeer
Eastern Ems
Borkum
Delfzijl
Memmert
RIVER EMS
Juist
Emden
Norddeich
Norderney
Baltrum
Bensersiel
Langeoog
RIVER
JADE
Spickeroog
Wangeroog
Neuharlingersiel

RIVER
WESER
Cuxhaven
Brunsbüttel
Hamburg
RIVER ELBE
KIEL CANAL
Flensburg
Schlei Fiord
Eckern
Kiel
ALS
Sonderbörg

Vixen 1897 outward route ———
return route - - - -

Statute miles
0 10 20 30

principle – had been worked out by the Germans' remains just that: a tantalising remark.

Two things, however, are indisputable. The first is that in the autumn of 1897, when he and Henry were cruising in German waters, he had no inkling that he was ever going to write a novel based on their experiences, nor did they see anything to suggest that the Germans were planning invasion. Secondly, when, five years later, he came to write the book, the plot was, as he said, pure invention, derived from putting together the rumours of invasion that were in the air and the vivid memories of that particular stretch of German coastline which he and Henry had explored so thoroughly that stormy autumn.

In this context it is worth remarking that until the signing of the *Entente Cordiale* in 1904 France was still considered as serious a menace to British power and security as Germany, and the possibility of a *French* invasion was being taken just as seriously as it had been in 1860, when the Spithead forts were built, and in 1802. Such fears were not allayed by the publication in French Service journals of various invasion projects.

'The most widely publicised of these projects', Professor Marder* writes, 'was the fantastic proposal in the *Revue des Deux Mondes* (March 15, 1899) that 1,500 pinnaces of small draught should be constructed and collected at different points on the navigable canals and rivers leading down to the coast. They would be armed with a quick-firer in the bows and a 1.8 inch machinegun, and would carry about twenty-four horses and half or a whole company of infantry. There would be little danger of these pinnaces, with their 170,000 troops, being sunk by gunfire, for they would be divided into watertight compartments, and if a hostile ship should attempt to sink them by running them down, the assailant would be blown up by the torpedoes, which would be part of the armament.'

Like all such schemes, French or German, the vital prior assumption was that the British Channel Fleet had either been lured away or destroyed in battle: and there was the rub. And behind them, and shared by all three countries, lay the fear of a preventive war, the 'pre-emptive strike' of current nuclear strategy or, in the terms then in common use, the German fear that the British were prepared '*zu Kopenhagen unsere flotte*'.†

---

* *The Anatomy of British Sea Power*, op. cit. p. 333.

† A reference to the British seizure of the Danish fleet at Copenhagen in 1807.

'For the next ten years', Andrew Boyle says in his biography,* 'Childers' book remained the most powerful contribution of any English writer to the debate on Britain's alleged military unpreparedness.' This seems to be pitching its impact a little too high, since references to it are extremely scarce in military works of the period; yet, because of its form – that curious combination of adventure story and patriotic warning – and its timeliness, it was widely read, by statesmen as well as sailors, and acquired both for itself and its author a kind of aura. Even today, even among people who have not read it, if you mention Childers' name the response tends to be 'Oh, didn't he write . . . ?'

Both certainly sprang into public notice again in 1910 when two British Army officers, Captain Trench and Lieutenant Brandon, went on trial in Leipzig, accused of carrying out espionage along the coast of East Friesland and the Frisian Islands. Brandon admitted during the trial that he had read *The Riddle of the Sands* three times, which in the circumstances, virtually amounted to an admission of guilt, and as a result Childers gave his views on the case in the *Daily News*. Since the two men were quite obviously spying, and were indeed found guilty of doing so, Childers' equation of their activities with his own perfectly innocent ones in *Vixen* thirteen years earlier has an unexpected speciousness about it; but he allows himself one characteristically wry comment: 'My own special interest lay in the intricate maze of channels which separate them [the islands] from the mainland . . . I took, perforce, many thousands of soundings, and tested only too many foreshores by involuntary stranding.'

He and Henry were not spying; they were, as he said in this same piece, exploring for their own amusement a part of the world 'which forms one of the most interesting and exciting cruising grounds I know.' But it is hardly surprising if, then and later, he was suspected of being a secret agent of the British government.

So much, then, for *The Riddle of the Sands*, its genesis, its writing, and its impact. It is time to return to Boulogne and August 1897, where the log entry for the 13th through 19th consists simply and eloquently of 'Contrary winds for westward and bad weather.'

On the 20th Henry arrived from the Tyrol and on the 23rd, Ivor Lloyd-Jones. The following day, 'Wind SW strong, glass falling.

* *The Riddle of Erskine Childers*, op. cit. p. 111.

dirty day. Gave up thoughts of the west and ran two-reefed in bumpy sea to Calais.' Two days later, with a fresh sou'westerly and sun for a change, they were off into Dutch waters. The log reads:

'*26 Aug.* Ran for the Wielingen lightship and thence across mouth of West Scheldt to the Roompot channel of the East Scheldt. When well inside grounded on the Onrust Sand with the plate down and had great difficulty getting off. Found the eight hour ebb tide very annoying as, though we went on at low water, it was two hours before the water rose. It was late when we got off, and we sailed and at dusk anchored under the shore of Beveland. Blew hard from SW with rain all night.

'*27 Aug.* Up at 7 and sailed to Zierickzee through a tricky channel among the banks. Wind SW strong, two reefs, sunny. Ran up 2 miles of very narrow canal to the town and moored by the quay. Ashore and found everything very pretty, novel and amusing. Views changed in the evening: brisk bombardment by small boys – missiles, mud and crabs – nearly caused a riot. (*– heavens! shall I ever forget those boys! A perfect murrain of them infests Holland; they seem to have nothing in the world to do but throw stones and mud at foreign yachts.* Riddle *Chap. IV, p. 43.*)

'*28 Aug.* Wind E very light, very fine. Under way early. Laborious tow in dinghy out of canal. Then drifted up the Keeten Mastigat, bound to Rotterdam. Took some art photos. No wind though, and finally anchored on the Mossel Bank in the evening. Rowed to a *schuyt*. "We have come from England and want bread." Were given a huge loaf with many expressions of sympathy.

'*29 Aug.* Followed some *schuyts* to Willemstad through difficult channels where charts ceased and we navigated by Baedeker. In lovely evening came up to the great suspension railway bridge, and found entrance of river to Dordrecht. Drifted on tide; found swing-bridge shut and anchored for the night.

'*30 Aug.* Ashore and saw Dordrecht; lovely old town . . . had first taste of Schiedam – effect good on Henry, bad on us. A 2 p.m. sailed up river towards Rotterdam. Wind NW strong and squally. Sailed in narrow river, well wooded and many houses; just lay closehauled most of the time, with a few tacks. Lost tide at 3 and anchored till 5; then it was a dead beat, soon in the dark, to Rotterdam. In Maas found dense crowd of anchored shipping.

Let go, and dragged on to a *schuyt*; made fast alongside; inhabitants came up and made merry with our whisky.

'*31 Aug.* Wind NW, strong. One reef (ought to have been three). Fearful morning. Dreadful business getting anchor, owing to being tied up in a knot with crowds of boats. Under way at last, but where to go? Book said Veerhafen – but where? Tacked blindly up and down among swarms of steam tugs, and finally got a tow through the great swing-bridge (towage compulsory, though we didn't know it). Were let go unexpectedly on other side – half a gale blowing – things went wrong ... !!!???! – towed into Veerhafen, and thence into a beautiful little basin, Westerhafen, among park trees, quiet and pretty – relief after morning's work. (Noticeable absence of paint on hull.)

'*1 Sept.* Found centreplate was twisted, so sailed to Zalmhafen a mile away and put her on slip for repairs. Stayed a week, during which incessant gales of wind and rain. Dullest place on earth.

'*7 Sept.* Wind NW, fresh, fine. (Bound to Amsterdam.) Sailed out and were towed through the big bridge, according to rule. First tried the Ganda Canal, but gave it up – headwind. So sailed up Lek River (to get to Amsterdam via Utrecht and the Vecht River). Got as far as Lexon village and anchored, strong adverse current stopping us. E. went ashore for supplies – the usual murrain of boys. Honey-cake a dream.

'*8 Sept.* Dead calm all day and strong adverse current. Spring-cleaning. Jettisoned three pounds of steak accidentally.'

For the next two days they towed *Vixen* laboriously, in turns, through Utrecht, on to Loenen, and finally to Muiden on the Zuyder Zee. In places weed and rubbish brought them to a standstill; but they finally escaped into open water.

'*11 Sept.* . . . Thence had a fine sail closehauled to the great breakwater leading to Amsterdam locks. Passed lock, and sailed to anchorage opposite station. Dined on shore; returning late, found a dinghy oar stolen – boys again. Paddled back somehow, cursing this tireless pest, and praying for a Herod to rule over this land. (*They want a Herod, with some statesmanlike views on infanticide.* Riddle *Chap. IV, p. 43.*)'

They then spent a couple of days in Amsterdam, and Ivor had to leave. The others worked their way to Ijmuiden via the North Sea Canal.

'*15 Sept.* Glass falling heavily. Sailed out at midday, but returned owing to threatening look of weather. Moored in the fishing harbour, which was nearly empty, but were most discourteously turned out. Spent a very pleasant evening at the Café Camperduin. Nice people, speaking perfect English, as most do in Ijmuiden.

'*16 Sept.* Wind SW light to NW fresh. Glass still falling heavily, but it seemed very fine, so we sailed out, with no plans, determined to follow the wind, whether it blew us to England again or the north. Found a SW air, so headed N for the Texel. Wind soon fell and we were becalmed till nearly 3 p.m. when it came up fresh from the NW. We could just lie up the coast on the port tack, so we called it a fair wind and held on. After dark we picked up the light on the point, and then the leading lights on Texel Island for the inshore channel. Found quite a race in the narrow part, negotiated it safely and ran up to Nieuwe Diep with the wind aft. A boat shot out of the gloom halfway and wanted to inflict a pilot on us, but as there were 20 fathoms everywhere we shook them off and made the harbour safely, mooring under the quay a good way up.

'*17 Sept.* [From *The Yachting Monthly Magazine*] The weather had broken at last, for we woke to a strong bluster of NW wind and promise of more, but were indifferent now, for we could run NE over the Zuyder Zee, behind the shelter of islands and banks. So we started double-reefed before the wind, hoisting our ensign at the peak according to the regulations of this naval port, as bawled to us by a gentleman on the bank who seemed to be in authority. It was fine at first, but we soon had to take in our third reef, while heavy rain-squalls fell on us in succession. It was our first experience of a kind of sailing to which we afterwards became quite accustomed. The channels were deep, narrow and complicated, and buoys and beacons of all colours, shapes and sizes seemingly innumerable. "We're lost" we concluded once, but we found the way in the end, and rounded the shoulder of the Great Oostwal Sand in weather now densely thick, with heavy squalls. But we could just see from buoy to buoy, and had a fine beam wind reach of 15 miles up the Inschott Channel, where the marks were simple enough, when visible. We were in the sea-passage between the two islands of Vlieland and Terschelling, and having had enough of it we tried to beat up to Vlie, but a sluicing ebb-tide driving us back, we ran east for Terschelling, peering for a big bell-buoy which, the chart informed us, marked the entrance. As luck would have it a blinding squall now blotted out everything, a very awkward circumstance as the North Sea swell was rolling in, speaking of the undesirability of running onto a bank. However, a compass course soon landed us among buoys, which the blessed Uniform System rendered intelligible.

'The mist cleared, and we were racing under scandalised sail down a narrow channel, between foam-washed sands, with a little red town before us, huddled white sandhills, and crowned by a noble old light-tower. We moored (in an excellent harbour) within a few yards of the missing and much execrated bell-buoy! It had run in for shelter apparently some time ago, but the chart had ignored its flight. I may mention here that our charts of all these waters, though the latest Admiralty editions, were altogether unreliable for the minor channels and swatchways.

'*18 Sept.* [From the log] SW gale. Stayed in port. Mr Fletcher, Lloyds agent, engaged in diving for treasure in the wreck of the *Lutine* outside, asked us to lunch and was very hospitable. In the evening met a lot of skippers, pilots etc at his rooms. The *Lutine* was an English frigate (captured from the French) and wrecked a century ago with £2M on board, insured by Lloyds. They have found no gold yet.' (*It seemed that off the western end of Juist, the island lying west of Norderney, there lay the bones of a French war-vessel, wrecked ages ago. She carried bullion which has never been recovered, in spite of many efforts. A salvage company was trying for it now, and had works on Memmert, an adjacent sandbank.* Riddle *Chap. XVI, p. 135, see also p. 140.*)

[From *The Yachting Monthly Magazine*] 'The weather was now hopelessly demoralised, and the North Sea was out of the question. A study of the charts showed us the long line of the Dutch and German Frisian Islands, stretching away for a hundred sea-miles and separated from the mainland by from five to eight miles of sand, in great patches which are mostly dry at low water. Whether this region is known to many English yachtsmen I do not know; for our part, in default of better, we found it delightful cruising ground, safe in any weather and a novel and amusing mode of getting to the Elbe and so to the Baltic, in a season when the North

Sea would be highly dangerous to a small boat. A light draught is indispensable, of course; ours of 4 feet is, I should think, nearly the maximum for comfort, though the channels are navigated by small traders loaded down to as much as seven feet. Occasional running aground is inevitable, so that a centreboarder which takes the ground comfortably when the plate is not in use is by far the best pattern of boat. Sound ground-tackle is indispensable, for gales must generally be met in open anchorages, though in shallow water, harbours (worthy of the name) being very rare. Of course for such events a careful choice of anchorage must be made, for the sea, when the banks are covered, can be very nasty, especially in the channels, where the tides often run with great violence. However, we rode out many a gale in safety, especially in November and December on our return journey, and found that a warm dry cabin to retreat to soon bred indifference to the elements. I said the navigation was "safe in any weather", but it is perhaps needless to add that great care is needed in crossing the gaps between the islands where the North Sea swell rolls up deep channels, and the chart is a broken reed. However, that precious institution the Uniform Buoyage [System], is one's sheet anchor there.

'The scenery perhaps requires some defence; for there is what most would call monotony in the long low line of mainland, and the white ribbons of sand which constitute the islands, each with its little red village on the sheltered side.

'*19 Sept.* We started (from Terschelling) before a strong north-wester, and had a splendid sail eastward along the islands for a few hours, most of which I spent at the masthead, picking up the elusive marks. About 2, I had just majestically coursed her to a black and white post, when we ran hard aground on a falling tide, and dried there after vain efforts at kedging off. This was off the eastern end of the island, and the post had been placed by some local humorist on the highest part of a big sand. After dark, at high water, we sailed to the deep channel and anchored in 3 fathoms in a strong tideway. Here we experienced our first gale in the open and, not being used to it, passed a wakeful night, for on the weather-going tide the sea was heavy, though with our 40 fathoms of coir we might have slept in peace.' (. . . *a misplaced boom* tricked us; kedging off failed, and at 8 p.m. we were left on a*

---

* Booms: perches, withies, or in Dutch and German, *prikken.*

perfect Ararat of sand, and only a yard or two from that accursed boom,
which is perched on the very summit, as a lure to the unwary. Riddle
Chap. XV, p. 130.)

'*20 Sept.* [From the log] Wind NW strong, and very thick, so
stayed at anchor, not liking to cross to the next island with
weather thick. In the evening it blew a hard gale with torrents of
rain and a nasty sea on the weather tide, in which we rolled
horribly. Very little sleep. Anchor held well with 25 fathoms of
grass rope.

'*21 Sept.* Wind SW to NW, rain. Under way with two reefs.
Ran across the West Gat to Ameland Island, and safely picked
up the channel behind it. Followed it about 6 miles to where
chart showed solid stone breakwater from island to mainland. We
could see nothing in the mist, but had heard vaguely of a gap, so
followed a line of booms which led us to a gap with 17 feet of
water in it. (We learnt that this gap had been here ten years.)
Ran on over very shallow flats hoping to make Oostmahorn on the
Dutch mainland (about 12 miles); but about 4 a black storm
broke on us from the NW, and we had to anchor suddenly under
the lee of a bank called Engelsmanplaat [Englishman's Flat],
where six smacks were also lying. It was soon blowing a heavy
gale, but the shelter of the bank was good. We were then
about 4 miles from shore, with nothing between us and Norway
but this bank; but that was enough!' (*As for breakwaters, you've*
got them all round you, only they're hidden. Riddle *Chap. XII,*
p. 110.)

'*22 Sept.* Wind SW, dull. Weather moderated, and we sailed to
Oostmahorn, which we found to be only a tiny hamlet with a
wooden pier along which we moored. . . . Officers in uniform
crept out of hovels with huge books and searched and classified us.
We bought all Oostmahorn's bread, butter and eggs, and in the
evening walked 2 miles to Anjurn, a large village where we did
some more shopping.

'*23 Sept.* Stayed in port for a rest after four days at sea. Walked
to Anjurn again. Took two small boys as guides, who quickly
swelled to about fifty, all yelling, till we were like the Pied Piper
of Hamelin.

'*24 Sept.* SW gale and rain. Stayed in port.

'*25 Sept.* [From *The Yachting Monthly Magazine*] We were under
way at 6, and had a fine run eastward before a whole-sail
westerly wind and in lovely weather, over the vast flats which

stretch for nearly 30 miles to the Ems, and which extend 9 miles to seaward, between the islands of Schiermonnikoog and Borkum, which are divided by a space of 12 miles, broken only by an islet named Rottum, inhabited, so we were told, by one lonely farmer who has grown fabulously rich by the export of seabirds' eggs. We hoped to make a record sail this day, but alas! the midday sun, after 20 miles, shone impartially on our entire hull as we lay high and dry on an awkward corner of sand, where the channel made a cunning twist. We saw this strange region at its best this evening, the setting sun reddening gloriously over the great banks and shining ribbons of water, and bestowing pink caresses on the distant sandhills of Rottum, and the feathery line of Frisian coast.

'At night, we sailed off into deep water.

'*26 Sept.* The same southwesterly wind, but a dull morning. We made the estuary of the Western Ems, skirted the great Rausel Sand, and then crossed the Eastern Ems and were now in German waters; Borkum, 10 miles from the mainland, being the first German island. For 15 miles here the navigation has to be very careful, for there is a considerable basin of deep water in which the tides run violently round various isolated banks. We now entered another great series of flats stretching over 40 miles to the estuaries of the Jade and Weser Rivers, where the islands end, and bounded at a distance of from 3 to 6 miles from the coast by the islands of Juist, Norderney, Baltrum, Langeoog, Spiekeroog and Wangeroog.* Between all of these the North Sea tide sets strongly in, and curling round each of them nearly encircles them with a practicable channel, but always leaves one shoal spot, about opposite their centre, which can only be crossed at half-flood or more. The flats themselves are for the most part dry at low water, but a new feature becomes increasingly common as you go east in the shape of minor tidal channels, leading from the main one to a series of little ports on the mainland. Wee, miniature basins [*siels*], presided over by pretty little villages which own a dozen or so of craft which frequent them, they stand at the outfall of small streams which have been canalised, and carry a modest traffic to towns in the hinterland. Being anxious to push east, we neglected these little places on the voyage out, but found two or

---

* 'Their names suggest *The Hunting of the Snark*', Erskine wrote to his sister Dulcibella.

three of them useful and amusing refuges on the return journey.*

[From the log] 'It slowly cleared to a lovely day, as we ran slowly up with a light wind against the ebb. At 3 we reached Slaper's Horn [Slapersbucht], a shallow bit where we had no water, so lay aground in the channel. Henry successfully long-spliced one of the grass warps, as it had chafed. Read *Esmond*. At 10 p.m. we were afloat. There was a nice NW breeze and the night was fine, so we decided to risk grounding and sail to Norderney, the next island, by compass, direct. It was three-quarters flood. A successful but not to be repeated venture, for we were often in but 5 feet of water, with the North Sea swell coming in and a wind which freshened a good deal. Found a fine deep-water harbour (the only one of its kind between Terschelling and the Jade, 120 sea miles), where we moored at midnight. A voice from the gloom made one or two perfunctory enquiries, and then all was silent.

'*27 Sept.* Our first German port. Change immediate and delightful. No boys, no bothers, no Customs. Great cleaning up, and then lunched ashore at a smart hotel. Bright, pretty, strangely southern looking town, just going to sleep again after the summer season. No fresh meat to be got. One shop had lots, but wouldn't sell it as they said it was New Year's Day. They were Jews. Terrible night – boat refusing to lie properly, and getting under quay piles; smashed the crutch thus. Finally got out two anchors into the stream fore and aft, and then slept.

'*28 Sept.* Started about 9. Wind E (foul at last), very fine. Had to warp out of port, and then made for North Sea. Found wind dead foul and light with a heavy swell, so gave it up and ran back and across the bay to the mainland side at Norddeich, where there is a ferry station which the Norderney steamers used. Found a queer harbour with two thin tentacles of deepish water on each side of the quay, buoyed, and apparently dredged constantly. Anchored and spent a quiet day. Ashore to a dirty village – strange contrast to Holland – for milk and stamps. Silent empty place, desolate, in sympathy with Norderney.

'*29 Sept.* Up at 6, but too late to get out before the flood tide came sluicing up our channel. Hot fine morning. Nearly towed her out but tide too strong. For exercise, kedged her on about 200 yards, tremendous hard work. Then anchored for breakfast.

---

* And, it might be added, even more useful when it came to writing the book five years later.

About 11 got off, but ran aground, and more kedging: finally started. Wind ENE fresh. Decided it was useless to beat on our course, so thought of running back to Delfzijl, on the Dutch shore of the Ems River. Reached the Ems, but then wind went north, so repented. Wished to take a new way back, so beat to the mouth of the Ems on a roaring ebb tide. Then tried for the boomed channel south of Juist Island, but here ebb was against us, and we were driven back. Let go in 13 fathoms with a tiny dinghy anchor* and 45 fathoms of warp. A tremendous tide swirled past, and the anchor held well. We were in a weirdly lonely place, just at the verge of the North Sea, close to a grotesquely dreary structure called the Memmert beacon.' (*a gigantic tripod, its gaunt legs stayed and cross-stayed, its apex lost in fog . . . Riddle Chap. XXII, p. 197.*) 'Tide turned after dark at 8. To our disgust, it had turned thick, and we had a difficult job to sail to sheltered water, with no help from Borkum light, which was not visible. Wind came up fresh from the SE with rain. We worked solely by the lead, and after two or three checks anchored in only 9 feet, vague as to our whereabouts.

'*30 Sept.* Thick fog. Overslept and woke to bumping – dashed out in pyjamas and tried to kedge off – failed and dried. Bed again. Off about 10 and groped about for our channel in the fog – found it at last and followed it to Juist, where we anchored a mile from the shore. About 1 fog lifted and we tried to go on, but wind easted so we returned to anchor and read *Esmond*. At 5 rowed in dinghy on falling tide as far as she would float inshore, and then walked over sand taking careful courses by grounded ships with compass in view of darkness returning. Found a brand new little budding watering place among the sandhills, empty now. Shopped and returned to dinghy, high and dry and undraggable, so anchored her and waded to the yacht, now in only 3 feet.

'*1 Oct.* Fog. Wind N light. At anchor all day. I went ashore in morning and found fog embarrassing, but was guided back by Henry with the foghorn.' (*The bray of a foghorn sounded right behind me.* Riddle Chap. XXII, p. 205.) 'Ashore again in the evening. Slight indisposition among the crew, so I landed again and bought champagne and beef-steak at the hotel.' (*Steak tastes none the worse for having been wrapped in newspaper and the slight traces of the day's news disappear with frying in onions and potato-chips. Davies was*

* Why is not made clear.

indeed on his mettle for this, his first dinner to his guest; for he produced with stealthy pride . . . a bottle of German champagne. Riddle *Chap. IV, p. 42.*) 'Blew hard in the night.'

'*2 Oct.* [From *The Yachting Monthly Magazine*] A fresh N wind and a lovely day. We started east to a beam wind down a most intricate channel, which we missed once and landed in a cul-de-sac of sand. However, we safely reached the end of Juist, and then had a short but anxious run across the interval to Norderney, trying hopelessly to decipher our useless chart in a nasty swell. We were very glad to be off the harbour once more and fairly in the next channel, over the flats behind Norderney. [This is exactly the route described in Chap. XXI, 'Blindfold to Memmert' – without the fog.] We now had a splendid run down the island with a beam wind, varied by an occasional short beat, and passed on behind Baltrum, the next island (only $2\frac{1}{2}$ miles long) to Langeoog, the succeeding one. Here we lost the flood tide, which had been helping us over the shoal spots, and found ourselves unable to stem strong ebb stream, so anchored in three fathoms in a broad, deep channel, off the head of a long, low pier running out over a mile from the shore. Every island has one of these jetties, which is intended as a landing-stage for steamers in the summer months. We found them quite useless for landing purposes, as they were never anywhere near the town or village. So scornful of them is the chart that they are never marked at all.

[From the log] 'Lovely calm night. Dinner – white soup, steak, onions and potatoes, champagne, black coffee, cigars – *Esmond*.

'*3 Oct.* Up at 4.30 so as to be ready to sail as soon as there was light to see the booms. Under way against strong ebb at 5.30. Reached the shoalest spot off the east of the island, and there stuck with no water. So had to wait till 2 p.m. Henry walked a mile over sand to a farmhouse carrying a big stone jar, and got water and milk. At 2 started. Wind SW to SE, fresh. Fine reaching wind past Spiekeroog, the next island to Wangerooge, the last of the islands, finding buoys at sea channels quite correctly by a chart of '96. Halfway wind freshened and veered to SE with rain. Passed a huge fleet of local trading boats, something like Thames barges but with better lines and much less canvas. Pouring heavy rain when we anchored off Wangerooge, out of the channel in shallow water where we grounded at half-ebb.' (*A low line of sandhills, pink and fawn in the setting sun, at one end of them a little white village huddled round the base of a massive four-square lighthouse – such was Wangerooge, the easternmost of the Frisian Islands, as I saw it on the evening of October 15th. We had decided to make it our first landing-place; and since it possesses no harbour and is hedged by a mile of sand at low water, we had to run in on the rising tide till the yacht grounded. . . .* Riddle *Chap. XIV, pp. 119–20.*)

'*4 Oct.* NE gale, very cold. Stayed at anchor. At half-ebb walked ashore 1½ miles over sand and found a pleasant little sand-embedded village crouching round a magnificent light-tower, showing at night a fine double-flashing electric light – the guiding coast mark for the Jade and Weser Rivers. Shopped – at the wrong shop! In afternoon at half-flood rowed in dinghy to nearest point on shore (about a mile off) to get water. Nasty sea running. I landed and got water and eggs at a sort of lonely shanty on the shore. Exciting run back in a heavy sea for a dinghy.

'*5 Oct.* Wind E by N, very strong. Fine and sunny. Dead foul wind, so stayed at anchor. Ashore at low tide. Shopped – at the right shop – and then walked to the west point of the island to see an old church tower which stands right in the sea at half-flood. It is big enough to be part of the cathedral of a large town, and looks most bizarre on the lonely verge of the North Sea.' (*most bizarre of all, a great church-tower, standing actually in the water, on the north side of Wangerooge, a striking witness to the encroachment of the sea.* Riddle *Chap. XV, p. 129.*) 'Decided to sail tomorrow, wind fair or foul.

'*6 Oct.* Wind ENE, fresh. Under way at 6 and beat through 7 miles of narrow channel till we made open sea in the estuary of the Jade River. Hence it was 32 miles dead beat to Cuxhaven at the mouth of the Elbe, rounding the great sands which run 15 miles from shore north of Cuxhaven. It was a lovely day, and the sea slight owing to the wind blowing off these sands, so we decided to do it. First took a long leg northwards down to the Rother Sand lighthouse helped by the Jade ebb stream. Then went about and stood SE across the stream of the Weser estuary where we found a nasty tidal jumble. Thence it was plain sailing in a fine whole-sail breeze, tack and tack, to the Outer Elbe lightship, which we rounded about 4 p.m. Thence we had hoped to lie direct S by E to Cuxhaven, but the wind easted more and kept us making short tacks up the Elbe estuary helped by a roaring flood tide. Halfway up it was dark, but the succession of lightships and the Cuxhaven light made it easy work. Had a close race tack for tack with a big fishing smack. At 8 p.m. ran into Cuxhaven and groped providentially to a cosy spot in a little-used corner of the harbour, where we anchored after the finest sail of the year, very tired and hungry. We couldn't but admire the fine system of buoys and lights which made the navigation of these sand-infested waters so easy.

'*7 Oct.* Being so near it, we now decided to go to Kiel by the Kaiser Wilhelm ship canal, which starts at Brunsbüttel, 15 miles up the river. It was not low water till 4 p.m. and quite useless to go against the ebb, so we had a spring-cleaning, and explored the town and got letters. The town is an extraordinary depth below the sea level. Behind a gigantic dyke on the north side stands a row of big hotels, right down in a hollow, to live in which must be a sore trial to the nerves. Season over, of course, and nothing doing. . . . At 3.30 sailed out, but found the ebb running like a millstream, which indeed it did till $1\frac{1}{2}$ hours after low water. It was 5 before we started, a dirty-looking evening. Wind S, light. Drizzle at times.

'It was soon dark, and being a thick night with crowds of steamers about, it was rather an anxious sail. The Brunsbüttel light was a wonderful piece of mechanism with five different sectors, and we found it almost too complicated. We should have crossed all sectors, but we missed one altogether, to our bewilderment. A blaze of many-coloured lights marked the canal entrance. We shortened sail and ran in, groping for a quay to moor to, but the darkness was made almost worse by the overhead electric dazzle. All was dead silent and seemingly deserted. Suddenly a wall loomed over the bows; we luffed hard up, tumbled everything down, and found ourselves by a sort of floating stage to which we moored. Same silence and desertion.' (*We rounded the last headland, steered for a galaxy of coloured lights, tumbled down our sails, and came-to under the colossal gates of the Holtenau lock.* [*The Kiel end of the canal, in fact, but the description holds good.*] *That these would open to such an infinitesimal suppliant seemed inconceivable. But open they did . . . and our tiny hull was lost in the womb of a lock designed to float the largest battleship.* Riddle *Chap. X, p. 92.*)

'I was putting off in the dinghy to explore when the lights ahead began a kaleidoscope shuffle, and I guessed the gates were opening. Hoisted foresail and steered in, but a gruff voice from the gloom above told us, in excellent English, to desist. Sailing forbidden. How it knew we were English I don't know. I went ashore and climbed a lofty quay and towed her into a huge lock where she lay, scarcely visible, in a corner. Ulstered official, only sign of life, conducted me to a palatial building where I passed through a long, silent corridor to a room and gave particulars to two sleepy men in uniform. Told to fill up a form which, being intended for vessels up to 10,000 tons, contained lists of unanswerable questions. Hitch over something which kept me making journeys between this and another office to another sleepy official, who had to be woken to see to it. Cleared at last, having paid 14 marks only for canal dues and towage through.' (*'Seems cheap,' said Davies, joining me, 'doesn't it?'* Riddle *Chap. X, p. 93.*) 'Returned and towed out of the lock (absurd contrast of our tiny hull and these mighty works) to the Binnenhaven, where a dozen or so dark hulls of schooners etc were lying as silent as the grave. Moored alongside one, lighted up, and turned in at 1 a.m. Told to expect tug at 6 a.m.

'*8 Oct.* [From a letter to Dulce] We have got into a far land now. This is the North Sea entrance to the Kaiser Wilhelm canal to the Baltic. They won't let us sail through it though there is a fair wind, and we are waiting in vain for a tug they promised early today, and it is now two. . . . We are sitting in the cabin by the warmth of an oil stove. Henry has been baking a pale flinty bread lovingly, also an apple dumpling, and inventing a pudding which "began with" Quaker's Oats and went on through condensed milk to apricot jam. . . . This is an immense canal only just made, and rather too grand for us. We are lying alongside a small schooner whence a funny little old man with spectacles issues occasionally and looks for the tug which never comes. There are thousands of these little ships in German and Dutch waters – coasters carrying vegetables, fruit and odd bits of cargo – all have in the stern the most exquisite little cabin where skipper, wife and family live, beautifully varnished and clean, with tiny dimity curtained windows on each side of the rudder. . . . We had a fine time in the Frisian Islands. . . . At low water you will find yourself the only living object on square miles of dry sand except for some sea birds and some mussels, which you may boil and eat, so winning a far-off communion with distant Whitechapel and Harry treating Harriet at a coster's stall in the Old Kent Road. If it is a fine evening the sunset will be lovely across the far sands to a fringe of trees and steeples on the mainland, or some red roofs among the sandhills on an island.

'*8 Oct.* [From the log] Up at 6 but no tug appeared till 4 p.m. SW gale blowing, heavy rain, and very cold. At last started,

Marguerite, *familiarly known as* Mad Agnes, *with Childers working on the foredeck.*

The cutter Edith, *owned by Childers' friend Walter Runciman.*

Walter Runciman at the helm of Waterwitch.

Looking back at Waterwitch *from* Mad Agnes, *on a cruise together in the Solent.*

Vixen in the Solent, taken in 1899.

Erskine Childers and William Le Fanu on Vixen *during the same cruise.*

Pricken (*withies or perches*), used in the Frisian Islands
to mark channels between the islands and the mainland.

The galliot Johannes, *a picture possibly taken by Childers himself during a cruise to the Baltic in 1906.*

The Westturm on Wangerooge, damaged in the war and rebuilt on dry land since Childers' day.

Found tucked into the account of the West Indian holiday.
This sloop in St George's, Grenada, could well be the Faith.

Hurricane damage in St Vincent.

Erskine Childers, William Le Fanu and Captain Charlton on board Sunbeam *in 1902, on the first Baltic cruise.*

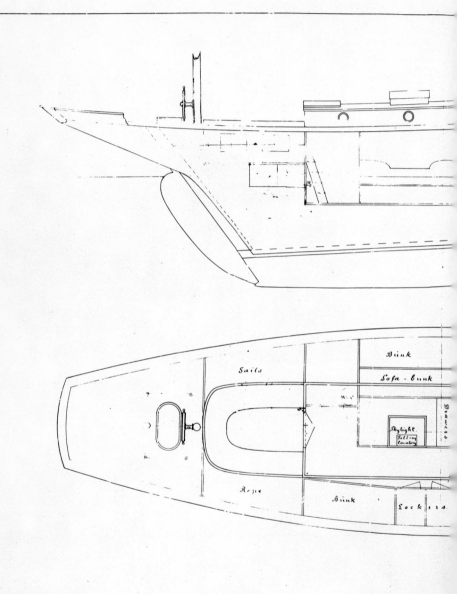

Sails

Bunk

Sofa - Bunk

Drawers

Skylight
Folding
Lavatory

Rope

Bunk

Lockers

128 63 0   1   2   3   4   5   6   7   8

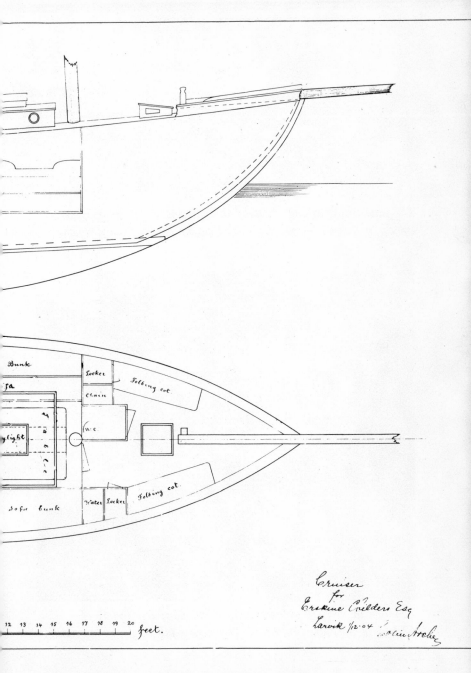

Bunk

sa

ylight

Sofa bunk

Locker

Chain

w.c.

Folding cot.

Folding cot.

Water Locker

12 13 14 15 16 17 18 19 20 feet.

Cruiser
for
Erskine Childers Esq
Larvik 1/12·04 John Archer

The yawl Sunbeam *on the wind in Southampton Water in June 1904; another photograph from William Le Fanu's family album.*

'A lesson in steering' says the album caption, of this picture of Erskine in Sunbeam *in 1902. The pupil could be one of his sisters.*

Sailing on Asgard, with Molly Childers at the wheel and Erskine directly behind her. The picture is undated, and there are no clues as to where it was taken, or to the identity of the other two.

Asgard in light airs near Aasens, September 1906.

Molly Childers and William Le Fanu in Asgard, running down Horsens Fiord in August 1906.

'The gun-runners' Molly Childers, Mary Spring Rice and Erskine row ashore at Cowes. No trio of people could look less piratical.

Childers, looking very tired after the gale the night before, with Mary Spring Rice on the quay at Howth as the guns are handed up.

Asgard *sailing from Howth under trysail after unloading the arms. The split mainsail, partly rolled round the boom, lies half across the cockpit. Molly Childers is probably at the wheel.*

Erskine Childers at the wheel of Asgard *after picking up the arms. Gordon Shephard, behind one of the ammunition boxes they had to ditch, obviously had no wish to be recognised.*

Asgard *in 1932. She continued in private ownership until 1961 when she was bought by the Irish government for use as a sail training ship for naval cadets. She was finally pensioned off in 1976, given the status of a National Monument, and has since been put on permanent exhibition in Kilmainham Gaol, Dublin.*

lashed alongside the *Johannes* schooner, bound for Kappeln in the Baltic. Skipper Bartels, a right good sort, who helped us a lot.' (*a little man in oilskins and sou'wester was stooping towards us in the cabin door, smiling affectionately at Davies out of a round grizzled beard. Riddle Chap. VII, p. 61 et seq.*) 'He began by a solemn present of pears. We replied with wax matches (an everlasting source of wonder and joy to all foreigners) and a clock which wouldn't go, also hot punch, very welcome on that bitter day. His boy steered for us both, and we had long yarns in our cabin.' (*'Karl shall steer for us both,' he said, 'and we will stay warm in the cabin.' Riddle Chap. X, p. 93. 'Karl was the shock-headed, stout-limbed boy of about sixteen, who constituted the whole crew of the* Johannes, *and was as dirty as his master was clean.' p. 94).* 'Splendid canal – lighted electrically at night, as well as Piccadilly and better than the parks. At 7 the cry of "*Fest machen!*" ran along, and we moored for the night at one of the passing-places by some piles.

'*9 Oct.* Long delay for some big steamer in the road. Went ashore to a farm and bought a big rye loaf, which lasted for three weeks and died soft. Stove in full blast, for very cold, but no wind. Photoed Bartels.' (*View there was none from the deck of the* Dulcibella; *it was only by standing on the main-boom that you could see over the embankments to the vast plain of Holstein, grey and monotonous under a pall of mist. Riddle Chap. X, p. 93.*) 'Arrived at Holtenau, the Baltic end, at 9 p.m. Towed out and made fast alongside a schooner at the polite offer of her skipper to save us the trouble of anchoring. His only entreaty was that our dinghy should not chafe against his ship's side, for with advancing years he found himself a very light sleeper. . . . Boarded *Johannes* and had *empressé* farewells with Bartels – more pears and matches.

'*10 Oct.* Up early. Wind SW light. Very hazy but fine. Beat in a light wind up Kiel Fiord. Nothing visible, till suddenly mists rolled away and showed a noble fiord, edged with tree-clad, villa-dotted hills, deep blue tideless waters all a-ripple and a-dazzle in the sun, and a long line of battleships moored in the fairway to where the town lay sparkling and glistening after the rain. A marvellous and magical contrast to the grey expanses of the North Sea, and the lonely levels of Friesland. It was only for half an hour or so, and the clouds were hurrying up from the SW with rain in them. We tacked in and out of the warships and anchored finally opposite the town on the east shore, among a forlorn group of dead yachts, hibernating, as were all we saw in this great yachting fiord. Harry went ashore for stores, and then we dropped down a mile to our anchorage off Folker's Garten.

'*12 Oct.* Henry had to leave for England. ['He has enjoyed himself awfully', Erskine wrote to their sister, 'and doesn't want to go, but has promised Stillwell and must . . . he is as keen as possible and would return in a month but that would be rather late.']* I determined to live aboard for a week or so and try to pick up some German ashore, leaving the future vague; possible return of Henry.

'*13–17 Oct.* Fearful weather. Stayed at anchor.

'*17 Oct.* Lovely day. Slight SW wind. No hesitation, set sails and started north to explore the Schleswig fiords and further if possible. Sailed to mouth of fiord in warm sunlight, 7 miles, and then took a course (18 miles) across Kiel Bay for Schlei Fiord. A thick haze and very little wind. Lashed helm and spent a lazy day. It was dark when I reached Schleimünde, the entrance to which is only 70 yards broad, though the fiord behind is 35 miles long. Groped in and unhappily took the ground – unkedgeoffably. No tide, so didn't bother but had supper. Then walked up to the only house visible (and indeed existing) and found a jolly inn, owned by the local pilot, a jolly old chap and his son and son's wife and children. Had a merry gathering round the fire. Pilot – in English – "Yes, we will first have a glass beer, then we will go and push off boat, then we will come back and have more glass beer." ' (*'Yes, yes,' he said, 'all right. There is plenty ducks, but first we will drink a glass beer; then we will shift your ship, Captain – she lies not good there. . . . Then we will drink another glass beer; then we will talk of ducks – no, then we will kill ducks – that is better. Then we will have plenty glasses beer.'* Riddle *Chap. VI, p. 59.*) 'Programme followed. Pilot had not talked English for twenty years and was rusty, but delighted to show it off. Spent a pleasant evening. Bed at 11 (moored to a tiny quay).

'*18 Oct.* Sailed at 12 in light S wind northwards for Flensburg Fiord. Another calm lovely day, but very hazy. Just made the mouth of the fiord, and anchored in a little indentation opposite the Langballig buoy, under the shade of deep woods. On the far side (it is about 2 miles broad) are gentle brown cliffs splendidly wooded, varied by pastures sloping to the water's edge; inland,

---

* They had considered the possibility of laying up for the winter in Kiel, but were deterred by the cost.

soft curves of hills and rich pastoral land.' (*From the shore we had left the hills rose steeply, but with no rugged grandeur; the outlines were soft; there were green spaces and rich woods on the lower slopes; a little white town was opening up in one place, and scattered farms dotted the prospect. . . . Spacious pastures led up by slow degrees to ordered clusters of wood which hinted at the presence of some great manor house. Behind us Flensburg was settling into haze. Ahead, the scene was shut in by the contours of hills, some clear, some dreamy and distant. Lastly, a single glimpse of water shining between the folds of hills far away hinted at spaces of distant sea of which this was but a secluded inlet. Everywhere was that peculiar charm engendered by the association of quiet pastoral country and a homely human atmosphere with a branch of the great ocean that bathes all the shores of our globe.* Riddle *Chap. III, p. 35–6.*) 'Navigation very easy – very slight current, sometimes a few inches rise and fall of water according to wind. Good holding ground everywhere, and always a wide choice of sheltered bays etc in bad weather. Decided that the southern Baltic was the finest yachting country I had yet seen.

'*19 Oct.* Thick fog and dead calm. A day to be hurried over. Calm, rain, fog, polings close inshore, towings in dinghy, all under a universal grey blur. Towed blindly in the evening into an inlet on the north shore, only 8 miles or so from starting point, and turned in after a chat with some friendly fisher folk, from a smack near, who gave me a bucketfull of fish.

'*20 Oct.* Glorious contrast to yesterday. Fresh NW wind and brilliant sun. Found myself only a mile from a seductive-looking inlet called Eckern Sound, so sailed in through a tiny slit in the hills and found a big stretch of water, fringed with woods in gorgeous autumn colours.' (*'That's Eckern Sound,' said Davies; 'let's look into it,' and a minute or two later we were drifting through a dainty little strait, with a peep of open water at the end of it. Cottages bordered either side, some overhanging the very water, some connecting with it by a rickety wooden staircase or a miniature landing-stage. Creepers and roses rioted over the walls and tiny porches. For a space on one side, a rude quay with small smacks floating off it spoke of some minute commercial interests; a very small tea-garden with neglected looking bowers and leaf-strewn tables hinted at some equally minute tripping interest. A pervading hue of mingled bronze and rose came partly from the weather-mellowed woodwork of the cottages and stages, and partly from the creepers and trees behind, where autumn's subtle fingers were already at work. Down this exquisite sea-lane we glided till it ended in a broad mere, where our sails*

which had been shivering and complaining filled into contented silence.
Riddle *Chap. III, p. 39.*) 'Breakfasted on deck. Then sailed out and
found I could just lie up Flensburg Fiord on the starboard tack.
Wind freshened, and I had a grand spin up to Flensburg under
shortened canvas, between fine hilly shores dotted with pretty
little villages and varied with bays and islands. Ran right up to the
town, but didn't much like the look of the anchorage for small
boats, so ran a mile back to a quiet spot under "Garrison Point",
and picked up a mooring. Ashore and walked in along prosperous
busy quays, lined with English steamers, to a big, bright town
humming with vitality. . . .

'*21 Oct.* To Kiel and back for letters. Left boat in perfect safety,
locked up, back at 9.

'*22 Oct.* Had still a week or more before Henry's return, so got
away to explore up Sønderborg way. Wind SW light. At mouth of
fiord it fell dead calm, and I had to anchor on the Krage Sand in
an exposed place. After dark wind came up from the SE, making
it a lee shore, so I got away and beat across in a fresh breeze to
Harrup Haven (about 8 miles or so), crept into a sheltered land-
locked bay and anchored about 1 a.m., after a long and ghostly
entanglement with a forest of fishing stakes which were invisible
in the dark.

'*23 Oct.* Woke up opposite a beautiful little village among trees
at an angle where the arms of the haven meet. Didn't land, but
wrote all the morning. At 3 sailed. Wind SE light. Ran lazily to
Sønderborg (5 miles NW). Narrow entrance barred by a pontoon
bridge which opened, and I glided up a narrow sound under a
quaint, old-world town, standing steeply on a hillside. A certain
amount of bustle on the quays. Moored at north end in a quiet
place, unobserved and unmolested. Ashore and strolled over town.
Wonderfully fascinating houses in the old part. The town is
Danish to the core, though German since '68. The very shop-
keepers speak German with reluctance.' (*Sonderburg with its
broad-eaved houses of carved woodwork each fresh with cleansing yet
reverend with age, its fair-haired Viking-like men, and rosy plain-faced
women, with their bullet foreheads and large mouths; Sonderburg still
Danish to the core under its Teuton veneer.* Riddle *Chap. V, p. 50.*)

'*24 Oct.* Wind E very light. Warm and sunny. Under way at 11.
Floated slowly north up Als Sound at whose entrance Sønderborg
lies, narrow as a river, and deliciously beautiful, with its reed-
bordered banks, quiet pastures, and background of gold and

russet woods. A fitful breeze was playing about and made sailing slow and lazy. About 4 miles from Sønderborg, caught sight of a little monument in a clump of firs. Landed and found a graceful little gothic memorial to those killed at that spot in 1864, when the Germans forced a landing and conquered Als Island. Good bas-reliefs showed scenes in the battle.' (*Opposite us on the Alsen shore there showed, clean-cut against the sky, the spire of a little monument rising from a leafy hollow. . . . Pushing aside some branches we came to a slender Gothic memorial in grey stone, inscribed with bas-reliefs of battle scenes, showing Prussians forcing a landing in boats and Danes resisting with savage tenacity. In the failing light we spelt out an inscription. . . . As for Davies, I scarcely recognised him . . . 'It was a landing in boats, I suppose,' he said, half to himself. 'I wonder how they managed it. What does* heldenmüthig *mean?' . . . He was like a schoolboy reading of Waterloo.* Riddle *Chap. V, p. 51.*) [The full inscription is carefully copied out in the log, and reprinted in the book.] 'It was a monument to the memory of the dead of both nations, and seemed to me singularly dignified and touching in its exquisitely peaceful surroundings. I boarded and went slowly on out of Als Sound, opening up new beauties at every turn, turned and sailed up the parallel fiord of Augustenborg a little distance, then retraced my way to the mouth of the sound and anchored off the little hamlet of Satrup.' (*'Come to Satrup,' they said; 'all the smacks are there, round the point. There is good punch in the inn.'* Riddle *Chap. V, p. 53.*) 'Visited a smack, had a long yarn, and then they conducted me ashore and introduced me to the village circle in the inn, where we drank a formidable beverage called coffee punch. Aboard again with a fine present of fish about 11. Lovely night – starry haze.

'*25 Oct.* Fog. Wind SE very light. Foghorned along east shore, back towards Sønderborg. Very thick. Moored in same place at Sønderborg. Fog all day.

'*26 Oct.* Fog all day. Stayed. In morning walked up to the famous Doppel Berg on the mainland shore, the scene of the last desperate stand of the Danes, taken by storm in '64.' (*The Dybbol of bloody memory . . .* Riddle *Chap. V, p. 49.*) 'Fog still, and no view of distance, but the great stone memorial was very interesting, so were the relics of the battle stored in an inn close by. In afternoon, fog cleared, so I hoped for a start next day. . . . [In fact the fogs and calms continued for another ten days. Unable to make Kiel to pick up Henry, the latter joined him on November 3 in Flensburg, bringing with him 'loads of guns, cartridges etc, big new double oil stove, and our fine old *Shulah* compass.' Plus, no doubt, a pound of Raven mixture!]

'7 *Nov.* Wind SE, bright, clear, warm, a welcome change. Splendid beam wind down fiord to Eckern Sound, then a long dead beat to the mouth of the fiord, whence we lay closehauled for Harrup Haven. Lovely night, full moon. Anchored at 7.30 on north shore.

'8 *Nov.* Under way at 5, moonlight. Wind E, light to fresh, very fine. Fine sail closehauled, southwards to Schleimünde – a glorious sunrise. Two miles from port, down came a thick fog; groped in and moored by quay at 9.30 a.m. Ashore and discoursed pilot on the subject of ducks.' (*Patriarchally installed before a roaring stove, in the company of a buxom bustling daughter-in-law and some rosy grandchildren, we found a rotund and rubicund person who greeted us with a hoarse roar of welcome in German, which instantly changed, when he saw us, to the funniest broken English, spoken with intense relish and pride.* Riddle *Chap. VI, p. 59*.) 'The question was whether to stay in the Baltic and try for them, or go back to Holland. Pilot was not encouraging, though he admitted there were lots of ducks, at first. In the evening we went out with him and his son and posted for them near a pond. Cold arctic. Pilot got one: we saw nothing! He said strangers weren't allowed to shoot in the fiord, but we gathered that personal considerations had much to do with this assertion. Anyway, we decided on Holland – via Kiel.

'9 *Nov.* Wind SE, strong. Dead foul for Kiel, so sailed up Schlei Fiord to explore. Lovely day and grand scenery. Four miles up came to Kappeln, pretty red town. Frequently found wind ahead in twists of the channel. Pontoon bridge at Kappeln; just squeezed through on port tack by an artful luff. Grieved remonstrance from the opener, who said we should have showed a flag in the main rigging if wishful to pass bridge. Fine beam wind to Arnis, a ditto of Kappeln, then opened a broad reach called Brednung Reach, several miles long, crossed at the further end by a railway bridge. A mile from this we ran full tilt aground on the edge of a steep-to shoal, and no kedging could move her. A little steamer tried to tow us off, but our warp broke and we lost several fathoms of it. A slight current was setting out, and we feared water would fall and leave us stranded for goodness knows how long. Nothing to do but take out ballast. No words to describe the exertion and loathesomeness of this job . . .! Filled dinghy, and then a friendly boat which we hailed. Took all starboard ballast out, and then she floated off; long before this it was a frosty moonlight night. Lay down among the ruins dog-tired, supped and slept.' (*a horrid business handling the pigs of lead, heavy, greasy and black. The saloon is an inferno, the deck like a collier's, and ourselves like sweeps.* Riddle *Chap. XV, p. 130.*) [The incident has been transferred almost verbatim to the Rute Flat, south of Langeoog, and the grounding described on September 19.]

'*10 Nov.* Wind SE strong, very fine, chilly. Spent till 10 putting back the ballast and cleaning up the unspeakable mess it had caused. Like sweeps when it was over. Then had a splendid sail – beam wind back down the fiord, and anchored at Kapplen to shop. Henry was asked by the baker (quite in a friendly way) if he was off a coal ship! Omelettes and beefsteak for lunch. Under way, and another fine sail to Schleimünde in a strong wind. Arrived there, decided to beat straight on to Kiel, feeling energetic; went a couple of miles, but found a nasty head sea and too much wind. Finally burst the foresheets, so turned back and ran into harbour – bet! Blew very hard in the night.

'*11 Nov.* Wind S. Thick fog all day. About midday heard step on deck, and next minute who should tumble down hatchway but our old friend Bartels, of the *Johannes.* He was on his way to Hamburg from Kappeln without cargo, and was fogbound as we were.' ('*I took my apples to Kappeln,*' he said sedately, '*and now I sail to Kiel and so to Hamburg where my wife and children are.*' Riddle *Chap. VII, p. 62.*) 'A joyous meeting celebrated in hot rum punch. In evening we heard duck in the fog quite near and followed them in the dinghy. Henry got two shots, but got nothing. Spent a pleasant evening at the pilot's house.

'*12 Nov.* Wind SSW, very strong and squally. Dull. We three-reefed and put on the storm jib and started for Kiel. It was a brute of a day, but we should be able to lie closehauled to the mouth of Kiel Fiord across the bay, so we decided to start. Lowered plate and had a very wet but jolly thrash with one tack to Kiel Fiord, in just about as much wind as she could possibly stand, and a short, very wetting sea. Wind moderated when we reached the fiord, and it was then a dead beat of 7 miles from Bulk Point to Kiel, seeming very long with no tide to help one. We shook out one reef and sailed well. A lovely evening. Passed a big steamer ashore. Where the channel narrows at Friedreichsort we were hailed from a Customs steamer to heave-to, and were boarded by an officer, who searched everything (a most unusual proceeding in Germany) and then demanded a table, pen and ink, embarrassing requests in view of the mess the cabin was in after our hard day's sail. He gave us a clearance paper and then left us. It was a tiresome delay, and we had to beat on to Kiel in the dark. Fouled a buoy and carried away bobstay and damaged stem a little.* Harbour full of warships (just before the Kiaochow affair†) whose launches were tearing about everywhere.

[The next four days saw them being towed once more through the Kaiser Wilhelm Canal, back to Brunsbüttel.]

'*17 Nov.* Wind SSW, moderate. Lovely day. Sailed on a roaring ebb to Cuxhaven: just lay closehauled the whole way. Tried to luff into the harbour, but in an instant were whirled past by the tide. Just let go anchor in time, paid out all the chain, and swung just clear of the quay and a steamer, with the tide foaming past. Read and lunched till slack water, then sailed into the same old spot. Herr Dieck (the ship chandler) appeared and talked fluent English at us. Ashore to find shops shut – St Peter's Day – could only get bread, and that by stealth. The great difficulty was water. After many enquiries, met with bewildered shrugs, we were led to a railway porter who, with great solemnity, lifted some mysterious flagstones inside the railway station, and lying on his stomach, filled our jars laboriously from a subterranean pool. No public supply at all. Being a saint's day made it worse.

'*18 Nov.* Wind W. Bespoke a carpenter to mend the stem, etc. Did a lot of rope jobs; bought landing nets and sponge baskets of colossal size to hold meat. Counted sorts of liquor on board. Result – thirteen, the best being Doppel Kummel, a Flensburg drink excellent in cold weather. Blew hard from W.

'*19 Nov.* Carpenter mended stem, etc. Blew hard from NNW.

'*20 Nov.* Same persistent hard W wind – dead foul for going west, so stayed in port. Dieck paid us a visit in the morning. Hot baths at the Handa Bad Hotel, followed by *Mittagessen*, and then a long walk along the sea dyke to the northern point of the land, coming back round by Dühnnen, a pretty little sand-side village. There were some tremendously strong forts on the point, to command the Elbe fairway. Back through northern suburbs of Cux-

---

* An incident transferred to Ostend, that 'filthy hole'. *Riddle*, p. 43.

† In November 1897 the Germans occupied the Chinese port of Kiaochow, as part of their drive for empire. 'The struggle for markets and spheres of influence in Asia and Africa had reached its most critical stage.' *The Anatomy of British Sea Power*, op. cit. p. 310.

haven, extremely pretty little boulevards planted with trees. Aboard to tea and *Pendennis.**

'*21 Nov.* Wind W, moderate. It was clear that we must beat against the winds if any progress was to be made. It was thick, unsettled weather, so we decided to cut in across the sands behind Newerk Island, following the boomed channels, as shown in some excellent up-to-date German charts we got here. Left about 8 on the ebb, and fetched about 6 miles down with a whole fleet of smacks. Then crept to the edge of the sands and explored for Sticker's Gat, our first boomed channel; found it, but also a strong ebb running out of it, and as it was a dead beat had to anchor about 12. It was quite dark before the tide turned, so we were done for that day. In any case a thick fog came on about 2, so we were glad we had not taken the outside route. Discovered we had only one jar of water. *Pendennis.*

'*22 Nov.* Wind W fresh. Grey day and thick haze. Took the flood and beat in short tacks northwestward along the booms. At last made out Newerk Island through the haze. Held on till the lighthouse and east beacon were in line, and then kept away west by south. Very thick, and booms ceased. Suspense – ended by a crash on the sand. Futile kedging.' (*Like lightning he had cast off the dinghy's painter, tumbled the kedge-anchor and himself into the dinghy, pulled out fifty yards into the deeper water, and heaved out the anchor. 'Now haul,' he shouted. I hauled, beginning to see what kedging-off meant.* Riddle *Chap. XI, p. 104.*) 'Dried 1.15 p.m. Found ourselves on Kleine Watt Sand, having just kept away 100 yards too soon. Long walk on sands.' (*For miles in every direction lay a desert of sand. To the north it touched the horizon, and was only broken by the blue dot of Newerk Island and its lighthouse. To the east it seemed also to stretch to infinity, but the smoke of a steamer showed where it was pierced by the stream of the Elbe. To the south it ran up to the pencil-line of the Hanover shore. Only to the west was its outline broken by any vestiges of the sea it had risen from. There it was astir with crawling white filaments, knotted confusedly at one spot in the northwest, whence came a sibilant murmur like the hissing of many snakes.* Riddle *Chap. XII, p. 106.*) 'Pendennis. Philosophy. Blew hard in the evening. Floated at 9 after severe bumping, and groped with the lead for the channel. Picked up the weather side of it and let go in 4 fathoms.

'*23 Nov.* Wind W, very strong. Thick haze – fog. Nasty sea

* *The History of Pendennis* by W. M. Thackeray.

when the bank covered. Great job to get up anchor. Started three-reefed about 11, high water, and groped from boom to boom closehauled southwards. Soon channel turned west again, and it was a dead beat against foul tide. Anchored about 2 under Grosse Knecht Sand in company with a schooner, which we visited and got water in exchange for cigars. We were here in a most desolate place, several miles from land, and nothing seaward but the sands. View none. Very bad night, with a heavy sea at high water and gunnel-under rolling. At midnight E. was flung out of bed.' (*to be pitched out of your bunk on to wet oilcloth* [linoleum] *is a disheartening beginning to a day.* Riddle *Chap. XII, p. 113.*)* 'Lockers burst open, and floor paved with honey, flour, broken glass and petroleum. At 5.30 wind shifted to N and we swung on to the sand and bumped. Took out a kedge and got her off.

'*24 Nov.* Wind N – moderate gale. Furious squalls. Our anchorage was now exposed to several miles of drift down the deep channel, and had to be left. Got anchor after great struggles.' (*I learned how to sail a reluctant anchor out of the ground.* Riddle *Chap. XII, p. 114.*) 'Three-reefed and reefed staysail, and sailed away west, now with a fair wind. Sailed about 10 miles, following booms at a tearing rate; once lost booms and got into 5 feet. At 1 reached the estuary of the Weser, and found a fleet of boats lying behind the edge of the bank. Weather too bad to go on, so let go in a heavy swell in 17 feet at high water. Quite safe, though, and swell fell with the water. A fine sail. Blew hard rest of day with hail squalls. Fine evening. Expecting swell at night we slept on the floor, but wind went down. Agreed that the plan was very comfortable, but caused too great displacement of things. *Pendennis.*

'*25 Nov.* Wind N by E, fresh. Lovely clear day. Started about 9 and sailed WNW slowly against the flood, closehauled, down the Weser channel, hoping to reach Wangerooge Island. Too clever in cheating tide and got into a *cul-de-sac* of sand, but discovered it in time. Further out found a heavy swell left from the gale. Tide slacked about 11 and we took fairway, edging from No. 7 black buoy to H red buoy, and so to the Weser lightship. Then bore away west for the Jade estuary, cutting over the Mellum Flat in 2 fathoms, where there was a very heavy swell. Passed a wreck here. Crossed Jade channel and headed for the Minsener beacon.

---

* See facsimiles to appear in separate plate section.

Thence easily picked up the boomed channel to Wangerooge and got into calm water, and familiar places. Lovely sail with wind aft behind the island. Ran her right in till she grounded a mile off the village, and let her dry there. [They were back where they had been on October 3.] Very glad to have done with what was the only difficult part of the return voyage. Landed with heavy load of water jars and oil-cans, etc. Warm welcome from our friends of the 'right' shop. Dark when we started back, loaded to the last extreme. Alas, we had forgotten to light the lamp, and we entirely lost the boat in the dark. Then remembered that we had also put no anchor out! Had to separate and search. E. found her at last, a long way off from where we had gone to. Relief. Lighted lamp and returned to help H. with the load. All aboard safely at 7. Floated at 11 p.m., and then sailed under jib to deep water and anchored. Glass high and wind NW – high hopes. [This incident is not used in the book: Davies would never have been so remiss!]

'*26 Nov.* Wind SW . . .! to our profound disgust, and glass falling heavily. Under way at 8 for the old game of beating. Lay closehauled on the port tack till nearly past the island, and then a dead beat across the sea-channel, helped by a strong flood which, against the strong wind, caused a drenching sea. Two-reefed. Heavy thrash along Spiekeroog, taking long legs over sand with the lead. At dark it looked very stormy, so we tacked over to the mainland side and ran her aground at half-ebb opposite the village of Neuharlingersiel. In view of a gale put out two anchors. Blew a hard gale in night with snow. Cabin quite warm with both lamps of stove alight and curtain up. Heavy roll on the weather tide.

'*27 Nov.* Wind SW moderate, rain and thick fog. When water enough, groped to the booms marking the channel to Neuharlingersiel and tacked up it by compass in the fog about 1½ miles. Suddenly the harbour (save the mark!) appeared a few yards off. Warped in and lay by quay. A tiny little basin set in a ring of cottages. Bought petroleum and 30 rolls and 5 lb sugar. Customs came along – chiefly for a drink. Found a jolly old sailor who had seen us off Cuxhaven. Pleasant people.

'*28 Nov.* Wind SW, fresh to strong (glass 30.0). As soon as afloat, sailed out to the basket-beacon and then (by direction of the people) stood away closehauled WNW over the sands in 5 or 6 feet towards Langeoog Island. Swell on the sea-entrance. Then a long dead beat along the island, tacking with the lead over the sands in company with six loaded boats. Wind stronger and rain. Two-reefed at 3, and, in view of dark, beat, as yesterday, over to the weather shore on the mainland and anchored under a bank in the Rute Channel. Glass began falling with frightful rapidity, almost visibly as you watched it. Two anchors out. Blew a heavy gale in night. Heavy sea at high water.' ('*It's been blowing a full gale, and the sea is at its worst now – near high water. You'll never see it worse than this.*' *I was prepared for what I saw – the stormy sea for leagues around, and a chaos of breakers. . . . The* Dulcibella *faced the storm as doggedly as ever, plunging her bowsprit into the sea and flinging green water over her bows.* Riddle *Chap. XII, p. 114.*) 'At midnight glass was at 28.50, having fallen $1\frac{1}{2}$ inches in 24 hours.

'*29 Nov.* Wind SW – gale abated but strong still. Very thick. Rain. Under way at light – determined to seek shelter at Bensersiel, a little place exactly on the lines of Neuharlingersiel, about 4 miles away on the mainland shore, approached by a boomed high-water channel. Fearful job to get anchor – found it bent! Groped three-reefed to the Bensersiel channel and anchored outside for water. Wind grew to an even worse gale, with heavy rain and a hurricane look in the sky. A waterspout passed us at a distance of about 400 yards. We were in the centre of a cyclone, we supposed, about 11, for the wind suddenly veered to the NE and blew a hurricane, making our anchorage and Bensersiel a lee shore. It was half-flood, and we decided to start, but how to get up anchor? Couldn't get in a link, as it was. In view of slipping it, we buoyed it ready: then got up sail, three-reefed, and tried to sail it out of the ground. Just giving it up when it came away and we got it up. [cf *Riddle* Chap. XV, p. 131, where they do let it go, accidentally.] Then bore away for Bensersiel. Got into the channel, but found booms almost covered by an abnormally high tide and very hard to see. Henry stood forward and waved directions, while E. steered. Soon got into breakers and found it a devil of a situation. Fearful work with the tiller under so much sail. One or two heavy gybes at turns of channel. When close inshore, sea less bad – missed booms altogether and grounded, but blew off again. Whole population on the beach yelling. Tide so high that all clues were obscured, but H. conned her skilfully on, and we were soon tearing into the mouth of the "harbour", about 15 feet wide, at about 7 knots. It was a tiny basin with not even room to round up. Tried to get sail down but peak jammed: let go anchor with a run, luffed, and just brought up in time with the bowsprit over the quayside, and received the bewildered congratulations of the people, who seemed to think we had fallen from the sky. [cf *Riddle* Chap. XV, p. 132. This is one occasion on which Childers, though using the scene in almost every detail, cannot improve on the reality. It seems as if he realised that he and Henry had made the wrong decision in running in before a gale, for in the book it is forced upon them when Carruthers lets the anchor run out and they lose it. Davies had intended 'running in behind the Jans sand, and not risking Bensersiel' – p. 131.]

'Boat and everything wet through inside and out. But she had done well, for she might well have broached-to in the breakers. Customs came aboard. Most hospitable chap. Insisted on our carrying all our clothes, bags, etc up to his house to be dried, and we were soon quite snug and dry below. [This functionary is sadly libelled in the book, where at first he is loaded with the self-important attributes of the 'gorgeous officials' of Oostmahorn, described in the log of December 8.] The crew of the Langeoog post-boat, lying just by, were also very friendly – stowed our sails, and asked us to pay them a visit.' (*The post-boat lay in her old berth at the eastern jetty, her mainsail set and her twin giants spitting over the rail.* Riddle *Chap. XXVII, p. 252.*) 'Underlying the general welcome we detected a slight current of disappointment connected with salvage operations which at one time had appeared probable! Sent for a carpenter and ordered a stout oak snubbing-post to be fixed in the bows. We had for long badly felt the want of it.

Tea with the Customs officer and his family. Beer later on in the inn. It is a small village of about thirty houses. Blew heavy NE gale in the night.

'*30 Nov.* Stayed in port. Rain and wind. Carpenter fixed post and made us a new crutch. Visited on board the post-boat. Cleanings and repairings. Customs man dined with us.

'*1 Dec.* Wind SW, light. No water to get out till afternoon so shopped, etc. Photoed Customs man and family. At 4 wind went suddenly round to NE making it impossible to sail out of harbour, channel too narrow in a headwind. After hasty discussion with all the village giving contradictory advice, and harbourmaster gloomily warning us to stay, we hurriedly chartered two men to tow us out as it was just high water, and soon too late and too dark. It was a long, tiresome business against a fresh headwind, and we grounded several times, but the men worked like niggers and at last we were in the open, and they left us in their boat. Unpleasant prospect as it was quite dark and raining and a lee shore. However, it was highish water, so we steered NW across the sands for Langeoog west point. After an hour's sail a boom loomed up, and the lead told us we were in 4 fathoms. So we let go, having not an idea where we were. Blew hard NE all night.

'*2 Dec.* Wind ENE, strong – a fair wind! Dull cold day but glass rising. Found ourselves just off Langeoog west point, two-reefed and ran cross sea-entrance and behind Baltrum, where we grounded at half-ebb with no water. H. fired at, but missed, a seal sleeping on the sand. Got off at 1.30, but kept repeatedly grounding and had no water as long as it was light. This was one of the shoalest spots in the whole region, and we found to our cost that E winds, though fair, brought much less water with them. Also the tides served badly just now: it was high water about 6 when too dark to sail, both morning and evening. Anchored near a loaded coaster and went aboard – very civil skipper – asked us to lie alongside, which we did. He said he hoped for scarcely 7 feet, even at high water (he drew 6 feet). Lovely evening. Frost.

'*3 Dec.* Wind NE, strong – lovely day. The only way was to start as soon as we could see anything and run on, on the ebb. Under way two-reefed at 7.30, but almost too soon, and lost booms and got into 4 feet 6 inches. Just found them in time and crossed sea-channel between Baltrum and Norderney, and ran into Norderneyer Watt (channel behind Norderney). It was now just a chance whether we could cross another shoal spot before the water fell too low. Ran on in a fine strong wind aft, Henry sitting on the bowsprit end to lessen her draft. She touched several times, but blew over and ultimately ran into deep water by the skin of our teeth. Saw a lot of ducks quite near, but no leisure to shoot. Splendid run to Norderney harbour, but went astray and stuck on a bank just off the pierhead and dried. A man came along who knew who we were, from a newspaper. Ashore and shopped. Welcome from the same grocer. Got a paper at an inn with large-type news of our stay at Neuharlingersiel. Town empty. Meat at the Jew butcher. Aboard and under way at 3.30. Wind fallen very light. Reached across to Norddeich and just got there when dark. Anchored in 12 feet.

'*4 Dec.* Wind ENE, light to fresh. Lovely day. Under way with daylight. Safely passed the shoal Slaper's Horn, where we had stuck on the voyage out, and had a fine run to the Ems estuary. Much puzzled by the disappearance of the leading buoy for the channel. After a false start, picked up the Ems fairway and breasted a strong ebb tide. Rounded the Rausel Sand, and then had to combat a strong flood, but wind freshened and at 4 we turned into our old boomed channel south of Rottum Island. Soon grounded, however, and after several attempts to get on, it grew dark and we anchored in only 7 feet (high water).

'*5 Dec.* Wind ENE. Dull, rain, thick. Two reefs. Under way too early and lost the booms: foolishly didn't anchor, but ran wildly on by a vague compass course. Ran for miles with but an inch or two under our keel through a grey inane.* Sighted one boom, ran to it, and found it a solitary specimen. At last sighted a row and thought we were safe as water was deep. About 10 yards from it ran hard aground at 6 knots, about. Unfortunately it was only about half an hour after high water. In two hours we found ourselves on a perfect Ararat, edge of a steep-to sand with a big sheet of open water behind it. [In the book Ararat suffers a geographical transfer from the Western Ems to the Rute Flat, SE of Langeoog, Chap. XV, p. 130.] Seemed the highest place for miles, and the peccant boom was bang on top of it. Took careful cross-bearings by Rottum and Borkum Islands, but couldn't identify our position. We were at the junction of two channels, the booms of the other being just visible in the south. Which was ours? After lunch, took a long walk with guns for miles in the direction of the mainland, and decided that the channel that ran that way was the right one. Had we not stuck, we should have taken the other one which led to the North Sea.' ('*The only way to learn a place like this,*' *he shouted,* '*is to see it at low water. . . . Look at that boom . . . it's all out of place.*' *Davies talking,* Riddle *Chap. XII, p. 107.*)

'Read *St Ives.*† Anxious moment at high water to see if she would float. At 8 she did so, or rather we scarcely waited but kedged her off stern first and anchored in 3 fathoms. Panic about water and

---

* Childers uses the word, unusually but correctly, in the book as well, to mean a void.

† Robert Louis Stevenson's 'tissue of adventures', as he described it, about a French prisoner-of-war in Edinburgh during the Napoleonic wars; unfinished at his death.

petroleum: found we had very little of either, i.e. warmth and sustenance. Rations of both.

'*6 Dec.* Wind SW, moderate. How we cursed yesterday's wasted day. Glass tumbling down. It was a dead beat against the tide, and we finally, in trying to cheat the latter, grounded again, in a good place this time. Walked further and identified our position exactly. *St Ives* getting very exciting. After dinner sailed into deep water. Water and oil very low!

'*7 Dec.* Wind SW, fresh, very fine but glass falling. Under way at 8, and lay closehauled for a mile southwards towards mainland. Here the channel turned along shore west and we had a long beat, with a good long leg on the port tack. A fine sail on a lovely day. Opposite village of Pieterburen, distant 2 miles, ran aground in the middle of a very big sandflat. Long walk. H. shot a bird resembling a small example of the smallest variety of the small jack-snipe. Cooked and eaten with due honour.' (*I stalked some birds with a gun, and obtained what resembled a specimen of the smallest variety of jack-snipe, and small at that . . .* Riddle *Chap. XV, p. 128.*)

'All the signs of a coming gale were present. Soon it came, and a very severe one from the SW with heavy rain. We bumped atrociously in leaving the ground and continued to do so after high water as the swell increased. Water swept over her in sheets just before she was waterborne. High water at 9.30 p.m. At 12.30 we took the ground again and had a good long sleep in comfort. At 3.30 a.m., when still dry, turned out and took out kedge with 40 fathoms of warp. It seemed to be blowing a hurricane then and we could barely walk along the sand. Oh! What a night!

'*8 Dec.* In morning wind had gone down. The boat seemed none the worse for her racketing, and never made a drop of water. Desperate condition of oil and water. Strict rations. Bread now almost gone, and couldn't spare water to bake more with! Wind SW, fresh. Dull. Under way at 8.30. Had a nearly dead beat to the Friesche Gat. Decided reluctantly that we must put into Oostmahorn for provisions. Seemed a fatality, as we had vowed never to go there again. Tested compass by Schiermonnikoog lighthouses in line NW¼N – exactly right. At 11 we reached the Friesche Gat deep water with wholesome red and black buoys to follow; slow beat against ebb to Oostmahorn, sustained by thoughts of oil and bread. A mile from the piers a heavy black squall struck us with a torrent of rain, and we had to scandalise and stumble in anyhow. Anchored outside and warped to south pier under gaze of entire population, as before. Same gorgeous officials came aboard, and this time there was a tremendous fuss because we were come last from a German port. Long inventory made of our stores, down to the salt in a little tin.' (*wanted to know our cargo, our crew, our last port, our destination, our food, stores and everything. . . . What spirits had we? What salt? Tin of Cerebos produced, and a damp deposit in a saucer. Riddle Chap. XV, p. 133.*) 'Then, "Where are you bound to?" "Terschelling." Great turmoil at this. Told we couldn't go there. Something to do with Customs – no office at T.; but we racked our brains to understand the thing as volubly explained in an incomprehensible language. "Where *can* we go?" They generously gave us a choice of ports, all utterly out of our way. Meanwhile our tempers were going. We were wet, tired and hungry, and had to sit in the cabin, chaffering impotently, while the curse of Babel brooded over all. At last it struck us that the whole thing was foolsplay, and only the over-zeal of official pedants to whom a ship in their port, of any sort, was a momentous event. "We will go where you please," we said. "Write it down – Harlingen" (a port down in the Zuyder Zee). They unquestioningly assented, and then wrote acres of papers, and took from us some unthinkable fraction of a threepenny bit.

'Once this was over, they were suddenly human and suggested punch. Being in a hurry, we gave them neat whisky, which they hate, and they withdrew, and we were free to warm, wash and feed ourselves, and fill up our water and oil cans and get stores. We had been five nights and six days at sea.

'After tea walked to Anjum, 2 miles, and renewed acquaintance with the polyglot Visser, innkeeper. He insisted on taking us round to see the two prettiest girls in the village. They were pretty, but it was rather an embarrassing visit as neither side knew the other's language, and we could not do much more in the social way than sit dazzled at so much beauty, while we drank tea with them. Shopped.

'*9 Dec.* SW gale and rain. Stayed in port. Visser and *fils* called, and the boy was instructed in the use of charts. Later we walked to Anjum again. He had some fine yarns. Had been a sea captain.

'*10 Dec.* Under way at 9. Wind SSW, fresh. Fair wind to Englishman's Flat, of stormy memory; then the usual beat, towards the breakwater. Passed it at 1, and beat on down boomed channel. Went astray and grounded at half-ebb, 2.15. Edge of a steep bank, out of the channel. *St Ives.* Lunch. In evening the usual gale got up and we had another terrific bumping, in rising.' (*She certainly had a terrific test that night, for the bottom was hard un-yielding sand, on which she rose and fell with convulsive vehemence. The last half hour was for me one of almost intolerable tension. . . . Sheets of driven sea flew bodily over the hull, and a score of times I thought she must succumb as she shivered to the blows of her keel on the sand.* Riddle *Chap. XIII, p. 116*.) 'At 11 p.m. turned out in fearful weather, meaning to sail to deeper water, but no power on earth could get the chain in, so remained where we were and made the best of it. It was a very exposed spot, several miles from any land. Wind gradually fell, however, and we got plenty of sleep.

'*11 Dec.* Woke to find dinghy gone! . . . One of us must have let go the painter in mistake for another rope, when setting sails in the dark and storm. Careful calculations showed it must have been blown to Ameland Island, 3 or 4 miles to leeward. So decided to sail there and make enquiries. Retraced channel nearly to break-water, and then turned west again, following a post-boat with passengers on board. The town, called Nes, is on the west end of Ameland, and we let go in very shallow water near the post-boat. E. landed among a crowd of natives and shouted for someone who spoke English. A diffident ex-sailorman was pushed out and proffered his few words. He turned out to be the inn-keeper, and we repaired to his house and I laboriously got into his head what I wanted, over weak Schiedam and water. He was very helpful, and sent out searchers at once. I offered a reward. Aboard again with him for a visit. Read Captain Cook's *Voyages*, and *Aeneid* Book VI.

'*12 Dec.* Sunday. Ashore, but no news of dinghy. Wrote and posted letters. After church the Amelanders sang hymns in the street in groups. A pleasant, pretty village, half-buried in sand, as in all Frisian islands. Huge square clock-tower. Seven hundred inhabitants. Two other towns in island, Hollum and Ballum – latter with 1,200 inhabitants. Bought some screws to mend rudder with. (We had found the lower end of it almost loose, screwplate having nearly come off.) Boat dried in the evening, and we had to mend it in the dark on the slushy mud by the lantern dimly burning and (by a fatality) continually going out. Screws were broken in the holes and we couldn't punch them out. A beastly job altogether.

'Floated after dinner and sailed to deep water (had left direc-tions with inn-keeper as to sending dinghy, if found, to Terschel-ling). Extraordinary tenacity of mud: though only 4 feet of water, had to get jib halliards onto chain to get anchor up, though no wind. (The dinghy turned up all right on shore of Ameland, and was sent to Terschelling after we had left for England.*)

'*13 Dec.* Wind SSW, fresh. Lovely morning. Delay of one and a half hours at a shoal place. Long beat against tide and wind along island and round the huge Vryhed's Flat to the sea-channel between Ameland and Terschelling Islands. Then a fair wind north to the mouth (buoys quite different to chart). Then turned into the old boomed channel, passed the white-headed post which lured us to disaster last time and our anchorage in the gale,† and on by a different channel this time. Suddenly at 1.30 a fog rolled up and we had to anchor. Gone by 2.15 and we started again, but it was now half-ebb with no water on the shoal places, and after some precarious progress from beacon to beacon (very far apart and hard to see) with H. on bowsprit end we finally stuck about 7 miles from the town of Terschelling. Threw out kedge and spent a pleasant evening reading Schiller (*Marie Stuart*). Usual gale at night, with heavy rain, but this time a comfortable berth. Glass falling heavily.

'*14 Dec.* Wind S, strong. Dull. Rain. Under way at 9.30, two-reefed. Splendid beam-wind sail to Terschelling. Entered harbour mouth and gradually shortened sail to bare poles and ran up gently into a snug berth by quay. Welcome from the crowd. Harbour crammed with Zuyder Zee smacks weatherbound, crews dressed *à la Turque*. Mr Fletcher had gone but had left word with Herr Schroo, British Agent, a man of note in the island, to look us up and give us help. He soon came aboard and proved a most useful and generous ally. We decided to lay up the boat here for the winter and go home for Christmas. Schroo offered to store all our gear in his own house for nothing, and boat would lie in harbour.

'Spent rest of day in skinning boat and transferring ballast to Schroo's, helped by Johann Schroo (nephew) and two other men.

---

* Childers told Walter Runciman of the loss in a letter from Oostmahorn, in which he described the cruise. Talking of the Frisians and the Baltic, he wrote: 'Both are jolly and indeed anywhere on the water, as I expect we both think! I have slept now over four months in this little cabin. . . . The boat though an ugly brute has proved fitted for the job and indeed has been roughly handled.' Runciman offered to replace the dinghy, and a new one 'magnificent to behold' was duly delivered to London in March the following year in one of the Runcimans' ships.

† See log entry for September 19.

Cleared all out and cleaned thoroughly. Slept at very comfortable hotel. Pleasant evening at Schroo's.

'*15 Dec.* Off by post-steamer at 6 a.m. Home via Harlingen, Stavoren, Amsterdam, Hook of Holland night boat.

'*16 Dec.* Befogged outside Harwich 16 hours – no bread. London next morning, a day late.'

End of Autumn Cruise 1897

V

West Indian Interlude 1898

Erskine Childers' 1897 cruise in *Vixen* was the longest and most arduous that he ever made. It was a notable achievement by any standards; carried out so late in the year it was remarkable; and, quite apart from the book that came out of it, is enough to ensure him an honoured place among the pioneers of small boat cruising. Its direct relationship with *The Riddle of the Sands*, of course, lends it a separate fascination: no one, I think, has created a work of fiction so exactly out of the events of a single cruise, and with such resounding success, and then enriched the stuff of a first-class yarn with a rousing patriotic message. It was a singular achievement.

Childers never drove *Vixen* so hard again. The following spring, having failed to recruit either Le Fanu or Walter Runciman to the enterprise, he went to Terschelling to collect her with a Burnham yacht hand, Alfred Rice. They found her 'ready for sea, but shocking bad fit-out – mast black, paint dull outside and evanescent inside'. It was blowing a gale when they arrived; but they got away after a couple of wasted days and fetched across in light weather to the Noord Holland Canal, which connects with the North Sea at Nieuwe Diep, by Den Helder. Here they bought a foghorn, which was money well spent in view of what was to come. Next day, becalmed in the canal, they chartered a horse and man at one of the locks and were towed to Amsterdam for seven shillings. In the canals they suffered the familiar plague of 'boy-pests', whom Rice swore at most effectively in rich Burnham dialect. The log also mentions lying alongside an immense iron transport barge; but whether this was later to suggest that lighter 'of well-proportioned and even graceful design, with a marked sheer forward' which Carruthers investigated (and slept in) in the Benser Tief, there is no means of telling. All Childers says is that while scrambling over her to go ashore he woke the skipper, who proved irascible.

It was now Friday, and he had to be at the House of Commons by 11 on Monday: progress was very slow. However, next day the weather relented; that is to say they had light airs and fog and were able to fumble their way south and west, heading for Dover. 'About 5 miles from South Foreland and growing dark another thick fog came on, with steamers about everywhere, keeping the foghorn very lively.' They finally crept between the piers of Dover Harbour, towing *Vixen* with the dinghy, at 8 p.m. on Sunday night, and Childers duly made it to his office next morning.

For the rest of a rather short season – he laid *Vixen* up at Moody's yard at Bursledon in mid-August – he strayed no further than from the Thames estuary to the Solent. Adventures were mild compared with the previous year's: having to drop the hook in a hurry to avoid being swept down on to an anchored steamer, or the following entry in July: 'Splendid sail up the [Southampton] Water, beating, wind having gone round to NW. Collision with a yacht which wouldn't give way when on port tack. Complete triumph for us!'

And this genial vignette: 'Fine beat past Cowes to Newtown for lunch. Parson sailed by in a dinghy under double-reefed Norfolk jacket and human mast.' But even if they did lose an anchor in Keyhaven, it was gentle work compared with Slaper's Horn in December. And in October he took passage in a very slow and more than averagely decrepit steamer, the SS *West Indian*, from Liverpool bound for Trinidad.

He very nearly missed her. 'Told boat was to start at 8.30 a.m.' his diary of the cruise begins. 'Drove up with Herbert at 8.15 and found her under way. Drove to the outer dock wall and boarded her. Luggage tumbled after and we were off.' The next day they had the southern coast of Ireland in sight. There were only three other passengers, a couple by the name of McCarthy and their daughter; 'golden-haired, eighteen . . . and a very good sort with no rot about her,' as he wrote to his sisters. 'The Captain and officers very pleasant, food indifferent, hours a nuisance, dinner at 5! Worst part – no electric light; out of order, and lamps too weak to read by.' Later other vital functions went out of order also; at best the old tub managed $9\frac{1}{2}$ knots. The eighteen day passage to Barbados passed pleasantly enough, however, with deck quoits, chess, brisk walks round the deck, yarning and reading, including reading Kipling aloud to the skipper. They saw two sailing ships bound home under a press of canvas; passed the Azores without so much as a sight of them; and were reduced at one point to 5 knots by a big sea and a strong headwind. Erskine tried developing his own films down in his hot little cabin – 'Indifferent results, under-exposed' – started to learn Spanish, and began *Lorna Doone* and Froude's *West Indies*, which he found interesting but shallow. He suffered considerably from indigestion.

They finally waddled into Carlisle Bay, Barbados on November 1: 'a low green commonplace shore, like the banks of the Thames in Sea Reach' was his first impression, soon to be erased by the dazzling novelty of sights, sounds, smells, the moment he and the McCarthys were rowed ashore by 'four mighty blacks' and into the Careenage, full of white schooners and small craft. Everything was new, strange, exciting: the squash made from fresh limes, the waving arrows of the sugar cane, the blinding white coral roads, the negroes' pathetic shanties knocked flat by the recent hurricane, the tailor's shop in Bridgetown under the sign 'Sartorial Artist'.

At Port-of-Spain, Trinidad, Childers left the *West Indian* and arranged a passage to Grenada in a 22 ton sloop. 'The idea of embarking thus for pleasure', he wrote in one of his *Times* articles ten years later, 'was received with a compassionate smile by the friend whom I consulted. Steam communication being very limited, an occasional traveller does, for some very urgent reason, resign himself to a sloop; but to West Indians in general these craft are a desperate resource, having an evil reputation for comfort, punctuality and safety. Sinister tales are told of their vagaries, and interesting statistics are quoted of their total disappearance.' What he had intended to do was charter a yacht and cruise among the islands of the Lesser Antilles, but there was none to be had. This is not surprising when one thinks that even after the war, indeed up until the mid-'50s, it would have been almost as difficult. Now it is a considerable industry; English Harbour in Antigua – Nelson's old base – is packed with charter boats, and

Grenadine islets like Mustique and Canouan and Bequia, which were hardly visited twenty years ago, are on every charter skipper's itinerary.

Undeterred by evil rumours and compassionate smiles alike, Childers duly laid in a stock of provisions for the voyage (Bovril, rum, bread and oranges), said goodbye to his friends, and had himself rowed out to the *Faith*, 'a little white-hulled sloop lying half a mile out. Dusk was falling on the crowded harbour and humming quays, and breadths of violet gloom were deepening on the mountains and the long curve of mangrove bordered coast and mingling strangely with the lamps of the big white town. The light was favourable to the *Faith*, and though loaded to the extreme she looked a shapely little craft, with a tall raking mast and a graceful stem.'

Thus he recalled it later: his diary, though less consciously wrought, has a greater immediacy. 'Brought down my luggage at 4 and found the skipper saying he couldn't start till tomorrow. Stormed back and called up his agent who said just "You *must* go", and he went. Rowed aboard at 6 and found a fairly good-looking boat, the deck piled with packages and passengers – four women, four men – all chattering and all good-humoured. How the crew were to get about to work the ship was a mystery. Two black pigs were strolling about forward and a hen fluttering.'

He had been promised the 'doghouse' as accommodation: this turned out to be 'a long low kennel standing on the starboard side – just room for a man to lie in' but 'perfectly sweet, clean, waterproof, insectless, and as comfortable as could be desired'. His diary continues:

'At 7 Captain boarded and we got under way in a scene of distracting confusion, and floated off in a dark still night with a young moon and a light easterly air. Order gradually grew, and we had our various meals by the light of a lantern – a queer, grotesque scene – showers soon fell, and I found the doghouse a secure refuge; the rest of the passengers disappeared into a small pit aft where sails were spread over the sugar bag cargo. The crew (six) had no resort that I could see. A wooden box amidships belched out smoke and seemed to be the galley, the black face of Napoleon the cook hovering over it like some infernal imp. After dozing I was woken at 10 by the heaving of the swell, and saw we were beating through the Bocas, high black cliffs towering on either side. Soon we were out in the open, steering closehauled to a NNE wind freshening.

'*16 Nov.* Woken by the roar of wind, shouting of men and beating of rain. Found her heeling to a fierce squall: crew shouting and hauling. Now saw that she was rigged with a whacking big mainsail, boom end far out over the taffrail, and a big staysail. In the squalls which followed very frequently, they lowered the halyards and roughly dragged down a reef-earring, leaving the sail in a bag till it cleared again. The boat was deeply loaded but behaved well in the nasty sea that was running. *Faith* was no idle name, for everything was eloquent of it, the rigging in a shocking condition of age and dilapidation. I expected the peak halyard to go at every puff. Things soon began carrying away: first the topping lift, hastily mended with a pathetically elementary knot; then the clew of the jib burst and had to be sewn up while we lay-to. The sails were dotted with holes, and I don't believe there was a single spare rope on board. There was an ancient compass in a cage, but I scarcely think anyone knew its properties: certainly there was no chart. Grenada was "somewhere over there"; the Captain vaguely indicated a large section of the horizon, and I suppose that was enough for his purpose – though many of these craft, I afterwards learnt, blown away in bad weather, turn up bewildered somewhere on the Spanish Main, short of everything, but no doubt quite careless. Such a happy-go-lucky concern I never saw. The Captain was the only man who could steer properly on a wind – we were closehauled on the starboard tack and so fetching a good deal to leeward of Grenada – the men letting her shake in the wind and sag away to leeward alternately, at night falling asleep at the helm! I unwisely break-fasted on sweet biscuits and oranges and was seasick, but happy enough.

'It cleared in the afternoon and I steered for several hours and earned compliments. It was very pleasant in the fresh trade wind and sunny sea. I also worked miracles, making soda water in my aerator in a scene of intense excitement, and bringing out my camera which they insisted on thinking to be a sort of telescope, and the Captain placing the lens to his eye said he could distinctly see land.

'Land – a blue haze on the horizon – did become visible on the starboard bow soon after. It was evident we should have a lot of beating to get to it. A lovely evening and moonlight night.

Niggers very gay. Woken up at midnight by the banging of the boom and shaking of sails, and found the helmsman asleep!

'*18 Nov.* At dawn land just visible a long way on the starboard beam, dead to windward. We fetched on the starboard tack for some hours and then went about when we could make it. I steered most of the day. Mine was the only watch on board and continually being referred to. Tried a ship's dinner: saltfish and yams, not at all bad.* My own provisions were much appreciated by everybody. A lovely day – sun and fresh tradewind. We had a smart beat up to the island, and at 2 were approaching the harbour. A lovely scene: high, tree-clad hills, white beach, palms and a little white town. Suddenly we dived into a deep little land-locked bay with high green cliffs, and soon were beating gently up to the quay.'

Childers spent a week in Grenada, staying with the Moloneys at Government House, making expeditions by pony all over the island, and ravished by its extraordinary beauty and luxuriance; and then took the mail steamer north, along the peerless archipelago of the Grenadines, to St Vincent. As they approached he 'could plainly see where the withering breath of the hurricane had passed. The hills looked brown and *ragged* and the bare poles of the coconut palms, shorn of their thick green crests, gave a curiously desolate look to the whole.'

It was the same when he was rowed along the coast to visit Souffriere, the island's active volcano which would erupt within the next five years and repeat, in a different form, the destruction wrought by the hurricane. His description of the trip, though only loosely connected with the sea, deserves quotation.

'Arrived at Chateaubelair, a village in a bay, in ruins mostly, but relief work and building proceeding rapidly. Procured a mule and a boy for bearer who took my mackintosh and provisions. ... Crossed a river, which the hurricane had evidently swollen to huge limits. It was now a mere trickle in a bed nearly half a mile broad, choked and littered with huge tree trunks, and in one place

---

* In the notes from which he wrote up his diary, Childers adds: 'We drank healths all round in weak rum and water and yarned. I caught the infection of irresponsible gaiety and wondered if, after all, life had any serious side.' He also lets out that his attendance at the dinner was by the Captain's invitation: 'I accepted courteously, but with resignation and inward despair!'

the ruins of a large sugar factory which it had mounted to and run clean through. Now a hard two hours' steep climbing up a crooked hog's back between two deep ravines: on either side lay the virgin forest – a yellow tumbled wreck, looking in the distance like a September stubble, and from near, like a game of spillikins. Hard to conceive the terrific forces that had worked to produce such appalling havoc. Gigantic banyans were lying tossed anyhow, roots in the air. Palms flung in fantastic postures and blackened like dead cigars. This was as far as eye could see, no nook or corner of the ravine, however sheltered, being spared, and so to the most distant peaks and ridges. A nightmare ride it was, through the valley of the shadow of death, in a grim and unnatural silence. . . . At 1.15, without any notice, I suddenly came on the crater, running sheer down three hundred feet* or so to what looked like a lake of milk tinged with emerald green. . . . By the time I was ready to start back, a heart of dark thick green had grown in the middle of the lake and was spreading out from the centre like a great blossom.'

A few days later he was off on another, very different, expedition.

'Long day on the sea in a cockleshell boat† with a negro – Dudley – to row. Went in windward direction. Round Cane Garden Point the strong wind against tide made a nasty sea. It looked impassable but Dudley was tranquil. Constant heavy bailing. . . . Potted harmlessly at pelicans with my revolver. Then got under some cliffs and fished. First was a "rainbow" fish – described by its name; then other strange sorts, of lovely colours, and queer shapes – all small except a big thing like a whiting. Lunch and a delicious bathe on a sandy strand. Smoked and read Browning. . . .'

He had one more island hop ahead, from St Vincent to St Lucia, for which he took the sloop *Flurry,*

'a 15 ton boat with new sails but the inevitably antique rigging. No cargo. Captain, two men and a boy about twelve, who was the

---

* After the eruption the crater was nearer a thousand feet deep, but the lake, infinitely sinister, still had that same milky, sulphurous tinge, with great, slow bubbles bursting on its surface.

† Almost certainly a dugout canoe, though he does not say so.

only able seaman, besides being cook and most other things. Weighed at 3 and ran down leeward side of island in a strong squally wind off the shore. No reefs in the big mainsail, primitive method of having two men always at peak and throat halyards and another hand at the jibsheet: in a squall, everything let go. I steered. At 6.30 were leaving the land and standing closehauled to sea in a NNE wind, not nearly making St Lucia. Rough night; heavy sea and strong wind. Continual messing about with sheets and halyards, accompanied by incessant yelling and confusion and quarrelling. *Flurry* a very appropriate name, as was *Faith*.

'Woken by a deafening quarrel between Captain and Mate in the middle of the night. There is no discipline, and master and man just screech execrations, till the one exhausted first retires with a haughty sulk, while the other keeps it up till breath fails him. . . . This time I stormed too till I daresay the united noise could have been heard all over the North Atlantic.

'*7 Dec*. At daylight we were about 12 miles to leeward of the south end of St Lucia. The two peaks of the Pitons standing up sharp and grey against the light. Long and tedious beat in with a foul tide and not much wind. It was 1 before we were under the land – rising in rich tree-clad ridges towards the interior, palms on the seashore, no signs of hurricane. Our port, however – Castries – is at the northern end of the island, and we had a long beat up along the leeward shore in smooth water and a freshening breeze, till forts on a headland appeared overlooking the narrow passage into Castries Harbour.

'The sun was just setting and it was a lovely scene – the harbour lying beneath a circle of green jagged hills dotted with villas and huts, and the town at the eastern end, white and pink in the sun. Two vast heaps of coal on the quay speaking of St Lucia's growing importance as a coaling station. . . . HMS *Pallas* was moored in the harbour. Unhappily we anchored just after 6 o'clock, too late for the harbourmaster to come off and examine, so, much to my disgust, I had to stop another night on board. The crew all went to sleep immediately, and I had a substantial dinner of tinned beef, apricots, and whisky and soda, and then meditated on deck over cigarettes under a still and starry sky and cool night breeze.

'*8 Dec*. Came to the quay and found a steamer coaling. Hordes of ebony amazons, mighty and massive of stature and magnificent of carriage, were hurrying up a gangway and through the ship in ceaseless clamorous streams, each carrying a heavy basket of coal on her head which the weaker sex filled from a black mountain on the quay and lifted on to the heads of their mighty partners. All worked with *acharnement* in a haze of coal-dust under the burning sky, for the pay was twopence for five baskets carried; the engineer giving every woman a brass disc for every basket thrown into the bunkers, the discs to be cashed later at the Company's office. Women can often earn seven shillings a day, it is said. The rapidity of the whole operation owing to the numbers, strength and discipline of the women is amazing: coal flows into the bunkers in a practically ceaseless stream, and St Lucia boasts that their coaling is the quickest in the world. They can, at their best, do 200 tons an hour. It was an extraordinary scene, with a weird, unearthly fascination in it – and it would prove a fearful shock to a theorist on the Dignity of Woman. Nevertheless, these thickset short-skirted giantesses have come as near complete emancipation as the most extreme of workers for Women's Rights could wish.'

The diary ends abruptly a couple of days later, without a hint of how or when Childers returned to England, but with a slightly wistful note that, according to Mrs King-Harman, the Administrator's wife, the Bahamas consisted of 'thousands of jolly little islands with splendid sailing'. He relished the Windward Islands, with their vitality and colour, and where one is never long out of sight and sound of the sea, so much that one can only regret that he did not write more fully about them. As to the inter-island passages by sloop, his article about them in *The Times* ends drily: 'It is impossible unreservedly to praise this mode of travel. Yet to anyone who tires of the gilded and secure monotony of a mail steamer and likes a good stirring sail, together with a glimpse into an obscure phase of West Indian life, the sloop may be commended. The best plan of all, given plenty of time and other favourable circumstances, would be to hire one of these craft, extemporise some sort of cabin accommodation, modernise the rigging, and sail with an amateur crew. But the hurricane months, July to October, should be strictly avoided.'

VI

Sunbeam and *Asgard* 1902-4

'In truth,' Childers wrote in a letter from Denmark, 'the only really proper way to get to places is in a sailing yacht by one's own efforts.' And again, in one of his *Times* articles: 'We cruise for pleasure, I suppose, but the ingredients of this pleasure defy rational analysis. There is a strong enough infusion, indeed, of abject physical misery to sadden a man for life on any logical theory of human tendencies'; and he quotes the experience of his friend and sailing companion, Gordon Shephard, 'hove-to for 30 hours through an icy northeasterly gale ... between Landsort and the southern entrance to Stockholm, a rock-sown shore a-lee and the broad Baltic to windward.' And he talks of 'a world of strenuous effort and infinitely varied emotions – high resolve, hopes, doubts, joys, depressions, ecstacies, torments, and every shade of suspense.'

Because the 'pleasure' is self-inflicted, and the emotions derive exclusively from the activity itself – weather, sea state, navigation, the vessel and her gear, the endurance of her company – these things overflow only slightly, and at a remove, on to the workaday world. We may all, as Childers himself once remarked, 'hunt in dreams'; but, in his normal daily life, the amateur sailor is businessman, engineer, civil servant, farmer or what-not and indistinguishable from his non-sailing fellow men. In the context of regarding Erskine Childers purely as a sailor, therefore, the separation of this aspect of his life from his everyday activities presents some problems, for the only sources of information on the former are his logbooks, the published accounts of his cruises, and occasional casual references in letters. Where these fail, one is in the dark.

Such gaps in the story occur most notably from 1898 onwards, and particularly to the blank years between 1907 and 1912. Logbooks end abruptly, or if they ever existed have disappeared; and other references are sparse. However, there are very full accounts of three of his cruises between 1903 and 1913, all of them noteworthy and one – that to Finland in the latter year – outstanding. Extracts from these follow in due course.

After his return from the West Indies at the end of 1898 Childers recorded only one more short season in *Vixen*, for April and May 1899, restricted to local sailing in and around the Solent. It is of no special interest, though old Solent hands may be intrigued by the following: 'took a pretty walk to Wootton . . . and later to Fishbourne at the mouth of the creek, and got a boy, Frank Young, to engage to look after the boat'. Could this be other than the weatherbeaten, sardonic, gruffly helpful Frank Young who until his death a few years ago was invariably on hand to scull out and direct visiting yachtsmen where to drop their hooks in the pool at Fishbourne?

Vixen's log ends suddenly on May 1 of that year, with the unrevealing entry 'Went to town by 8.02', and that is that.* A clue as to why he packed up sailing so early that year is to be found in Andrew Boyle's biography†: the crisis that led up to the South African War continued all that summer and early autumn, and kept Parliament, and therefore the clerks at the House of Commons, busy. Childers' mood is expressed in the letter which he wrote to Walter Runciman in July, and from which the title of this book is taken:

'All this year I have had the sea-thirst on me . . . but after many vows of weekends on the Thames nothing has happened. . . . As it is, my most exciting cruise has been in a sailing boat upriver on a dead calm day. Great is the sea!'

---

* According to R. M. Bowker ('*A Historical Postscript*' to *The Riddle of the Sands*, Bowker & Bertram, 1976) *Vixen* was sold in 1900 for £12, but he does not reveal the source of his information.

† Op. cit. p. 84.

And in October, instead of sailing, he and William Le Fanu went cycling in the Dordogne.

That winter Erskine Childers joined Basil Williams, who had already applied as a driver in the special battery of the City Imperial Volunteers, an emergency unit of the Honourable Artillery Company financed by private subscription in the wake of the string of British defeats in December, known as 'Black Week'. His service in South Africa is vividly described in his first book *In the Ranks of the C.I.V.*,* and although it has no place here, from several points of view the experience was both formative and useful.

The CIV, and Childers with them, were back in England in the autumn of 1900; but there is no record of his doing any sailing until 1902, when he bought the thirty year old 15 ton yawl *Sunbeam*† in partnership with William Le Fanu and A. H. Dennis. The following summer *Sunbeam* headed north and east for Terschelling, Cuxhaven, Brunsbüttel and the Baltic.

Dennis, three friends, a paid hand, and 'a small cabin boy who had never even *seen* the sea before' took her as far as Flensburg on the east coast of Denmark, where Le Fanu, Ivor Lloyd-Jones and Erskine – those three musketeers of many an East Coast and Solent adventure – joined her and replaced some of the others. With a Captain Charlton and the crew, they set out to explore waters which, over and over again, Childers refers to as 'the most beautiful, varied and interesting of all cruising grounds'.

The itinerary of the voyage took in that dazzling archipelago which lies between Denmark and Sweden, and divides the Kattegat from the Baltic proper. There are three main channels north and south through it: the Great and Little Belts, and Øre Sound on which Copenhagen is situated; and *Sunbeam* and her complement carried out an irregular figure-of-eight round the two main islands, Fyn and Sjælland. The weather, on the whole, was against them; indeed, it would not be too much of an exaggeration to say that it was a hell of a cruise. The following passage, from the account of it in the RCC *Journal*, gives the general flavour.

'*August 31.* A most depressing morning. Pouring rain, glass tumbling down, nowhere to run for, an open roadstead and a gale

---

* Published by Smith & Elder, 1900.

† Ex-*Zephyr*. 38 × 10 × 5 ft. Her owners are given in *Lloyd's Register of Yachts* as, in 1902, Erskine Childers; from 1903 to 1905, he and Le Fanu.

brewing. In due course the sky cleared, the wind veered to the west, and the blow began. Our berth became a lee shore, and we weighed hurriedly in company with quite a fleet of smacks and coasters who were in the same box as ourselves. We hoped the change of wind would allow us to proceed south again, so with three reefs down we fetched round the Head and tackled the open. No use; found the wind ahead, and an impossible sea. Back again and sailed slowly up and down under the lee of the cliff while some terrific squalls passed over. This cliff, by the way, was the finest we had seen – a towering wall of chalk, but crowned with magnificent woods, and cloven at intervals by ravines wooded to the water's edge. Finally we anchored together with all the other vessels in a spot which promised good holding ground, well round the shoulder of the cliff, and under shelter of it; a heavy ground swell running in, and we rolled horribly. At 9 p.m. the wind veered still further round to NW and blew a heavy gale. As we were, however, the land was still just – and only just – a protection, and we rode it out there all night, the anchor holding well, though the sea was considerable. Some of the other vessels, including a German yacht, dragged and got sail up and shifted still further round. We kept anchor watches, and the night was a rather anxious one, but all turned out well. None of us will forget the scene that night: the little *Sunbeam* plunging her bows into the short white seas and the great pale cliff rising above.'

The cruise, though strenuous and covering 1,870 miles, does not call for more extended quotation, for it was something of an interlude between Erskine's dashing introduction to the Baltic with and without Henry in 1897, and his further exploration of its tideless waters with Molly later. What it did do, despite the weather, was to confirm its appeal for him. The visual beauty, the abundance of natural anchorages and pleasant harbours, the sense of history, vivid but quiescent – except for the ships of the German High Seas Fleet which they always seemed to meet at Kiel or in the Canal – and the intricate navigation, all matched his ideas of what cruising should be. The demands for technical challenge and aesthetic reward, for that extension, physical, mental and emotional, on which he thrived best – never 'to rust unburnish'd, not to shine in use' – were utterly fulfilled there.

And after he met and married Molly Osgood of Boston in 1904, he could hardly wait to take her there. 'We are approaching my beloved and lovely Baltic,' he wrote to her family from Rensburg, on the Kiel Canal, in 1906, 'where I hope to show her some of my favourite places.'

But first he had to introduce her to his kind of sailing. Her father, Dr Hamilton Osgood, had promised them a boat of their own choosing as a wedding present; but the choosing was not something to be done in a hurry. 'Then as to the yacht . . .' he wrote to 'The Commodore', the honorary and light-hearted title by which he always addressed his father-in-law, 'we have thought a great deal about it. . . . It would be impossible to find and fit out *your* yacht this spring. . . . We have decided to take a fourth share in the *Sunbeam*, our old yacht, with Le Fanu, Dennis and Colomb (a colleague of mine here). . . . It is only experimental, as I am not at all sure that Molly will find it quite comfortable. This plan is for "weekending" principally, and if we want a long cruise in August we can settle about it later.'

So, during that first summer of their marriage, *Sunbeam* remained in home waters. Nevertheless, after one or two small preliminary sallies they set off for the West Country and got as far as Falmouth.

'It was a test day,' Erskine wrote to The Commodore from Plymouth; 'a strongish wind, lumpy sea, heavy rain all day, and a long sail with a headwind most of the time. She sat in her oil-skins and seaboots and sou'wester by the mizzen all day long, looking such an able little sailor-girl.' Although Molly Childers was usually seasick at the start of a cruise, it was not long before she had thrown off any need for such protective concern: indeed, even on that occasion she soon found herself in the galley, and it was not long before she was taking the helm and standing her watch with the rest.

Some time during that summer they decided the kind of boat they wanted, and they commissioned the Scottish–Norwegian naval architect Colin Archer, of Larvik, at the mouth of Oslofiord, to design and build her. Archer, designer of Nansen's ship *Fram* as well as of many of Norway's lifeboats and fishing vessels, had a reputation for building boats, usually double-ended, of great strength and rugged beauty; and for the kind of cruising that Erskine Childers had in mind he could hardly have gone to a better man. Whether he ever went to Larvik, whether they ever met, one doesn't know; but by December 1904 the original plans for a 'Cruiser for Erskine Childers Esq.' had been drawn. With a number of modifications, building went ahead; and in the summer of the following year she was delivered to Bursledon by a Captain Knüdsen, with Ivor Lloyd-Jones on board as Childers' representative. They had a rough passage – in a complimentary reference written for Knüdsen, Ivor mentions his 'resourcefulness and care . . . in some heavy weather which we encountered': nevertheless the boat was delivered safely to Bursledon in August.

On the 30th Molly and Erskine, with a friend, Laurie Rainsford, joined their brand-new ship. They had christened her *Asgard*, which in Norse mythology was the Home of the Gods; a kind of Scandinavian Olympus, approached by a rainbow bridge and containing, among other establishments, that eternal banqueting-hall for warriors slain in battle, Valhalla. A good name, eloquent of hard nor'easters and driving spray, and incidentally embodying, as Burke Wilkinson points out, a sly complimentary pun on the name of her provider, Dr Hamilton Osgood.

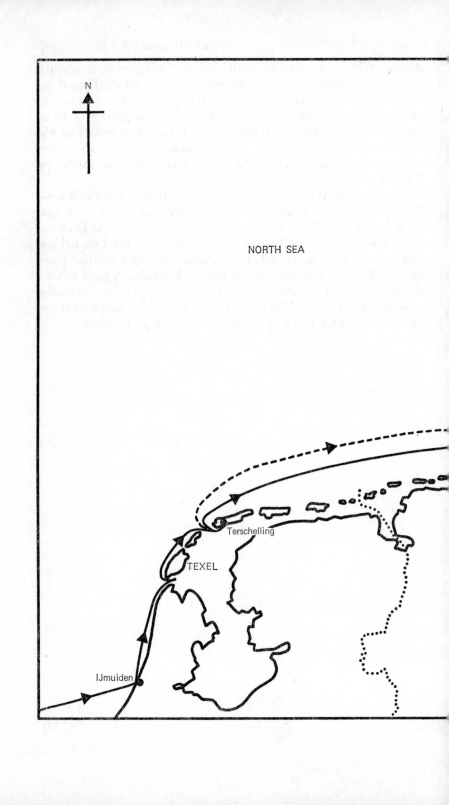

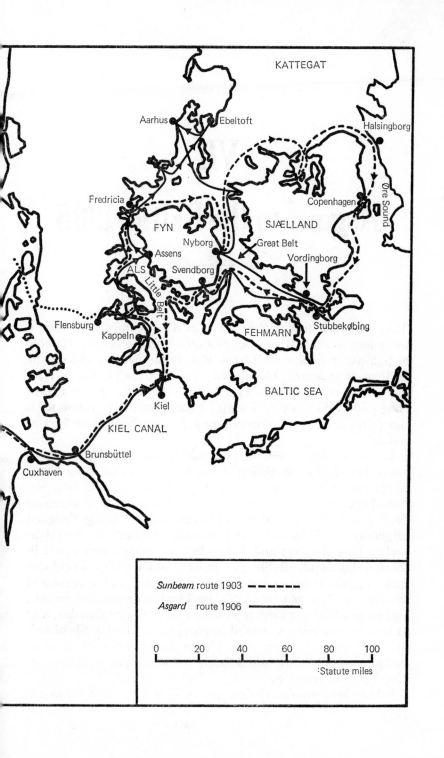

KATTEGAT

Aarhus Ebeltoft

Halsingborg

Fredricia

Copenhagen

FYN

SJÆLLAND

Nyborg

Great Belt

Assens

Vordingborg

ALS

Svendborg

Little Belt

Flensburg

FEHMARN

Stubbekøbing

Kappeln

Øre Sound

Kiel

BALTIC SEA

KIEL CANAL

Brunsbüttel

Cuxhaven

Sunbeam route 1903 — — — —

Asgard route 1906 ——————

0   20   40   60   80   100

:Statute miles

VII

Asgard to the Baltic 1906

They had their first trial in her next day. It must have been a tremulous moment when they cast off and ran down the Hamble at half-past four that afternoon, but, in the manner of logs, the excitement is muted. Conditions were ideal: wind NE to NW, light. 'Ran out of river and beat up Southampton Water against ebb; yacht sailing well. Went up Itchen, touching ground for a short time at dead low water on east side. Anchored near ferry at 8 p.m.'

Later, as they roved further afield, they quickly came to appreciate *Asgard*'s qualities: strength, stiffness and, for a heavy displacement boat, a good turn of speed, even in light airs. She had the Colin Archer stamp: a powerful spoon bow sweeping back (an indication of her northern origins, being designed originally to ride up on ice and smash it) to a fairly short straight keel; a long counter; and a fine, but not exaggerated sheer: in short, a thoroughbred. She was 44 feet overall, with a short bowsprit, 13 feet beam, 7 feet 6 inches draught, and a registered tonnage of 18.44. She was gaff-rigged on both main and mizzen, and set in addition a main topsail, two headsails, a spinnaker, and at least once a mizzen staysail improvised by Gordon Shephard. She had wheel steering with a tiller for emergencies, a small cockpit, two skylights, and a forehatch which got washed overboard on one occasion.

Below, her accommodation was divided into three cabins: a

two-berth sleeping cabin with its own wc to port; a companion-way with another bunk to starboard leading to the main saloon with two more berths, and a fo'c'sle with a couple of folding cots. On the original drawing there is no indication of the galley, but in fact it was in the fo'c'sle. She had, of course, no engine. In lieu, she carried sweeps which, that first summer, they used to propel her in through the southern entrance [now closed] of Portland Harbour – against the tide!

During that same shakedown cruise there is the gratified note in the log: 'Overtook and passed a 200 ton schooner which had outsailed us earlier in the day, because we could sail so much closer than she'; and, beating across to the Yealm from Plymouth, 'Molly steered the whole way. Yacht quick and handy in the narrow places.' They were taking the measure of her then; and on the run from Prawle Point to the Solent under all plain sail they logged 86 miles in 12 hours, which is good going.

Although Erskine would never be a skipper to spare his crew, for he suffered acutely from that restlessness which afflicts all true cruising men ('Be the anchorage never so tranquil, the port so congenial, the day so fair, he must be up and off', he wrote later), the mood of the *Asgard* logs is subtly different from those of his previous boats. The tacit discipline of cruising, the *raison d'être* of which is still to visit as many places as possible, is tempered by a new warmth and gaiety. Erskine's anxiety over Molly soon gave way to respect for her skill as a helmsman, and her exceptional sharpness of sight; and, added to the sheer joy of cruising, there is the joy of introducing his young wife to a sport, and to places familiar and unfamiliar which he longs to share with her. One catches also the merriment and camaraderie of a company of friends thoroughly enjoying a well run, at times quite exacting, but wholly invigorating adventure.

The atmosphere aboard can be detected in the mock-insulting remarks which Molly appended to the crew list in the log. In 1905 Erskine is classified, under the heading 'Capacity', as '*de trois hommes*'; she herself as 'nil'; and Ivor as '3 gallons neat'. The following year, the skipper is 'slave-driver' and, under 'Remarks', 'very severe'; she is 'charwoman' and 'fractious'; Ivor is 'the driven slave, patient but complaining'; William Le Fanu is 'a barnacle, sticks to everything' [a reference to his ancient and adhesive oilskins]; and William Amor, their ex-naval paid hand, 'would cook while sinking'. And so on. The impression is of a taut ship which it would be fun to be on, as long as you pulled your weight and your face fitted. One, that of an American friend of a friend, did not. 'An altogether speculative proposition', Erskine wrote to his favourite confidante, Aunt Flora, 'who turned out not exactly a success and not exactly a failure – a sort of negative who came and went and left no trace. He was terribly nervous at first and used to wake me up and implore me to order sail to be shortened!'

Once, that first summer, they even risked the hazardous experience of taking other people's children to sea with them. They were 'very merry and active all day, scrambling, climbing, laughing, eating and drinking, nearly falling overboard, etc.... For the last hour there had been a substantial pandemonium of shrill noises, whether of gaiety or agony difficult to determine. Baby crawling at large all over yacht, stepped on occasionally by owner. Now an unearthly silence has succeeded; probably all dead. *Requiescat*. No! – the baby lives. A splendid day!' Whether they ever took their own two boys to sea is not clear: their names certainly do not appear in the crew lists in the surviving logs. One feels sure that young Erskine, at least, must have accompanied them on some of their Solent weekends during those years from 1907 to 1912 for which the logbooks are missing, when he would have been between two and seven years old. No doubt he too got 'stepped on occasionally by owner'!

At all events, by the time they laid up early in October they had done enough to be certain that they had a good boat, stiff in a breeze of wind, quick in stays, weatherly, strong, roomy and comfortable. Erskine also knew that he had a wife as eager for new and farther horizons as himself, and capable not merely of coming with him but of acting as a useful member of the crew. 'Little Molly, sitting in her oilskins and seaboots and sou'wester by the mizzen all day long' becomes the Mate, who can keep a watch and cook, and has eyes as keen as the sea-eagle's.

Their first son, Erskine Hamilton, was born in December of the same year; the following August they left Bursledon 'in a perfect deluge of rain, the weather having unfortunately just broken after a long period of cloudless summer days', with Ivor and Amor, and raced along the South Coast and across the North Sea bound for Ijmuiden, Texel, Terschelling and the Kiel Canal. Molly was 'shamelessly' seasick, she told her parents, but recovered and was soon taking the wheel. 'I am so excited to think that I am going to see *The Riddle of the Sands* country,' she said; and the remark nourishes that curious sort of mental displacement which tends to affect readers of the book. When, a little later, going through the canal, they find themselves tied up to a galliot the skipper of which 'knows Bartels of the *Johannes* well', that misty frontier between fact and fiction seems to take on a quality of mirage. Will they see von Brüning smiling down on them from the lock wall, or spot the *Blitz* among the triple ranks of the German High Seas Fleet anchored in Kiel Fiord?

In fact, fictional realism is overtaken by reality: they are pestered by midget torpedo-boats, and fired on by a cruiser which opens up on its target without warning as they pass her. 'We had to put about quickly,' Childers notes in his customary undramatic way. But they were in his 'beloved and lovely Baltic' with, as he wrote in *The Times*, its 'clear tideless waters, delicious scenery, a vast variety of sheltered anchorages and snug harbours, friendly, hospitable folk'. And behind these delights there was always the tingle of excitement as he exercised the skill he enjoyed most:

'Indeed, the artistic joy of sailing up the reaches of some winding sound at night by working in the sectors of successive leading lights is often a full reward for the hours of calm or contrary wind which have prevented arrival by daylight. But in weighing risks we must make up our minds never to run aground. Since there is no rise and fall of tide, stranding may involve heartbreaking labour, if not considerable peril. For my own part, I suppose I shall never cease to be chaffed for an error of judgement which resulted in "piling her up" in Fæno Sound and imposing on my friends and myself the work of removing several tons of ballast in the dinghy before we could float her off.'

This unfortunate contretemps does not appear in the account he wrote of the cruise for the RCC *Journal*, only this lyrical description of Baltic cruising's other face.

'The evening was fine and cloudless. A full moon shone down clearly, and everything in sight was reflected in the still water. A great barge, all sails set, and standing unusually high fore and aft, came slowly down the fiord, slipping silently with the gentle current. She dropped anchor and headsails close by us, but left her great mainsail up, and lay there looking like a powerful bird about to take flight.'

Like most well-conducted cruises by competent sailors, this one lacked drama, but not incident. As they were careering along past the Frisian Islands double-reefed and with a big quartering sea, the spinnaker boom, which was stowed up the forward side of the mainmast, suddenly broke adrift and crashed over the side. Still made fast at its lower end, it 'bent and bent and creaked furiously under the fearful force of the water', as Molly described it in a letter. 'We luffed instantly, but it broke and had to be cut away . . . Erskine and Amor were forward right near it, but it fell clear.'

Others were less startling. On their way to Flensburg, with a strong WNW wind and one reef down, 'we had two annoying mishaps, for one of which we were prepared. Our tiller ropes, which had showed signs of wearing, went about 3 p.m. We immediately shipped our emergency tiller, which fits on over cap of rudder head. Next, at about 5 p.m., the mainsail began to tear and in a few seconds had split about two yards. We luffed, dropped mainsail, and Amor at once began to mend it. In $1\frac{1}{2}$ hours we were able to set it again. Meanwhile, with headsails and mizzen, we made good progress notwithstanding, and came into the more narrow and sheltered waters of the beautiful Flensburg Fiord.' In his account of the cruise for the RCC *Journal*, Childers continues: 'Like many of the places referred to in this log, Flensburg is an old sailing haunt of mine. It grows more modern and German at every visit; everywhere new and gaudy though not unattractive buildings are going up; but the old quays remain, and a few fascinating old Danish streets are still unchanged, with their red-tiled roofs and plastered walls.'

Ebeltoft, up on the northern peninsula of the Danish mainland, remained unspoiled, however. 'The only modern feature', Childers wrote, 'is a large co-operative steam dairy like that possessed by nearly all towns and villages in Denmark. It is not enough to walk down the street to discover the quaintest old buildings. One must dive down into crooked alleys and old courtyards, whence one gets splendid vistas over the blue waters of the fiord.' Their arrival there had not been entirely straightforward. 'However, we made entrance to New Harbour without mishap, and once inside dropped anchor to reconnoitre. It is well we did so, for the quay along which we planned to moor, marked with a depth of 16 feet on the chart, has now only 4½ feet depth by it! Finding this out just in time, we warped alongside a big brig which lay moored on the south side. A hospitable crowd assembled and offered obstructive help, and the brig's cat boarded us and refused to leave. We had to remove her forcibly the next day before sailing.'

Not that departure was easy. The log reads, 'This morning I found the wind had veered to the NW, so that it blew straight into the harbour. After breakfast Le Fanu and I went out in the dinghy and sounded round the channel outside, and found it too narrow and tortuous to tack in. So we engaged one of the small petrol fishing boats which abound in all Danish harbours to tow us out for a few shillings. We made ready, cast off, and then there was a long delay caused by the boatman stupidly losing his head. He backed suddenly and fouled his screw with our towrope. We at once dropped anchor. At this moment an excited little man on the quay, dressed tightly in obviously his best Sunday clothes with little patent leather boots, rowed off and boarded the petrol boat, taking charge in a tremulous manner and with a white face. He was not much more efficient. Finally Amor leapt on board the boat, and with fine British arrogance assumed unquestioned control of the whole business, driving the shrinking occupants into the bow while he endeavoured to get our hawser clear. But it was too late. We had to cut and lose a part of the warp.'

Through Molly's eyes, via her letters to her family, we catch occasional glimpses of Childers as navigator. Approaching Assens, in the Little Belt, all he concedes is that 'Unlike most Danish harbours, the entrance . . . is badly marked, and it was a somewhat delicate manoeuvre to work our way in by the lead through a number of confusing groups of stakes.' Molly's account reveals rather more. '*Very* tricky navigation. Erskine really has genius. It went perfectly. I was in terror and could not imagine how he knew the way. First time too. Chart no help. Absolutely without squeak.' It was, no doubt, what he referred to in another context as 'a most *enticing* bit of navigation'.

By now their cruise had taken them north through the Little Belt as far as Aarhus, and south into the Great Belt to Nyborg. On the whole the weather had been kind; but now, halfway through September, the wind shifted to the east and blew with a hard tiresome persistence, interspersed with rain and the odd gale. They had hoped to slip round the south of Sjælland through a difficult channel known as the Storstrøm, and so head north for Copenhagen. The account in the *Journal* describes the attempt:

'*At sea – September 18.* Still the same baffling E wind, and stronger than ever, but clear weather. Determining this time to battle our way to the Storstrøm, we started at 9 a.m. battened down fore and aft, under mizzen and headsails, and hoisted double-reefed mainsail just before we cleared the fiord. Outside we found a steep hollow sea, through which we thrashed to Omø Sound. Here in the narrow channel between two small islands we had a brief respite, but at 1.30 p.m., when we once more faced the open, we entered on the heaviest thrash of our cruise.

'At about 2.30 p.m. in the course of a long board SE by S½S towards Veiro, the wind increased to a gale with severe squalls. We hove-to, took in a third reef in our mainsail, and lowered foresail. We had too much canvas even then, but it was absolutely necessary to make all the progress we could to the east so as to get within the sector of Vordingborg lighthouse (at the mouth of Storstrøm) before darkness fell. *Asgard* was pretty well smothered, but she behaved magnificently. We made long tacks to and fro between the dangerous banks which lie north and south . . . for a somewhat anxious period we thrashed on with no marks to guide us, but at 9.30 to our great relief we distinguished the Vordingborg light, whose white sector leads a vessel clear through all dangers to the Storstrøm. The nearer we got to our weather shore the less vicious the sea became. But we now became conscious that a strong current was setting out of the Storstrøm against us so that we made exceedingly slow progress. About midnight the wind decreased, and we gradually shook out our reefs. It was 2 a.m. before we made the mouth of the Strøm and proceeded with the help of a beautiful series of leading lights, which made navigation far easier by night than by day, to tack our way up its various arms. At dawn we were off the little town of Stubbekøbing, and at 6 a.m. we turned into its snug and crowded little harbour. We breakfasted, shifted our berth at the bidding of the harbourmaster, and then had the joy of donning dry clothes and sleeping till 3 p.m.'

That is the skipper's version: the mate's fills in the picture:

'You must picture us to yourselves at this time with a close beat of

30 miles before us, the sun shining, the sea rising like lightning, and the *Asgard* simply laughing with the rollick of it. Smothered in spray, clinging to our positions, and simply loving it. The crew worked hard at the sheets, and I at the wheel. We had rather difficult navigation before us ... the sea was high and hollow, very short, which continually stopped *Asgard*'s course. She could dance over two, but the third often caught her. Nevertheless they all said they had never seen a boat so buoyant and so quick. . . . It was very hard tacking. Once in a while she wouldn't do it, if two or three huge seas struck her bows. Erskine lowered topsail and took two more reefs in mainsail – making three for the first time. It was a question as to whether to lower mainsail, but we had to try hard to get somewhere before dark and pick up these *very* important buoys off sands, etc. He decided rightly; the *Asgard* was splendid under that rig, and simply made us love her ten times more. . . . Poor William, coming aft from the sheets, had to wade over his knees in water and his boots were two wells ... Mr Thompson and Amor worked like heroes, and Erskine was three men in himself ... navigating, steering, at the ropes, reefing – he was everywhere at once. We took brandy several times as lunch was slight, tea nil, dinner nil too, and that and biscuits kept us going.* Even Erskine took brandy. I made him.'

'At 8 I went below,' Molly's letter continues, 'in answer to Erskine's *comments*, undressed, found myself soaked through and through ... I rubbed myself dry, put on dry things, was seasick, and got into my bunk cold, hungry, exhausted, despairing. In five minutes I was glowing and hot all over, rested, happy and deliciously sleepy, too sleepy to want to eat, and seasickness forgotten. I was seasick only because everything was on its head below, and I was so miserable. But I loved it all the time on deck and had not one qualm.'

The reaction, after a punishing eleven hours of hammering to windward, was natural enough; and in her next letter Molly reveals a little more of their feeling for the sea.

'Whenever Erskine says I have done well – as he sometimes does – then I feel proud. . . . But I have so much to learn still . . .

---

* One is reminded of R. T. McMullen, crossing the Channel singlehanded in *Orion* thirty years earlier: 'I continued to support myself, at intervals with brandy, champagne, granular magnesia or claret'.

and of course I am no good at the ropes, for they are so heavy. I pull once in a while, and often coil up and tidy after, but I am of little use except at the wheel, of which I do at least three hours a day, and often more – and spying for buoys. Apparently my sight is extraordinary, for I seem to see just as well without glasses as most people do with them. William has splendid eyes too, and he and I do it together very often. Erskine is very remarkable in his sailing; he seems to have a gift for *diagnosis*. He knew yesterday about touching [approaching Stubbekøbing they had grounded in the middle of the channel] and had us off, or going off, before we knew. We saw it, of course, by the boat's slowness in going off the wind, but he knew in plenty of time. And he seems to live as part of the boat and to keep his ear always listening to the sounds she makes. If the wind changes when we are below, he knows it when the rest of us don't. He is a splendid sailor. One feels absolute confidence in him.'

The plain skills of sailing can be learnt by any reasonably practical person, but that extra sense, that 'living as part of the boat', with its corollary, making the instant right response in any situation, is an instinct and a gift. It was one that Erskine Childers had, and one which gave him a profound satisfaction.

In the conditions, Copenhagen was beyond their reach: in any case they had already decided to lay up for the winter somewhere in the Baltic. By chance, the yard to which they were recommended was at Svendborg, which they had already visited and which lay to leeward. 'If we took her back to England', Molly wrote to her father, 'we should not be able to get farther afield than this, whereas leaving her here, we can go to the Gulf of Finland next summer and the year after either sail her home or, if there is a constitutional government in Russia by then, sail in Russian waters. We cannot afford weekend sailing at home, and it is only for the cruise we can use her.'

And so, after two days of being trapped in Stubbekøbing, they sailed back to Svendborg. 'We look to find a splendid winter berth for *Asgard*', Molly wrote, 'in a sheltered cove a mile below the town. The man there lays up sometimes forty yachts . . . she will be hauled up and have a roof built over her to keep off snow.'

So ended 'a very delightful cruise'. They had sailed over 1,100 miles; and Erskine had been able to show his wife something of that fickle but entrancing inland sea which he always regarded as unmatched as a cruising ground. That Molly too had fallen for its clear tideless waters, there is no doubt. 'It is so unlike any sailing I have known,' she wrote to The Commodore. 'Strong winds often, water which grows rough or smooth in a minute, fascinating old-world harbours, scarcely any yachts or fashionable life, every-where the most divinely salt atmosphere, and everywhere welcome to greet us, which is warmer and more personal than elsewhere. The greetings usually are "Where do you come from? This is a good place to lie. You are the first English yacht we have had here for two years, three years", etc.'

No wonder they had ambitious plans for future seasons. Mean-while, during the raw evenings of a London winter they could look back and remember, not only that hard thrash across to Storstrøm in the teeth of an easterly gale, but moments of pure idyll as well. '. . . at about 9.30 p.m. the others turned in, and Erskine and I took our watch until 2.30 a.m. It was a marvel-lously clear night, the sky deep with stars and an old gibbous moon which rose about 12.30, pink and golden out of the waves. Part of this time Erskine slept by me while I steered, but mostly we two just sat and talked together and loved it together. It is always a great experience, night sailing.'

VIII

Return to the Baltic 1913

The Childerses' cruise to Germany, Finland, Sweden and finally Norway in 1913 was the longest in distance – 2,500 miles – which they ever made, singly or together; the toughest – 1,000 miles to windward on the return voyage; and, of all that Erskine Childers ever carried out, one of the two or three on which his claim to fame as an outstanding cruising yachtsman most securely rests. He himself said of it that it 'was the best of my life, bar perhaps the *Riddle* cruise'. In a summary at the end of the account which he wrote for the RCC *Journal*, he notes that: 'nineteen complete nights were spent at sea. The longest halts (in complete days) were: at Texel, three days; at Stockholm, two days; at Kalmar, three days.' In all it lasted from June 26, when they slipped their mooring in the Hamble, to August 22, when they left *Asgard* in Oslo (known in those days as Christiania) for Gordon Shephard to cruise in and then bring home. It seems to have been the cruise which Erskine and Molly planned for 1907.

Of their sailing between the two dates there is virtually nothing to be said for, as has been remarked, no evidence has appeared in the Childers papers as to those years. The fact that Molly was twice pregnant; and that until 1910 Erskine was not only serving as a Clerk in the House of Commons but also writing books as well, might well explain why they undertook no extended summer cruises; and odd hints suggest that instead they were restricted to weekend sailing with, perhaps, a brief cruise to the West Country after the House had risen for the summer recess. It is strange, nevertheless, that there should be such a complete absence of letters or logbooks or any reference whatever to sailing during that period. Certainly there is nothing in the various accounts of their 1913 cruise to suggest that they were visiting familiar waters, once they were clear of Kiel Fiord. Regarding Stockholm, for example, Childers remarks in a letter to Aunt Flora that 'it too won our hearts this time. We were there before, but not yachting, and hated it.' According to Burke Wilkinson,* Shephard 'often borrowed *Asgard* from them': it is possible, as the two men became great friends as soon as they met in 1909, and though Shephard owned an 11 ton yawl *Sorata*; he brought *Asgard* back from Oslo in the autumn of 1913, leaving her in Holyhead. That is just about all that can be said on the matter.

Gordon Shephard was with the Childerses when they set off for the Baltic in June 1913. In addition there were two Americans, Barthold Schlesinger and Samuel Pierce, and a paid hand, Robert Nowell, who had sailed with Shephard. The first week was occupied inevitably in fetching across the North Sea and passing through the Kiel Canal – an all too familiar route, even if they had not done it for seven years. There is little of note in it, though it is interesting that twice in the early part of his account in the *Journal* Childers feels it worth mentioning that they had 'no motor or other means of mechanical propulsion'. This emphasis suggests that the auxiliary engine must have been steadily gaining acceptance in sailing yachts during the intervening years: earlier it would have been taken for granted that they would not have had one. (The yachting press started to run features on motors from about 1908.)

One other point is worth a passing reference. Childers rarely took on pilots, and had no luck with them when he did. One remembers the sour remark which he put into Davies' mouth in *The Riddle* after Dollman had tried to drown him: 'So ended that little trip under a pilot.' On their earlier Baltic cruise a pilot employed to take them through a short-cut from Terschelling, in order to save fifteen miles, chose instead to lead them through the perfectly straightforward Stortemelk channel which he was being

---

* Op. cit. p. 76–7.

paid to bypass. On the present occasion the circumstances were different, but the result was even more unsatisfactory.

'At 1 p.m. made out the Haaks lightship, having previously identified the big pilot-vessel which always lies near it, about 12 miles to seaward of the Texel mouth. It was now so thick and the sea on these dangerous outlying banks so heavy that I decided to ask for a pilot, and hailed accordingly. Answer, that they could not board us in a boat, but would sail ahead and guide us in. This they accordingly did. . . . But the arrangement, made by shouting and gesticulating in a high wind, while dancing about in the sea, included a compulsory corollary which we had not understood or bargained for, namely that on arriving off the harbour of Nieuwe Diep we should take on board a harbour pilot to moor us. Since the harbour itself presents no difficulty whatever, we regarded the arrival of this gentleman, who boarded us in smooth water about 1 p.m. after the passage of the banks and bar, with amused impatience. I blame myself, resplendent though he was in gold lace and brass buttons, for not divining from his first questions and orders that he was an incompetent young novice, who had no business to be piloting at all. But I was tired and off my guard. He took charge, gave his orders, chose our berth alongside the naval quay, and the next minute we were foul of the boats and davits of a gunboat, with a sprung mizzenmast. At least we suspected it to be sprung, and thought it safest to procure a new one and take no risks. Our friend, who smiled with undefeated assurance throughout and seemed to regard this manner of berthing a vessel quite normal and satisfactory, then requested me to sign a paper to the effect that I had been "well and safely" piloted to my destination; a lie with which I declined (not without some vigour) to blacken my conscience. . . . This was our first and last pilot during the cruise.'

They just made Brunsbüttel, by tearing up the Elbe in the dark under spinnaker, in time to pick up a tow through the canal before the Sunday closure ('*Warning* –' Childers noted, 'beware of the ships' brokers on this canal. They are apt to introduce themselves as officials and thereby make big commissions.'). Then, from Kiel Fiord, instead of the usual route to Schlei Fiord and Flensborg and the Little Belt, they turned east, to follow the North German coast and its off-lying islands towards Stralsund. 'The scheme we provisionally settled now was to follow the German islands to Rügen, then sail north to Wisby in Gotland, and thence to Helsingfors [Helsinki] in Finland. Return journey by Stockholm and Denmark to Christiania [Oslo], where we would leave the yacht towards the end of August.' This programme they carried out to the letter.

Their first port of call was Burgstaaken, on the sound which divides the island of Fehmarn from the mainland, 'and no pleasanter one could be found'. *The Times* account, published in two parts in November, goes on:

'Rügen, our next destination, is the kind of place that looks almost unapproachable on the chart, so narrow and exposed are the channels which lead to it from the open sea and divide the island, or rather islands, from the mainland. It requires faith in German thoroughness to tackle the Gellenstrom, or western channel, in a dark rainy dawn before a fresh sou'wester with no visible landmarks. But the faith is justified for the buoyage, even in thick weather, is foolproof, though it can give exciting sport. A headwind up the first long southerly stretch means a succession of lightning tacks and such absorption in tiller and sheets as to leave no time to observe the features of vast ghostly sandbanks dimly emerging out of nothingness and closing in on either hand. The next pair of buoys is the limit of thought and vision, the next 'ready about' the end and aim of life. Suddenly comes one of those magical revolutions which are the supreme joy of the sport and make one swear (what is after all the literal truth) that the only rational way to go to any strange place is in a small yacht.'

After this lively spell of short-tacking – 'holding the sheets till the yacht just gathered way, and then going about again' – they rounded the weathermost buoy and had 'leisure to take breath and look around. Just then the western sky brightened, with a momentary fleck of blue in the racing clouds. The leaden vapours roll away to leeward, revealing a vast shallow mere through which straight as an arrow runs the double line of buoys marking the dredged channel, in a far perspective of tiny dots. Behind us the mere is locked by the banks we have threaded, as it were blindfold. On the left are green islands, with here and there the vivid red spot of a village or farm, and far away ahead, where the mere narrows to a slender sound, Stralsund, dominating all the low wooded country around with its three mighty spires, and already beginning to glow and sparkle in the sun. Warmth, peace, and freshness succeed to the fatigues and rigours of the night. We can breakfast in luxurious tranquillity, with one hand at the helm, till the yacht is comfortably moored beneath the shadow of the Stralsund spires.'

The very essence of cruising under sail is expressed in that passage; and, more particularly, the essence of Erskine Childers' delight in it. However, they had made one mistake, for which they had to pay.

'There is, it appears, a Customs vessel stationed in the Gellen-strom, where incoming vessels are supposed to heave-to for examination. With no eyes for anything but the buoys and the navigation, we had not seen it or the signal which it was said to have made to us. Hence a small fine, after some to-do with officials headed by a dazzling being with a clanking sword!'

Getting out of Stralsund was almost as tense as getting in. The *Times* account continues: 'Nor is the eastern approach to Stralsund – the door by which we left it on the following day – any less beautiful. Here the Sound broadens into quite an inland sea, with an opening to the Baltic five miles in width, but so blocked by shoals as to offer only two navigable channels barely fifty yards broad in their narrowest parts.' However, the buoys 'all lettered or numbered like the houses in a street' and a fresh quartering wind saw them safely through, and now 'the whole of the open Baltic stretches away northward' to Helsinki, over five hundred miles away.

'So, leaving the Landtief leading buoy an hour after midday with a spanking west-nor'wester just abaft the beam, we were abreast of Bornholm Island at dark, and off the south point of Öland next morning. Another day of lighter and more baffling winds and calms brought us early on the third day to the ancient capital of the Hansa League [Wisby]. A summer haze veiled the heights and showed us only the lower part of a picturesque old Swedish town looking down on a harbour so exposed in outlook and restricted in size ... that one could hardly believe it to have played so great a part in the commerce and politics of a past age. It is only when you climb up to the mighty fortified wall and see the still noble ruins of great cathedrals and castles that you realise the power and majesty of that vast organisation which, for more than two centuries, wielded its influence from Novgorod to London, and could make so unpromising a site as Wisby a centre of trade and government.

'We have now covered 960 miles since Hamble in fifteen days, of which six days and six nights were spent in port: the rest at sea.'

Despite the weight of its historical associations, they did not linger in Wisby but beat on northwards along the coast of the Swedish island Gotland. They were now approaching 58°N, on the same parallel as Aberdeen though it sounds ten times more remote.

'Never really dark tonight,' Childers logged on July 13. 'The red glow of sunset changed almost insensibly to the pink glow of dawn. Hove-to off the entrance to Fårö Sound about 1 a.m., and at 1.30 bore up for the entrance. Just hit off the buoy on the Svingrund shoal in the twilight and ran on through the narrows (only 10 yards broad; strong S current). Floated almost becalmed up the peaceful sound; low piney shores and seabirds screaming. Used sweeps for a mile and at 5 a.m. tied up on the little jetty of Fårösund village. Blazing sun, but silence and desertion everywhere. All slept till 8 a.m. . . . then went ashore and got the local merchant to open his store and sell us eggs, bread, butter and matches.'

They were away next day, and hoping 'for at least a partially fair wind for the long passage north, but it settled into the NE, dead ahead and light.' Although it relented for a time, they had to work for their northing: the following *Times* account summarises what must have been a long and rather tedious haul.

'From the southern exit of the [Fårö] Sound, one steers NE to pass outside the point of Dagö Island [now renamed Hiiumaa] in Russia. With time, of course, one would not pass by Riga Bay; but, Riga excepted, this part of the Russian coast is not specially beautiful or interesting, and it is better to sail straight on and make sure of Helsingfors. The long summer nights now begin to make their full influence felt. In fine weather indeed there is only an imperceptible transition from the warm afterglow of evening to the paler radiance of dawn, with blendings of colour in sea and sky which the benighted cruiser in Western Europe has hardly dreamed of. In what passes for our middle watch, from 10 to 2,* one can watch the whole marvellous process and extinguish the almost superfluous sidelights before turning in.

'Another brisk nor'wester, picked up halfway to Dagö and carried well into the Gulf of Finland, left us becalmed somewhere off Reval [Tallinn in Estonia], so that it was late on the second day out of Fårö that we made the outer Helsingfors lightship, and after midnight before we had groped with the lead to an anchorage in a secluded part of the inner bay. We had tacked our devious way in a NE breeze from light to light, dimly aware of craggy islands, beaconed rocks, and once a dark sleeping town above a cliff – Sveaborg – but it was not till we turned out for the morning bathe that we saw what a beautiful place we had come to: a spacious land-locked fiord interspersed with islands, and alive with shipping, small and great, with the capital city standing proudly on the northern shore.'

They picked up a yacht club mooring, and spent 'a delightful day, shopping, bathing, sight-seeing and feasting in this beautiful and interesting town. No Customs examination, or bother of any sort.' It may have been, as Childers says, the Mecca of their pilgrimage, but they only allowed themselves one clear day there, all the same. The next log entry reads:

'*July 17*. From Helsingfors. Under way at 10.30 a.m. bound west for Hangö, 80 miles. Wind NE, light. Showery. We had no time for Petersburg [Leningrad], and now turned west, resolving if the conditions permitted to travel some distance through the islands which fringe the Finland coast.'

'No yachtsman,' Childers wrote in his description of the cruise in *The Times*, 'should leave Finland without having enjoyed a spell of navigation behind the islands which border the coast in profusion, melting on the west into the vast Åland archipelago and extending thence, after a break of only twenty miles, right down the east coast of Sweden. Seen on a general chart of the Baltic these islands look like a "stoneyard" of impenetrable rocks. It is only on an engraving of the largest scale that the navigability of

---

* The middle is traditionally kept from midnight to 0400.

this strange region seems to be anything more than a joke. Certain dotted lines now appear, wriggling with an evident purpose through the fine lacework, and certain scarlet dots indicating lights. Even so it is apparent that for the subtlest intricacies the mariner must rely not on the chart, but on the excellence of the lighting and buoyage.

'Experience soon shows that this reliance is justified. Coastal communications depend largely on the navigation of the islands, and certain selected routes have been minutely surveyed and marked. These routes are marked by the dotted lines; and the first and last rule for a stranger who enters the maze is to grasp one of these clues and never depart an inch from it. If he does so depart, he will probably repent his rashness, at the best losing himself in a pathless wilderness, at the worst "piling her up" in a position exposed to the ocean swell, out of sight and earshot of human help. Holding her nose to a dotted line, he will find little difficulty either by day or night, less perhaps by night than by day. . . . The lights are ensconced in little huts or stone towers, which in the daytime make good guides to navigation. One, which will remain long in our memories, was let into the face of a cliff near Helsingfors, where it opened and shut like a great eye. There is also a multitude of small beacons and cairns and of white squares and other diagrams painted on the rocks. In one limited area which we entered, some inhabitants with sympathy and a sense of humour had painted the name of each island in large white letters on a prominent rock, just as some country station-masters adorn their embankments.

'It must be understood that for a craft without mechanical power a leading wind, or at least a reasonably fair wind, is almost essential. The writer has not come across any spot positively too narrow for a 27-tonner to tack in, but there are many – and generally the most beautiful – so confined that you lose most of a fair wind and are nearly powerless on a foul one. In any case short-tacking is apt to become intolerably tedious. Hence an element of speculation which is one of the more dubious charms of the game. For, once in, it is not easy to get out. The open sea is never very far as the crow flies, but there may be no dotted line to it from anywhere near the scene of your entanglement, so that it is a case of turning back (which is unthinkable), or of stopping still, or of involving yourself yet more deeply in the tangle.

'A dilemma like this – though it led to a happy result – befell

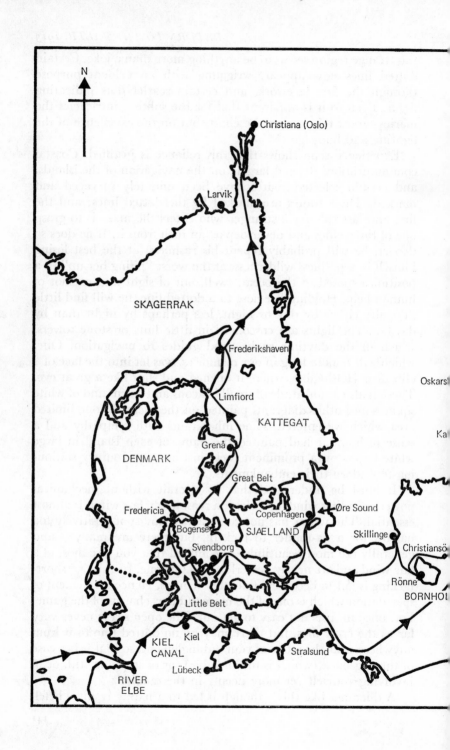

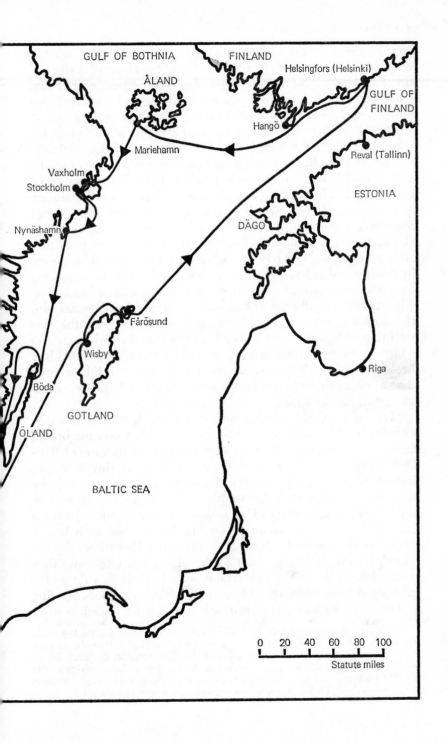

ourselves on our first night westward out of Helsingfors, whence we plunged direct into the islands, bound for Hangö [at the SW tip of Finland]. After twenty miles of gentle progress in light airs, footing it delicately among pine-clad islands and bare reefs, we found ourselves at dusk headed by the wind in a position where we could neither anchor, owing to the depth of the available water, nor reach the open Baltic. We had counted too carelessly, in case of a hitch, on a tempting outlet across a bay to another part of the islands; but a close inspection of the chart now showed no dotted line, but instead certain sinister pinpoint specks, hinting at pinnacles of rock, which would have rendered the passage hopelessly hazardous. "We are committed" said one of us grimly (he had been to Finland before*); and committed we were to a wide sweep round our bay through a mass of rocks and islets ever increasing in density. Very strange it seemed at first to be tacking through this labyrinth in the dark, now close under a black bluff with the pines rustling overhead, now slanting across a lagoon with the snouts of rocks dimly perceived to right and left; the eyes straining after some spectral perch or fixed on the vivid sparks of white, green, or red which were our guides when the perches had become invisible. Yet so accustomed and confident did we grow that at midnight only two hands were left on deck to steer, navigate, and handle sheets.

'The new watch, turning out at 4 a.m., had a memorable experience. The sun was already warm, the air pure, the breeze faint, but at last fair. We were approaching the narrows of Barö Sund, the crux of the passage, its entrance so tiny a notch, indeed, that the sleepy navigator, bereft of lights, passed it by unnoticed, and only woke to his error by finding himself in a *cul-de-sac* of ugly shoals. Our steps retraced, we turned into a homely little stream between two low islands and then into a gorge, where you could throw a biscuit onto either shore. For the most part the rocks rose sheer to the pines; but sometimes they were cleft by a little grassy strand with browsing cattle and a glimpse of farm buildings or by a creek with shady pools, bending out of sight. In and out from reach to reach we glided in utter

---

* Gordon Shephard who in 1911 left Ramsgate on April 30, 'pushes on to the north, is the first sailing vessel to pass the ice in the Gulf of Bothnia, ascends the Gulf to its apex within forty miles of the Arctic circle, descends by its eastern shore, threads the intricate Åland Archipelago, circumnavigates the Gulf of Finland, and pays his respects to the Petersburg Yacht Club.' Erskine Childers, writing in *The Times* of the exploits of members of the RCC.

silence, even the ripple at the forefoot stilled, only the loftiest angle of the topsail catching the breeze, our lifeless mainboom almost grazing the tall red and white spar buoys; till at last the sound widened, the mainsheet straightened, and we shot out under a strengthening wind into more open lagoons.

'But this day proved like the last, the wind backing to the west in the afternoon; so that after some hours of laborious tacking we struck out for the open sea by one of the rare buoyed outlets . . . [and] sailed away for our next port in the Åland Islands. (Our sound rule throughout the cruise being not to make a harbour at night unless we could spare the next day for seeing the place.) This was to be Mariehamn, in the western part of that huge and intricate archipelago, roughly a hundred miles by fifty, which stretches across the mouth of the Gulf of Bothnia. Most of it is unsurveyed, much of it unsurveyable . . . weeks could be spent in exploring this fascinating and beautiful country. Unfortunately we had no time even for Abö, and had to content ourselves with Mariehamn, whence there is easy egress to Sweden on the west.'

'This is a dangerous stretch of coast,' Childers wrote in the RCC *Journal*, 'for the rocks extend for many miles from the main islands. It is a lonely sea, too. We saw no traffic whatever. . . . Suffice to say that at 7 p.m. the outlook improved, the wind freeing southerly, and at 8 p.m. we sighted Grimsoren beacon, one of the huge beacons on outlying rocks which are the principal means of identifying one's position in this eerie region.' At three in the morning they at last picked up the Fastorne beacon which marks the entrance to Fögle Fiord and the passage to Mariehamn. 'At 5.15 [we] passed between it and the buoys marking a group of ugly shoals. No land was visible yet, and the scene was grim enough, but before long the nearest islands were sighted, and henceforward it was a case of running from buoy to buoy between them, rather hampered by rain and mist. The scenery grows more and more beautiful, and the land higher as you approach Mariehamn' – but the town, when they finally got there, they found disappointing, 'a cheap seaside holiday resort for Russians'.*

* Maldwin Drummond, writing in the RCC *Journal* (now called *Roving Commissions*) in 1968, found differently: 'This little port, more than any other, can lay claim to be the last stronghold of commercial sail. The towering spars of the four-masted barque *Pommern* dominate the busy harbour, and next door . . . is the best maritime museum of its type in the world. It tells of the golden age of sail and Mariehamn's great part in it.'

But their visit was not entirely without either interest or excitement. 'In the evening a fiery Finn drove us in a hired motor-car at headlong speed to see Bomar Sund and the forts and town bombarded by the British Fleet in the Crimean War. It was an act, alas! of purposeless brutality, which gives to the shattered ruins in their exquisitely peaceful surroundings a most painful interest for Englishmen. Indeed, we almost felt that our fiery Finn was planning for us the Austerlitz we had escaped outside, as he whirled us to and from this sad scene, up and down precipitous hills, bump! into a ferryboat over a sound, and finally, at appalling speed, round a hairpin curve down to the quay and bump! up to the yacht's side.

'From Mariehamn it is only thirty miles, of which twenty-one are in the open, to the Söderarm entrance to the Stockholm archipelago (or Skärgard); and with a fair wind on the next day we were soon racing up that magnificent avenue, over sixty miles long, towards the Swedish capital. Magnificent, yet without the peculiar charm of the wilder Finnish and Åland channels. Much of the famous Skärgard is a suburb of Stockholm, and wears a suburban air with its hundreds of little villas, bungalows and hotels, and its hosts of butterfly yachts and buzzing pleasure steamers.' 'Had a long race with another yacht from Söderarm on', adds the account in the *Journal*. She passed us in Furo Sund but turned out to have a motor.'

The Times account goes on: ' "Operatic" one of us called it; and oddly operatic it felt that night when, after pushing on till near midnight in a deluge of rain from the north . . . we navigated by the leading lights in torrents of rain, a small square of the chart being cut out and used on deck till it was pulp [A case of nature imitating art: see *The Riddle of the Sands* pp. 190 and 213] . . . we ultimately rounded up, half blinded with dazzling electric lights, into the very doors almost of a gay restaurant, and moored not ten yards from a supper party and a band, under the eyes of curious revellers. This was Vaxholm. An irruption of bustling ferry steamers drove us out betimes the next day, and on we flew under short canvas to Stockholm.'

In Stockholm Gordon Shephard and the two Americans departed, arranging 'to sail to Lübeck tomorrow in the *Svithiof*, our old friend of 1911 and Captain Bori'* – 'a sad parting after a

* This presumably refers to their previous visit to Stockholm 'not yachting'.

really magnificent cruise. We have now made good from Hamble 1,505½ miles in 27 days. We have been thirteen nights in harbour, including the night at Brunsbüttel, and fourteen at sea.'

Their new crew were lined up, ready to join ship as and when directed. 'Telegraphed to Maitland to await instructions at Gothenburg as we purpose to push on south, if it seems possible', which meant that Erskine and Molly and Nowell would work the boat south between them. But in the meantime they would make the most of this, one of their few decent spells in harbour. 'E.C. and M.A.C.' (thus the log) 'dined luxuriously both nights at the Operahallen and sat on the upper terrace afterwards for coffee and music. There can scarcely be a pleasanter place for coffee in Europe, but Helsingfors is hard to beat. In crossing the gangway from the yacht to shore E.C. dropped M.A.C.'s silver-handled stick into twelve feet of water. E.C. dived in vain for it. Asked at the ships' chandlers for a diver, and one of the shopmen came over on the evening of the 24th, put on a pair of my flannel trousers and a vest, and dived persistently for about twenty minutes. Large crowd collected. Finally he found it. Loud cheers. Hot whisky punch. Friendship sworn for ever. He is a delightful boy of about twenty-three; speaks English with a strong American accent.*

STOCKHOLM TO CHRISTIANIA

'*July 23rd, Stockholm.* Our next crew of three were not due to meet us till August 1st. But a week's idleness, however attractive the scene, was little to our taste, so we decided to sail south, short-handed as we were, and meet them at Kalmar.'

Two days later they set off with about 220 miles ahead, 100 of them, from Nynäshamn to Kalmar Sound, in open water. Winds were light and variable to begin with; but on the 28th the glass started to drop fast.

'Wind slowly freshening. Topsail down and jibs shifted at first dawn. A short, hollow, stopping sea into which we bumped and jumped with annoying vehemence. At 10 a.m. wind settled into W by S, fresh, nearly but not quite to the reefing point, and as we had just made a long westward board we could now lie close-

---

* This story only appears in the log: the fact that Molly was partially crippled is never mentioned in the published accounts of the cruises.

hauled for Öland Point. Weather now grey and dirty-looking. At 2 p.m. sighted Öland lighthouse right ahead and low down. . . . It was a wild-looking showery evening, with the glass galloping down. We were tired and averse to another night at sea, especially with the difficult Kalmar Narrows as a climax, so we bore up for Böda Bught, 5 miles down the east coast of Öland, in the hope that the inevitable gale would begin and blow itself out in the night.'

For this part of the cruise, Childers notes, 'we took singlehanded watches in turn,' and that 'M.A.C. took her full watch alone on deck in the night and was as efficient as a man.'

'En route (for Böda Bught) we passed Grankulla Viken, a tiny inlet near the north point but with only 4 feet . . . in the entrance. At 5 p.m. we were working into Böda Bught, but did not like the look of this exposed bay, and just now discovered in a Swedish pilot book that there was 9 feet, not 4, into Grankulla. So back we went, only to discover that we should have to beat in by a passage 45 yards broad! Baffled, we returned to Böda, and at 7 p.m. let go in 4½ fathoms, with a long scope of cable a mile from the shore. A lonely, dreary spot.'

The glass continued to fall, and it blew hard in the night. Next morning 'the wind was only moderate, though the sky was bad. Under way 10 a.m. Wind NW moderate, to NNE moderate gale later. We reached out of bight under plain sail and second jib and made a long board to N to clear the north point of Öland. At 12 got well up to the N of Öland, when a change of weather began. The NW wind fell very light, and then suddenly veered to NNE with a deluge of rain. There was already a highish swell, and the sea now rose with amazing rapidity; but it was the long healthy sea that *Asgard* revelled in.

'At 12.30 p.m. we tacked, freed sheets, and raced away W¾S, meaning to go to Oskarshamn 20 miles off on the mainland opposite. Wind rapidly increased. Mizzen lowered and mainsail rolled up a good bit. We travelled very fast. . . . Then E.C. decided that in this wind and weather it was unsafe to attempt Oskarshamn, a lee shore full of intricate shoals, and decided to turn and run up Kalmar Sund for Kalmar. This meant a gybe, which we could not do short-handed, so we wore and bore up, lying about WSW.

'We now got in trouble with the dinghy, which ever since Nynäshamn we had been carrying in the davits swung outboard. In a vicious sheer to windward, she got well down into the sea and so caught the crest of a wave that the wave in arrogance turned in on the yacht and filled the cockpit, so that E.C. found himself gazing into the compass card through pale green limpid Baltic water! Forward davit was lifted out of its lower socket, and a boathook in boat broken and lost, and forward [davit] guy parted. Cockpit soon emptied, but it was necessary to get boat inboard; and Nowell succeeded in heaving her in on davits and placing her upright, resting on deckhouse and bulwarks. . . .

'From this time we had a really tremendous run under close-reefed mainsail and jib before a very high sea. Squalls of great strength at intervals, and sometimes heavy rain with them. Clear intervals. *Asgard* was thoroughly at home, but the helm was heavy work. Our course of WSW brought us towards the Öland shore, so that another gybe was necessary. Did it all-standing by accident, but so nearly checked her that it was a light affair. To our annoyance, however, the lashing of the peak of the mainsail gave way at the gaff end and the sail began to come unlaced, but brought up, luckily, about 4 feet from the gaff.

'We had a memorable 8 knot run up the broad part of the Sound, passing Borgholm, on the Öland shore, at 5 p.m. Approaching the narrows formed by Skägganas Island, I decided that it was unwise, at this speed, to take the orthodox, and very narrow, passage under the Skägganas shore, so we took the longer but broader passage by the Öland shore. . . . Once inside Skägganas we were in sheltered water, but it blew harder than ever, and the buoys were hard to distinguish in the tumbling foam and bad light. . . . But for my wife's extraordinary sharp sight and unruffled coolness in such situations, we should have had a very unpleasant time. As it was, all went well . . . and we entered the harbour (of Kalmar) at 7.30 p.m. – just as a big steamer did, and made for mouth in company. Very embarrassing for us as she wouldn't give way. Scraped in somehow, and after much tacking about to look for a berth, with the mainsail unlacing itself gradually, got into inner dock . . . and lay alongside a small schooner. An English yachtsman appeared on the schooner and most kindly helped with our warps. Turned out to be Carson of the RCC, 7-tonner *Lone Wolf*, who had started the season from Copenhagen and been round by Wisby, Helsingfors, Stockholm a few days ahead of us. Crew, he and his sister. . . . An exacting and exciting day, successfully ended. 63 miles, 9½ hours.'

Their new crew, two novices, Alfred Ollivant and R. C. Woodhead, and one near-novice, F. W. Maitland the constitutional historian, duly joined them a day late at Kalmar, and on August 2 they set off south again, 'bound for anywhere we could get to!' Which was not far; 'an excellent day for training beginners, but otherwise tedious work'. With light airs, invariably from ahead, they worked their way out of Kalmar Sund and headed for the island of Bornholm. On their course, and fifteen miles short of it, they 'sighted high land with a queer castellated summit', the Danish island of Christiansö, where 'there was an anchorage, according to the pilot book. At 2.30 we were close up and tacked between the islands and rocks . . . and headed in. Realised then that the place was ridiculously small. No room to round up. So tumbled down all sails and let go, swinging close to fishing boats on either side. On the east, above us, lay a high rocky islet crowned by a huge dismantled fort (now the lighthouse) and covered with the remains of massive fortifications, two huge embrasures for cannon looking down on us. Trees in crannies, houses among them, and beyond, overhanging the sea, what looked like a big brown barrack which, in fact, was the main street. On the west was Frederiksö Island, much lower and very barren, with a few poor houses, and a red circular tower with sugarloaf roof. Spanning the sound a swing footbridge. At either end of this little sound the white-capped swell was tumbling and booming, and between, stillness and calm. The whole effect in the afternoon sunshine was wonderful.

'After tea landed and walked round both islands. The larger is one mass of old fortifications, built of gigantic granite stones, but now dismantled. The island was fortified in 1684. Rough cemented walks have been made among the rocks, with trees in little dells – all of them touched with frost and with half-withered leaves. The shore itself is wild rocks. Surprised, and watched, a children's game of rounders – superb play and very exciting. Bought half a loaf (all they had) at a tiny little inn. The pilot said we were the first English yacht to visit this place.

'*August 4th*. Under way at 6 a.m. Wind W, moderate. Dull. (Wherever we turned on this homeward cruise the wind headed us with most extraordinary punctuality.) With all its charm one is glad enough to get safely out of Christiansö, and the skipper certainly slept badly with the surf booming so near. A motor fishing boat gave us a pluck out for a couple of kroner, and we were soon beating over to Bornholm in showery, dull weather.'

Once round Hammer Point, 'the magnificently bold and rocky promontory, the finest far that we have seen in the Baltic', they passed 'numbers of snug little harbours . . . and went straight on to Rönne, the capital' where they tied up alongside an old brig. Ollivant asked the skipper 'Do you speak English?' to which the answer came: 'Speak English? By good God, damn!'

They were away next day, dogged by the same headwind, to Skillinge, and so, next day, to the mouth of the Sound which leads north to Copenhagen. 'It was rather a wild-looking morning, but the wind held steady and good, and we sailed fast to Dragør, where the narrows of the Sound begin. Here the wind freed still more, and we raced in fine style to Copenhagen', tying up to a buoy opposite the brewery – 'the familiar fried buttery odour filling the air!'

They dined ashore. 'Dinner good but inadequate in bulk. Waiter maddeningly slow for a famished crew. Presently he placed a basket of rolls on the table. Five greedy hands pounced like vulture's claws, and it was empty in an instant! Two others fared alike!'

They had now been away and sailing hard for six weeks and had covered nearly 2,000 miles, with another 500 between them and Christiania. They could have shortened that considerably by heading north from Copenhagen and slipping through Øre Sund into the Kattegat: instead they picked up their old track of 1906, across the mouth of the Great Belt to Svendborg, south of the big island of Fyn, and up through the Little Belt once again, putting in at Fredericia at its northern outlet. The monotony and weariness of constantly thrashing to windward is reflected in the log, which is laced with entries such as: 'another hard night's sailing', 'under way at 6.15 a.m. . . . all ready for a heavy thresh to windward', 'wind very strong WNW . . . hove-to and reefed, sea very steep and choppy and we got a thorough *salting* all day'. They reached Fredericia on the 13th. 'Entered harbour at 7.15 p.m., tired, wet, hungry and rejoicing, after a memorable beat to windward.' But they were not finished with contrary winds yet.

'*August 14th*. From this point to the Skaw (on our way to Christiania) our course lay roughly north, and we had reckoned that now, at last, we should have fair winds in this type of persistent westerly weather. But at this precise moment the wind went to the north, and remained there for a week! Our philosophy was equal to the test. Our crew, new to yachting, thought it all quite normal, and all of us enjoyed the life under any circumstances. [Which speaks well for them, their crew, and their philosophy!]

'Our time was now very limited, and there was no question of choosing ports otherwise than by the dictation of the wind. Our first happened to be Bogense . . . the queerest and quaintest harbour, half a mile long, but so narrow that even *Asgard* could hardly turn in it. . . . A perfectly lovely little town; the old architecture quite beautiful, and a splendid white church with a black steeple. Exquisite colours in the late evening, and a peaceful night, but wind still NE and fairly fresh.'

And so it continued: to Grenå, their next port of call – 'all to windward'; to Limfiord, a 'dead beat'; to Frederikshaven, 'the usual dead beat north'; and, as they cleared the northern tip of Denmark and met 'the great heaving swell of the Skagerrak', after a brief respite 'very soon it veered to the old quarter'. They took a long board across to the Swedish coast. 'And now began a curious day. Very slowly but steadily the breeze backed, so that without changing from the port tack we described a semi-circle, and at 10 p.m., wind SW fresh, we were back on the north-and-south line Skaw and Christiania Fjord. . . . We had hitherto intended to go for Larvik, where *Asgard* was built and Colin Archer, her builder, still lives. But the fair wind decided us to go through to Christiania.'

Next morning they were actually able to set the spinnaker. 'Difficult to describe the strange and ecstatic sensation of running like this after weary weeks of beating.' This favouring wind, although buffeting them with heavy rain squalls, carried them at last to Christiania and, in thick weather, to an 'exposed, dirty and uncomfortable berth' at the wrong end of the town.

'This was practically the end of the cruise,' Childers wrote; but they still had Maitland with them (the other two had left) 'and we planned to get back 70 miles south, as far as Larvik, so as to leave the boat there, at Archer's yard. . . . But the weather said

"No!" It rained and blew from the S all the 23rd. Glorious weather on the 24th, and we set sail down this wonderful fiord with the largest fleet of little pleasure yachts we had ever seen. But the wind, after a long calm, again set in due S. We feared to miss our steamer to England, *and were also at this last moment sick to death of beating to windward.* At 4 p.m., therefore, after tacking for about 12 miles, we turned back, anchored at Dronningen, and made arrangements with . . . the Christiania Yacht Club to take charge of *Asgard* until Shephard came out. We spent two laborious days in stowing sails and gear, varnishing, painting, repairs, etc and on the 27th left for Hull by the Wilson steamer. The thousand-mile voyage from Stockholm to Christiania was the longest bout of windward work I have ever had to tackle. The distance made good between these capitals was 996 miles, of which, counting every little slant of fair wind, 285 at the utmost were made with free sheets, and 110 of these were in the final passage to Christiania.'*

This, though Molly and Erskine could hardly even have imagined it as they left *Asgard* that day to catch the steamer back to England, was to be their last cruise in her. Never again would they lay off that familiar course from Dover for Ijmuiden or Texel or Terschelling, race up the estuary of the Elbe to Brunsbüttel, arrange their tow through the Kiel Canal and, with expectation and delight, fly out of Kiel Fiord with 'the whole of the open Baltic stretching away northward' and a thousand new islands, anchorages and channels to explore, ahead of them. For them, as for a considerable proportion of mankind, a strange and dangerous future was already forming round them, events more sombre, and more anxious in a quite different way, than a rising gale and a lee shore impended, and their nautical skills would be required for more important purposes. But it was a rattling good cruise to end on.

Gordon Shephard duly picked up the boat in October, and with Robert Nowell and two friends, one of them a novice, set off for Bursledon by way of Bergen, the Shetlands, and the west coasts of

---

* The log includes detailed accounts, both of the preparations for, and of the voyage itself. The former, including the yard's bill for fitting out – £23.19s.19d – and Nowell's wages of 30s per week, came to £77; the latter, including all stores, harbour dues, repairs and replacements over nearly two months, came to £44.11s.8d.

Scotland, Wales and England. The cruise was one that Childers himself would have relished: four weeks of hard sailing at the stormy end of the season, and a route that would demand the utmost from both boat and crew.

The first week, working up the Norwegian coast, was uneventful; but then, as Shephard headed *Asgard* west for Lerwick in the Shetlands, the weather turned on them and his log of the voyage from then on is a tally of high winds, heavy seas, burst sails and damaged gear. On October 20, when they were hove-to somewhere off the Butt of Lewis, he noted: 'We had now during the passage lost three sails, besides sundry minor damage to gear', and worse was to come. They lost the kedge anchor in Stornoway in the Hebrides, and the main anchor (though they recovered it) in Tobermory; and as quickly as they repaired their tattered sails they blew them out once more. The climax came on November 2 in the Irish Sea off the entrance to Carlingford Lough: in winds of hurricane force – 75 m.p.h. gusts were recorded that night – *Asgard*'s bowsprit carried away, the sheets of the storm jib parted, and the foresail halyards became so thoroughly snarled round the mast they could not be untangled. Under jury rig Shephard ran off southeast for Holyhead, where he had a new bowsprit fitted and they sorted out the shambles aloft. They left the boat to be laid up for the winter in Conway, having had, ironically enough, a delightful sail with a light sou'westerly wind, from Holyhead.

For this eventful cruise Gordon Shephard was awarded the Royal Cruising Club Challenge Cup. It certainly helps to explain why, when Childers went to pick up *Asgard* in July of the following year, he was depressed by the state in which he found her. But that was a detail. He and his crew had an appointment to keep off the Belgian coast, and it had absolutely nothing to do with yachting.

IX

'A Voyage with an Object' 1914

I

'I was in black despair when I got down,' Erskine wrote to Molly from Conway on June 17, 1914; 'no men, no news, and the yacht in an appalling state, but things look rather better now.' The mainsail was split and had to be unbent and sent to the sailmakers; sheets, halyards, topping-lifts all needed renewing; the clock, the barometer and *Vixen*'s old compass were missing, and everything was in a muddle. They had not sailed *Asgard* that year, and she was a long way from being in commission. As he had just offered the boat, with himself as skipper, for running a cargo of arms for the Irish Volunteers from the Continent to Ireland, and they were due to sail in less than a fortnight, he had reason enough to feel dispirited.

The scheme had been born the previous month, in response to a similar, and extremely blatant, bit of arms-smuggling by the Ulster Volunteers in the North. Mention has already been made in Chapter I of Erskine Childers' evolving personal commitment during these years to the cause of Home Rule for Ireland, and the arms run may be seen as the watershed between thought and action, between sympathy and participation. But before the voyage begins, some brief reminders may be useful about the people involved, the action which they were planning, and the context in which they were acting.

To dispose of the last first, it is necessary, though difficult enough, to remember that in 1914 Ireland was still a single country, and as much a part of the United Kingdom as Wales or Scotland. But the Act of Union of 1800 had never been accepted by the majority of Irish people and opposition to it, with its corollary, pressure for national independence, grew steadily through the nineteenth century. Nurtured by men of the stature of O'Connell and Parnell, it became, from the foundation of the Home Rule League in 1873, an increasingly powerful demand for some form of self-government.

But as one Home Rule Bill after another was rejected by Parliament (two, those of 1892 and 1913, were passed by the Commons, only to be rejected by the Lords) extra-constitutional means seemed the only practicable alternative. Opposition to Home Rule for Ireland from another quarter began to grow in strength, determination and violence; and when in 1911 the power of the House of Lords to reject bills passed by the lower house was reduced to delaying their passage for two years – thus ensuring that Home Rule would become law sooner rather than later – that opposition became intransigent. Given cohesion and a polemical voice by Sir Edward Carson, and support verging on sedition from Andrew Bonar Law and the Conservatives in Parliament, the predominantly Protestant Irish in Ulster mobilised themselves to fight it by every means, including force. The Ulster Volunteers numbered 100,000 and were drilling openly under the command of a British general, and received on April 25, 1914 a large consignment of rifles and ammunition which, in flagrant defiance of the law and with the connivance of the army and the police, were landed at Larne on the Antrim coast, twenty miles north of Belfast.

The mood was ripe for civil war between north and south, but with all the advantages on the Unionist side since no such connivance was extended to the newly formed Irish Volunteers in Dublin, who were drilling clandestinely with wooden weapons. 'We must have rifles' became the battle-cry of MacNeill and O'Rahilly, their leaders.

They found constructive support among a group of friends – of each other and of Ireland – who formed a committee of Home Rule sympathisers and met for the first time in London in May 1914. The members included Alice Stopford Green, widow of the historian John Richard Green; Sir Roger Casement; the Honourable Mary Spring Rice, daughter of Lord Monteagle of Mount

Brandon, Co. Limerick; her cousin Conor O Brien; and Erskine and Molly Childers.

Mary Spring Rice is credited with the practical suggestion as to how MacNeill and O'Rahilly's plea might be met. She knew of a smack, the *Santa Cruz*, which had been trading on the Shannon and might be suitable for carrying a decent quantity of arms (which at that time they did not possess), and a few days later she, O Brien and Childers went and had a look at her in Foynes Harbour, down river from Limerick.

'A fine powerful smack, very old but sound enough for sea with certain repairs,' Erskine wrote to Molly; 'of course in an awful state of mess and confusion.' They estimated that it would cost £70 to make her ready, and the committee's funds, raised by voluntary subscriptions from its members, would run to that; but they rejected her all the same. For one thing, it was doubtful if the work could be done in time; for another, as Conor O Brien said, 'nothing could make her look like a craft with legitimate business in the North Sea . . . [but] nobody asks what a yacht's business is anywhere.'

It was decided instead that *Asgard* and O Brien's smaller *Kelpie* should be used for the work; and Childers went to Hamburg with a member of the Volunteers, Darrell Figgis, to try to buy the arms. Figgis, tea-buyer turned writer, combined a gift for self-dramatisation with a bent for conspiracy: that peculiarly Irish refusal to recognise any rift between poetry and action, out of which, as Yeats noted, 'a terrible beauty is born'.

Together they visited a firm of arms dealers, Moritz Magnus. Negotiations hung fire until Figgis, on a sudden inspiration, explained that the guns were for Mexico. 'No-one in their senses would mistake us for Mexicans,' Childers whispered while the Magnus brothers were out of the room. Almost certainly nobody did; but it gave the dealers the excuse they needed, since the German government had imposed an embargo on arms sales to Ireland; and a deal, for 1,500 old-fashioned Mausers and 45,000 rounds of ammunition, was agreed. The two men then went to Antwerp to try to arrange for a tug to ferry the stuff out to the yachts.

Childers returned to North Wales to get *Asgard* ready for sea, while Casement briefed Bulmer Hobson (code-name Dolan), a member of the Irish Republican Brotherhood and an old friend of his, to organise the landings on Irish soil. Childers and Hobson later met in Dublin. 'He is pessimistic about all the ordinary sort of plans,' Erskine wrote to Molly on June 21, 'and produced a very daring one of his own which took my breath away.' Figgis, meanwhile, was to return to Hamburg and tie up the arrangements at that end. Casement, travelling constantly between London and Dublin, acted as courier between the several members of the enterprise, over which was draped, rather conspicuously, a heavy cloak of secrecy.

II

The rendezvous arranged between *Asgard* and *Kelpie* and the tug *Gladiator* was the Ruytingen lightship,* eight miles north of Gravelines and about twenty-five miles east of Dover. O Brien, characteristically, adopted a sardonic stance towards the expedition. 'In those good old days,' he wrote many years later,† 'all the best people were engaged, on one side or the other, in the contraband trade; so I, to be in the fashion, had put my yacht and my services at the disposal of the other side. If I were asked which other side, I should have to admit that I knew as little as my employers did, so obscure were Irish politics in 1914; by the other side I mean not Ulster.'

He was an architect by profession, a sailor to his finger ends, a wanderer by temperament, and an excellent writer about the sea. After the war, during which, like Erskine Childers, he served in the Royal Navy, he built the 42 foot ketch *Saoirse*, sailed her round the world, and lived aboard her until 1940. He was awarded the RCC Challenge Cup three times.

'All my happiest memories of the sea', he wrote, 'refer to voyages undertaken with some object, other than the search for pleasure.' He had a volcanic temper which, as one of his crew on this particular venture, Diarmid Coffey, confessed with delightful understatement, 'made life aboard a bit exciting'; but his squalls of impatience and vituperation passed as quickly as they arose. It is difficult to imagine two men less alike – except in their shared passion for salt water – than O Brien and Childers; even the love of adventure, which was also common to both of them, seems to spring from a different source.

---

* Variously spelt Ruytigen or Roetigen in different accounts. The light-vessel has since been replaced by a buoy.
† *From Three Yachts* (Edward Arnold, 1928) p. 6.

It must not be forgotten that for all its splendidly amateur organisation, its cloak-and-dagger aspects, the operation was unquestionably and specifically unlawful – as, indeed, though it was winked at, had been the smuggling by 'the other side' at Larne – by virtue of a Royal Proclamation of December 4, 1913 forbidding the importation of arms from any source into Ireland. In one of her letters to Alice Stopford Green, Molly mentions as a very real possibility that *Asgard* might be confiscated if they were caught.

Conor O Brien's complement was made up of his sister Kate, Diarmid Coffey, and two Foynes men, George Cahill and Tom Fitzsimons: they left the Shannon 'quite unnoticed' at the end of June, and were to meet *Asgard* in Cowes on July 7. *Asgard*'s crew was to be Molly, Mary Spring Rice, Gordon Shephard, and two Donegal fishermen, Pat McGinley and Charles Duggan, who at the start had not the faintest idea of the purpose of the voyage.

III

Asgard's sailing date was twice postponed. Mary did not join the vessel until July 1; and although by prodigious efforts Erskine had got her ready for sea, he was exhausted and had injured his hand, below decks everything was in chaos, and two of their crew, Charles Duggan and Gordon Shephard, were adrift. In their place, as a desperate resort Childers had managed to recruit a lad from the Volunteers' office, but he knew nothing whatever about sailing. Nevertheless, and unready as they were, Childers decided that they must sail next day. The weather, which had been hot and sultry, broke up into a thunderstorm that evening, and the following morning it was thick and the glass was dropping. They thrashed about for an hour, and then gave it up. The decision proved wise. Duggan arrived during the day, Erskine and Molly got some rest, and next morning the 'friend' or 'Mr Gordon',* as he was referred to, turned up, having spent the night in a station waiting-room.

He was just in time. As soon as he had scrambled aboard with his bags they weighed anchor, and as the wind was light from ahead got a pluck out over Conway bar on a falling tide. The date was July 3; Cowes was over 400 miles away, and they were

---

* Gordon Shephard was, of course, a serving soldier, so could hardly associate himself openly with such a politically and legally dubious venture.

supposed to be there by the 7th to join up with *Kelpie*. If they were late, Conor would go spare. 'I thought of him storming round Cowes,' Mary wrote in her account* of the trip, 'talking to the Lord knows who.' She knew her cousin with his wild mocking tongue, his explosive temper, as well as the good heart underneath.

Because of the delay in starting they were under tremendous strain, to which the weather did its best to contribute. For the first twenty-four hours they jilled about, getting nowhere. Then when the wind did come it was from ahead, picking up a short choppy sea. They were all sick – except Gordon Shephard, who did not help by assuring Mary that 'it wasn't really rough'. He and Erskine decided to make a board in towards Fishguard and put in if things got worse; but next day, Sunday the 5th, things improved a little, though the wind was still heading them, and they were still struggling to round Strumble Head, the Welsh point to the west of Fishguard. Nevertheless, Mary wrote: 'It was a perfect afternoon and one began to feel like settling down. Erskine lost the look of tense anxiety which he had when we started, though still greatly preoccupied with the problems ahead – times and seasons, transhipping, etc – and that afternoon we assembled in the cockpit, the men being safely below,† while he unfolded to us the landing scheme.

IV

This scheme, the one that took Erskine's breath away when he first heard it, is best described in Bulmer Hobson's own words.

'On thinking the matter over I decided that 1,500 rifles would not go very far in solving our problem, but that if we could bring them in in a sufficiently spectacular manner we should probably solve our financial problem and the problem of arming the Volunteers as well.

'With this in mind I decided to land the guns during daylight in the most open manner and as near to Dublin as possible. I

---

* Erskine Childers wrote nothing about the voyage: his rough log has not survived. This account is based, therefore, on the full, light-hearted, rather gossipy story written by Mary Spring Rice, a number of letters written by Molly to Alice Stopford Green, and the various versions of events collected by F. X. Martin o.s.a. in his book *The Howth Gun-Running, 1914* (Browne & Nolan, 1964) including a separate account by Conor O Brien.

† They were told later.

personally examined every harbour between Greystones and Balbriggan . . . and only turned down the North Wall in Dublin because I thought that we might not get time to unload before the authorities would appear.

'I decided that Howth was the most suitable harbour, and that the best method was to march a large number of Volunteers to meet the yacht, to arm them on the spot, and march them back. . . . I met Casement and Childers . . . one Sunday about the end of June, and proposed my plan, with which they both agreed. Childers and I went out to Howth next day and looked at the harbour, and settled just where he was to come in.* At that meeting it was fixed that Childers should sail into Howth Harbour at twelve noon on 26th July and that I would have the Volunteers there to meet him. Childers then went off to keep his appointment with Figgis in the North Sea.'

The timing was absolutely critical, for two reasons. One was that it had to coincide with the arrival of the Volunteers; the other that Howth is a drying harbour, and *Asgard*, normally drawing 7 feet 6 inches but nearer 9 feet with the arms on board, would only have a very short time in which to enter, unload and escape. If the yacht, or the Volunteers, were late, either she would not be able to get in or she would not be able to get out. This was perhaps the most audacious aspect of a plan the very essence of which was audacity. So that Sunday, while Childers was unfolding it to the others as they desperately bucked wind and tide no more than 85 miles from their eventual destination – but with almost a thousand miles ahead of them before they came to it – the Volunteers set out on the first of a series of Sunday route marches. 'The police were enormously interested in the first,' Hobson wrote, '. . . at the second they were not so active, and the third week they were indifferent.' The psychology was brilliant.

In the meantime *Asgard* had two other appointments to keep, one of them at least as precise and mandatory as that later one at the top of the tide at Howth; and as things were going it seemed fairly unlikely that she would be keeping either, for next day, the

---

* The carefully hand-drawn plan of the harbour, containing all the relevant information, is among Childers' papers; unfortunately it is not suitable for reproduction.

6th, the wind, such as it was, deserted them and left them rolling
mercilessly on the Bristol Channel swell.

'We only seemed to have averaged about 2 knots', Mary wrote,
'since we left Conway. At last we got up nearer to the Smalls, and
Erskine decided to go inside through the passage with a bubbling
tiderace and horrible looking rocks. Altogether it looked a wicked
place, however of course one felt a sublime confidence in
Erskine's steering and we got through alright. Then the wind got
up and we were soon humming along.' They were moving at
last; and on Monday morning Mary went on deck to find 'the sun
shining on the purple coast and white cliffs of Cornwall'.

Suddenly everyone was more cheerful. They contemplated
putting into St Ives to sit out the foul tide, and Gordon Shephard,
who like many active men had an insatiable appetite for sleep
and food, was already planning his lunch ashore; but the Skipper
was adamant. However slow their progress, they must keep going.
The breeze was southerly, so it was slow, but one by one the great
outliers and headlands of that harsh extremity of England came
abeam and were put behind them: the Longships, Land's End,
the Runnelstone – whose buoy they passed too close for comfort in
a misty twilight, its bell tolling through the murk – and at last
the Lizard.

That was the greatest moment for now, after four days of the
keenest frustration, they were able to free sheets and go romping
up the English Channel. Never mind that Erskine's hand was still
painful, that Pat McGinley had been knocked senseless by a
swinging block and received a nasty cut above the eye, that
cooking in the stuffy fo'c'sle was a penance: Shephard insisted on
cramming on all sail, and *Asgard* picked up her heels and flew.
They roared through the edge of the race off Portland Bill,
averaged 8 knots across Poole Bay to the Needles, caught their
tide through the Narrows, and anchored in Cowes at 1 o'clock in
the morning on the 9th – forty-eight hours late.

They had hardly finished breakfast when they were hailed:
'*Asgard* ahoy!' They darted up on deck, to be met by 'a torrent of
abuse' from Conor O Brien. Why were they so late? Why had they
never written? He had run out of money and was in a lather of
impatience and rage. 'If all Cowes and Dublin, not to say the
Castle, do not know of our expedition, it is a miracle,' said Mary
ruefully. But the squall passed. 'He came back later and worked
hard helping us,' Molly wrote to Alice Stopford Green. 'Every-

thing has been carrying away, and our day in Cowes has been spent with sailmakers and carpenters on board.' Part of O Brien's ill-temper stemmed from the fact that he felt *Kelpie*, shabby as she was, looked a lot too conspicuous among the well-polished concourse of yachts at Cowes. 'We made some demonstrations with holystones and paint, realising, however, that it was not usual to fit out in the Roads ... Cowes in early July is not so busy that it cannot speculate on the origin and destination of strange yachts, and we did not want it to speculate on ours.'

This brief spell in the very heart of fashionable yachting epitomises the ironies implicit in the whole adventure. *Asgard* and her owners, if not *Kelpie* and hers, were well known; they were flying the RCC burgee at the main masthead. After their cruise to Finland the previous year, duly written up and published, there must have been quite a lot of curiosity about their plans for that season. Gordon Shephard, writing to his mother the day they arrived, sets the vague, evasive tone: 'They have this year two fishermen from Connaught as crew ... Miss Spring Rice is a wonder. She has never been far to sea before, yet she was hardly ill at all and looks and is most useful. ... The Childerses had an appointment here with some Irish people on another yacht. They have not yet decided where to go, but do not expect to hear from me till my leave is up.'

They knew very well where they were going, and when they had to be there. A letter from Darrell Figgis was waiting for them in Cowes: providentially the rendezvous at the Ruytingen lightship had been postponed till the 12th, three days ahead. It would still be tight, but given even a little luck they should be able to make it. Feeling more relaxed than at any time since they left Conway, they all went ashore for a huge lunch, and later a huge dinner, at the Marine Hotel. Mary spent all her money and had to borrow two shillings from 'Mr Gordon'. Conor, Diarmid Coffey and Kitty joined them for coffee after dinner; and later they went aboard *Kelpie* and settled the final details of the next, vital stage of the enterprise.

V

Kelpie sailed early the next morning to carry the east-going tide out of the Solent; *Asgard*, her repairs completed, followed in the afternoon. The wind had gone round easterly and freshened. 'Mr

Gordon insisted on setting the topsail, much to Molly's disgust', Mary noted. 'I rather agreed with her at the time as I struggled into my bunk, and sighed that all men were alike about setting topsails on all possible occasions, but we sped along, so perhaps it was as well.'

That was Friday. On Saturday, with a fickle breeze still from ahead, they crept along the Sussex coast, and by 8 o'clock that evening were still not round Beachy Head. It was very hot: a perfect day, in fact, for lazy holiday sailing, and the worst possible for passage-making. 'A depressing day, full of doubts and anxieties', Mary wrote in her diary; and Sunday was little better. 'I came up on deck to find Erskine steering in a calm sea with a light breeze ruffling the water and the fog just lifting and letting the sun through – a heavenly summer morning – if one had no gun-running appointments at the Ruytigen lightship, 45 miles away, at 12 noon.' 'Headwinds, slow progress, despair' was Molly's summing-up. They had intended to call in at Dover to see if there were any last-minute changes or instructions from Darrell Figgis, but there was no time for that. All they could do was make the best progress possible, and pray the arrangements held. In the meantime they could start the job of turning a cruising yacht into a cargo ship.

'This meant cutting up the two saloon bunks, and Molly, Pat and Mr Gordon were soon hard at work chopping and sawing. . . . We were keeping right inshore . . . and I saw Folkestone beach within a stone's throw, full of the "smart set" parading their best clothes in the brilliant sunshine, while on the starboard side lay four or five warships with their bells ringing for church.' *Asgard* slipped quietly along between them, to all appearances a well-found yawl on passage, perhaps for Dover or, as on previous occasions, for Texel or Terschelling and the Baltic, while down below she was being swiftly and noisily gutted.

Noon came, and they still had twenty miles to go. Would the tug wait for them? And what should they do if it had given up? Was there, even now, a letter sitting in Dover, altering or cancelling the operation? The suspense was acute. Then a catspaw came rippling over the calm blue sea, a breath of moving air over the skin, a creak and rattle of blocks as, at last, a breeze from astern filled *Asgard*'s sails and the water began to make its music at her stem. Shephard and the two men ran up the spinnaker, then ran it down again as the breeze shifted from aft onto the beam. At the same time the visibility started to go, and soon they were in dense haze that was almost fog.

They heard the East Goodwin fog signal, then the Sandettie, and knew they were on course. Anxiously they peered ahead. A buoy – Molly was the first to spot it, as always – then the light-ship; but no sign of the tug or *Kelpie*. A shape came drifting out of the haze, but it was only a fishing smack. 'A cry from Molly . . . "Conor and the tug! Do you see? A steamer and a yacht mixed up – lying close to one another – now the tug is coming towards us." ' *Kelpie*, black-hulled, had at that instant finished loading and cast off; a wave from Conor, and she vanished into the mist. The timing was perfect. And there as the tug came alongside was Darrell Figgis with his little pointed beard, shouting at them that Conor had only been able to take 600 of the guns, instead of 750, and less than half the ammunition. That meant that somehow they had to find room for 900 rifles and 25,000 rounds in *Asgard*'s accommodation. It seemed impossible, but there was nothing for it but to try. As soon as they were made fast the tug's crew started to pass down the big bundles, ten guns in each, wrapped in straw and canvas, to McGinley and Duggan who passed them on down through the main hatch, to the human chain below.

It was obvious almost at once that the only chance of stowing them all was to strip off the packing. 'I wish you could have seen the scene,' Molly wrote. 'Darkness, lamps, strange faces, the swell of the sea making the boat lurch, guns, straw, everywhere, unpacking on deck and being handed down and stowed in an endless stream . . . the vaseline on the guns smeared over every-thing; the bunks and floors of the whole yacht aft from the fo'c'sle filled about 2 feet 6 inches high even from side to side, men sweating and panting under the weight of the twenty-nine ammunition boxes . . . a German face peering down the hatch saying "they will explode if you knock them or drop them". A huge ship's oil riding light falling down through the hatch, first onto my shoulder and then upside down into a heap of straw – a flare-up, a cry, a quick snatch of rescue – the lamp goes out, thank God, work again, someone drops two guns through, they fall on someone; no room to stand left save on guns, guns everywhere. On and on and on.'

The last ammunition box was transferred from the tug to *Asgard* at about 2.30 in the morning and added to the jumble on deck. 'Erskine's one thought was to take everything,' Mary wrote; for

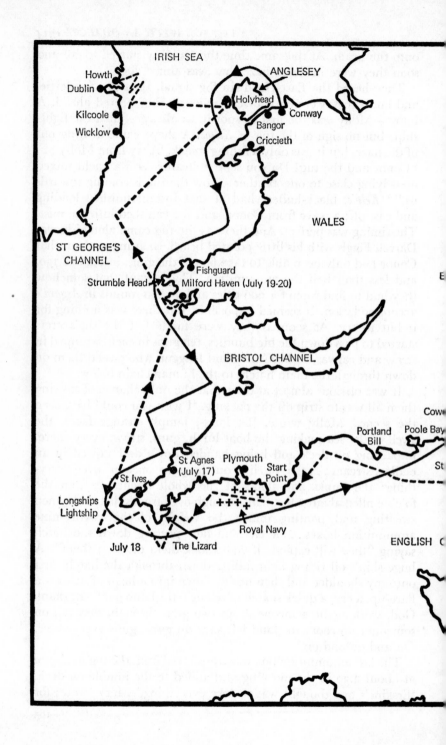

IRISH SEA

Howth
Dublin
Kilcoole
Wicklow

ANGLESEY
Holyhead
Conway
Bangor
Criccieth

ST GEORGE'S
CHANNEL

WALES

Fishguard
Strumble Head
Milford Haven (July 19-20)

BRISTOL CHANNEL

Cow

Portland
Bill
Poole Bay

St

St Agnes
(July 17)

Plymouth
Start
Point

St Ives

Longships
Lightship

Royal Navy

July 18   The Lizard

ENGLISH C

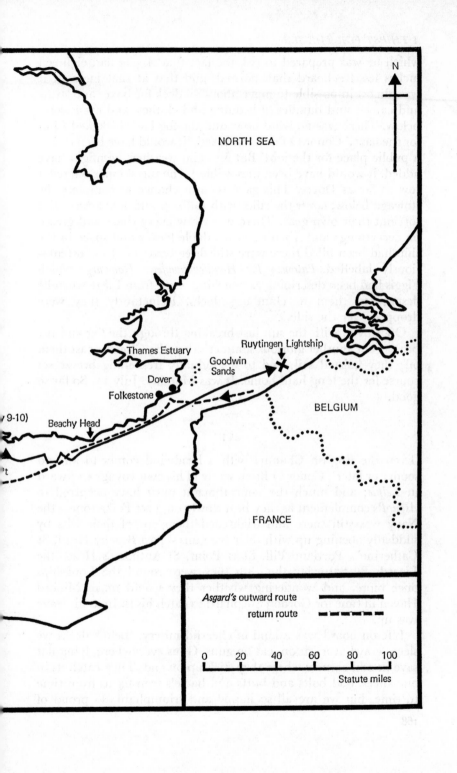

North Sea

Thames Estuary

Ruytingen Lightship

Goodwin Sands

Dover

Folkestone

BELGIUM

(9-10)

Beachy Head

FRANCE

Asgard's outward route

return route

| 0 | 20 | 40 | 60 | 80 | 100 |

Statute miles

which he was prepared to risk the fact that *Asgard* had eighteen inches less freeboard than normal, and that at that moment it was almost impossible to move about on deck for boxes and straw and canvas and bundles of bedding and clothes, and even worse below. There was no wind now, and the fog had thickened ('but for the haze,' Conor O Brien remarked, 'it would have been rather a public place for the job!' But for calm weather, he might have added, it would have been impossible.) The tug skipper offered a tow as far as Dover. This gave them a chance to complete the stowage below, cover the rifles with sailbags and mattresses, and sort out their own gear. There was straw everywhere and grease on everything; and when every available locker and space in the ship had been filled there were still three boxes on deck, ostentatiously labelled *Patronen für Handfeuerwaffen: Hamburg*, which Figgis had been describing as 'machine parts' from Liège when he despatched them to Hamburg docks. Reluctantly they were dropped over the side.

Off Dover, with the sun just breaking through the fog and the prospect of another glorious summer's day, the *Gladiator* cast them off; they hoisted sail, and to a gradually freshening breeze set course for the long haul home. It was Monday, July 13. So far so good.

VI

'Even the English Channel with a headwind comes to an end sooner or later', Conor O Brien wrote of his own voyage westward in *Kelpie*; and much the same thought must have occurred to *Asgard*'s complement as they beat slowly on, past Folkestone – the Navy was still there and frightened them out of their wits by suddenly opening up with their big guns – past Beachy Head, St Catherine's, Portland Bill, Start Point, St Anthony's Head, the Lizard. By Saturday the 18th they were round the Longships once more, and wondering whether they would make Milford Haven in time for Gordon Shephard to catch his train as his leave was up.

Life on board was a kind of cheerful misery. 'Below decks we sleep, crawl over, sit on, eat on guns. Guns everywhere, lying flat save in odd corners where they stick up on end. They catch us in our knees, odd bolts and butts and barrels transfix us from time to time, but we are all so happy and triumphant, so proud of ourselves, that we swear we are comfortable. Mary and I sleep on mattresses laid across our cabin over the guns. One can kneel anywhere but can stand only in one place about nine inches square.'

'How Molly manages to get about with her leg is a constant wonder to me,' Mary said in her account; 'the difficulties for her now are, of course, enormous.' And she goes on: 'The odd thing about this sort of life is that one spends such a lot of time cleaning up, and yet one is always dirty. Crawling is not good for the clothes, or gun grease for the hands, and doing one's hair squatting like a Red Indian is rather a job.'

Nevertheless Mary still managed to cook them two hot meals a day. 'I generally crawl into my clothes between 7.30 and 8 with sleepy remonstrances from Molly . . . and calls from Erskine as to when breakfast will be ready. He usually takes the second watch and is very hungry by 8 o'clock . . . I crawl to the fo'c'sle – Pat generally has the Primus going and if one has not to tie the pans on with string, and hold on while you do everything, breakfast doesn't take very long.' The main problems were Erskine, who always found something to do on deck just as everything was ready, and Gordon, who never got up a minute before he was forced to. It was also uncommonly stuffy below.

Off Plymouth they had their third brush with the Royal Navy. 'They seemed to be executing some night manoeuvres,' Mary said, 'and were all round us with their great lights towering up; it would have been very picturesque if one had been looking on from a safe position on shore.' Worst of all was when a destroyer suddenly broke away and headed straight for them, only altering course at the last minute. For a moment fear of discovery was outweighed by fear of collision.

After a hideously uncomfortable sail in light airs and a big swell across the mouth of the Bristol Channel, they made Milford Haven early in the morning of Sunday the 19th and anchored in order to put Gordon Shephard ashore. Of course, he could not find his hat and boots – one has a sudden glimpse of the domestic helplessness of this intrepid soldier/sailor, who would not get up in the morning, and had to have his bath, had a passion for Golden Syrup, and obviously adored being made a fuss of by the two women – but at last he was bundled ashore to catch his train, which then did not leave until half-past six in the evening. So he and Mary, who had gone ashore with him to buy victuals, had a vast breakfast, to be quizzed by a stranger at the next table as to how they fared on board, and what sort of cook they had.

' "Oh, we've quite a good cook; we really manage very well," said Mr Gordon, looking at me over the marmalade, convulsed with suppressed laughter.'

There was now exactly a week before they were due at Howth. On that Sunday, while *Asgard* was in Milford Haven, the Volunteers carried out their third route march; and Bulmer Hobson kept an uneasy eye on HMS *Porpoise* which had come in and lay at anchor in Dublin Bay and showed no signs of departure. Somehow, if she did not leave of her own accord, she would have to be lured away. Hobson set his inventive mind to work on the problem.

On Monday it blew hard from the east, and at 2 p.m. *Asgard*'s anchor started to drag.

VII

They had promised themselves a second unbroken night in harbour: now, being forced to get sail up, Erskine could not bear the thought of a fair wind running to waste, and so they cleared the harbour and turned north along the Welsh coast for Holyhead. Almost immediately the wind dropped and they had twenty-four hours of calms and light airs. When the wind came back, it was with a bang on Tuesday night: by Wednesday midday they were safely anchored in the outer harbour at Holyhead. Erskine went below to get some sleep; Mary was in the saloon, sewing 'when I heard Pat's voice on deck saying "Yacht *Asgard*", evidently answering someone. . . . "Erskine," I shouted, "wake up, you're wanted; they're asking her name!" But Erskine is very hard to wake and I was just meditating shaking him when he turned over and said sleepily, "What?" "Come on deck!" and I dashed up, he after me. There were the Coastguards in a boat close by, calling out questions: "last port – destination – registered tonnage – owner's name?" Erskine, now thoroughly awake, shouted prompt answers, some of them truth and some of them fiction, and to our immense relief they rowed away and we breathed again.'

They did not breathe freely for very long. When they woke on Thursday morning – Erskine demanding to know what had happened to breakfast, as usual – it was blowing and raining from the southwest, and the glass was still falling. It was still blowing on Friday, but there was nothing for it: they had to be across the Irish Sea by the following night, to be sure of making Howth by noon on Sunday. They hadn't been going very long when a tear developed in the mainsail. They put back, and Molly and Mary got to work on it, on deck, in a downpour of rain. In a couple of hours it was mended, and they set off once more. The wind veered to nor'west, dropped for a time, and then towards evening freshened to near gale force.

'It was an awful night,' Mary wrote. 'Erskine stayed on deck the whole time; the waves looked black and terrible and enormous and though everything was reefed one wondered if we should ever get through without something giving way. For about half the night I crouched in the cockpit or the hatchway, then crawled into the cabin where Molly and I lay, half on top of one another – which seemed to make the elements less terrible, but hardly slept a wink all night.'

They not only survived, they made progress; and by daybreak the Irish coast was in sight. They worked their way slowly inshore, and when they were ten miles or so off Howth, hove-to. They were all dog-tired, none more than Erskine, who still carried, alone now, the responsibility for bringing the ship in at the exact time next day. That was supposing that the arrangements that he had made with Hobson nearly four weeks before still held good, for they had had no contact since. The relief of being within a few miles of their destination was offset by sheer weariness and by a dozen unanswerable doubts. For a moment Erskine was tempted by an exquisitely simple solution.

'Shall we just go boldly into Kingstown Harbour?'* he said to Mary. 'It's the most natural thing for a yacht to do after a storm like this, and ten to one against any questions being asked.' It was tempting, indeed, the thought of lying quietly at anchor, out of the turmoil of the sea, to rest and regain their energies; but then they thought of the apprehension which would make rest impossible. The Navy might be there; word might have got round, Conor's wild talk might have found a ready listener. What an unbearable anticlimax, to be searched and arrested a bare seven miles from success. What a betrayal!

The Irish coast was a weather shore and the sea was calmer.

---

* Now Dun Laoghaire, the harbour for Dublin.

Under reduced canvas they sailed slowly north beyond Lambay Island, paid off and ran gently back again, and continued so all that night. Next morning they were all about by 6 o'clock. The wind was still northwest and fresh; no danger of them being becalmed. At 10 a.m., according to the plan, a motorboat should come out to tell them if all was well; but no boat emerged from Kingstown Harbour. Back and forth they sailed, and still no boat came out to meet them.

Eleven o'clock. Two hours to go. The mounting doubts and fears of those three weeks seemed all too valid now, and the one reassuring signal that would dispel them was not forthcoming. The decision rested, as all the decisions had done, with Erskine. Boat or no boat, they would go in.

Twelve o'clock. They could see all Dublin Bay before them, and at its northern arm the hump of rock to seaward of the entrance to Howth. Now they could see the entrance itself, and the quay beyond. Was there a crowd to meet them and accept the arms which they had carried so far and guarded so carefully? Molly stared and stared: the place looked deserted. Nearer now. Mary came up on deck wearing the red skirt which was the signal to those ashore; Molly took the wheel; Erskine, Pat and Duggan stood by the halyards. In they surged; Molly luffed; down came the main, followed by jib and mizzen. Carrying her way, *Asgard* swept in towards the wall. And there, suddenly, was a group of men to take her warps and draw her in.

The time was a quarter to one; and at that moment came the sound of marching feet as a long, rather ragged column of Volunteers came swinging on to the quay towards them.

VIII

As soon as *Asgard* was alongside unloading started. There was a scramble for the first of the guns to be handed ashore, and Childers held up proceedings until some system was enforced. Soon the rifles were being passed from hand to eager hand along the ranks. The ammunition was spirited away in a fleet of taxis specially hired for the occasion – another of Bulmer Hobson's brainwaves.

Among the excited throng was Gordon Shephard, who had tried in vain to persuade the owner of the motorboat to go out to meet them, and then organised a mooring party to catch their warps since, as he wrote to his father, 'nobody there knew anything about such matters'. Then he went aboard.

'Molly and I and Mr Gordon stood by the mizzen', Mary wrote, 'and looked at the scene; it still seemed like a dream, we had talked of this moment so often during the voyage.'

HMS *Porpoise* was no longer at anchor in Dublin Bay. She was in Wicklow twenty miles away, sniffing after a red herring – a rumour of an arms landing down the coast, cunningly trailed by Hobson. But the Howth Coastguards were on the alert and came rowing across the harbour to investigate, only to find themselves staring into the barrels of a number of purposeful-looking rifles and revolvers. With understandable discretion they retired, and contented themselves with firing off distress rockets instead.

In half an hour the job was done.* The Volunteers, armed at last, formed up and yelled their cheers, then set off to march back to Dublin. On *Asgard* sail was hoisted – the main split again and the trysail had to be set instead – the warps were cast off, and Erskine and Molly, alone now but for Duggan and McGinley, swung *Asgard* round and headed out between the piers for the open sea, weary to the bone but buoyed up, triumphant.

In one of her letters, written on the homeward voyage, Molly had written of 'the peculiar, fascinating savour of it, the discomfort, the glory which makes up for everything'. Now the reaction set in. The vessel was a shambles; the decks filthy, a skylight broken, the cabins and the saloon like a battlefield, with woodwork battered and ripped out, the cabin sole littered with straw and broken glass, not to mention the various personal possessions which had slipped irrecoverably down between the stacked rifles.

But the job was done; and now, with the same brisk nor'wester on her quarter, and restored to her normal trim, *Asgard* flew across the Irish Sea. The weather worsened and they put into Bangor, in behind Anglesey. There they left the boat – and there she stayed. A week later Britain and Germany were at war, and soon after that Erskine Childers, Lieutenant RNVR, was joining the seaplane carrier HMS *Engadine*, as an Observer in the Royal Naval Air Service.

Though neither he nor Molly were to know it then, their cruising days were over.

---

* *Kelpie*'s cargo was also landed successfully, at Kilcoole, between Bray and Wicklow.

Envoi: The Yachting Mood

Schön thut das Meer sich mit erwärmten Buchten
Vor den erstaunten Augen auf.—Goethe

For many a trim little cruiser from the Crouch to Falmouth or the Clyde the winter's sleep is at an end, and her owner's pent-up longings for fresh adventures are soon to be satisfied. His is no ordinary thirst. Most of us 'hunt in dreams', but there is no imaginative restlessness so acute as that of the cruising yachtsman during the long night of inaction when his little vessel lies in her mud-berth and he himself, only a degree less inactive to his own ardent thinking, tramps the mud of the drab city or tastes the insipid recreations of the land folk. This is partly because he carries everywhere with him, even when the immediate use of it has lapsed, the habit of studying the skies and winds and all the baffling phenomena of what people call the 'weather', and of adapting his outlook to their unending caprices and vicissitudes. Thus every breeze and shower, every calm and storm and fog, has its peculiar train of intimate associations, past and prospective.

In some devoted enthusiasts this tenacious habit of thinking, even on land, in terms of a wind-driven seaborne vehicle, has been known to have strange psychological results. It is an obscure region of research, because the most truthful and sensitive souls, unlike the charlatan masters, are reticent about such experiences. But there are undoubtedly those who, especially on blowy days,

By Erskine Childers, published in *The Times* May 1913.

note that it is a dead beat to the City or a broad reach to Westminster, and unconsciously, even direct their path to the goal by working eddies in back streets, hugging the weather shore of a major thoroughfare, sounding carefully along an uncharted alley or court, or luffing to squalls in circuses. Coming home, they steer for the Park as for a friendly offing, and there stream the log, heave-to to reef, or run with a gloriously bellying spiritual spinnaker from Apsley Gate or the Marble Arch to Kensington Palace or High Street. Navigating thus, one is lost to the outside world, save for a dim resentment at the anarchy of the streets – sidelights misplaced and mis-screened, the rules of the road defied, sound signals a meaningless babel, a dazzle of unauthorised lights – together with a dim wonder that he has not in the midst of this lawless confusion foundered by collision. Daydreams are apt to become night-dreams. There is a nocturnal hallucination peculiar to amateur skippers that the house is rushing through the night towards shoals with nobody at the helm, and at least one of these persons has been known to summon his family and domestics on deck with the news that the flat is dragging its anchor and must be brought up with a kedge.

These are perhaps questionable vagaries – though the scientific inquirer is bound to take note of them – but whose memory and imagination are not normally and wholesomely stirred by the varieties of wind and weather which mean so little to the uninitiated, or at the most mean something pitifully trivial? Motorists, golfers and what-not – aye, and the whole race of Adam in its *terra firma* valetudinarian mood: 'Lor', what do they understand?' 'Bitter east wind' complains a shivering friend. 'Petty blasphemy' we inwardly reflect, gazing wistfully at the packed regiments of clouds racing across the sky and recalling the brilliant passages made in the honoured company of that lordliest of the North European winds – whose correct name, by the way, should be northeast, for at his best he nearly always has a dash of the Arctic in him. One by one those passages leap to mind. There was that tearing, double-reefed run, short-handed, from the Clyde to Dublin Bay, when we so nearly in sheer fatigue put into Donaghadee, with the narrow midnight shave of fouling the smack while straining our eyes for Rockabill, and so to the leaden-eyed arrival in Kingstown. And then that other run in late October from Wexford to Penzance, with a whole-sail breeze on the quarter so steady that we never stirred a sheet or shifted a jib from the Tuskar to Land's End, and that never-to-be-forgotten first dim view of the Longships rocks, starkly jutting into the Western Ocean, a spectral surf keening around their feet. There is a piercing chill in the air. Decks and sails and oilskins reek with icy dew. The limbs are numb with steering cramp, and the eyes ache with long absorption upon the glimmering compass card or, latterly, upon the Longships light. Then comes the memorable moment that makes the scene live so vividly. The light strengthens in the eastern sky and grows golden over the Cornish hills, while the man-lit lamps to west, south and east – the Seven Stones, Wolf and Longships – pale their ineffectual fires. Headland by headland the coast reveals and defines itself, first towards Trevose, then towards the Lizard, and the infinite ocean broadens into view, specked by the Scillies in the west. Lastly the grim rocks close to windward take wonderful colours – swarthy violets, umbers, fawns and gold; while, as if in sympathy with all this vital change, our genial friend the northeast wind suddenly freshens with a halloa, pushes our lee rail into the flying foam, and teases and cuffs the great good-natured swells until they are all fussy and fuming. Incongruously, but inextricably, mingled in the memory with these perceptions of eye and ear is the taste of the peculiarly virulent brand of tinned coffee and milk – a nauseous beverage in most circumstances but ambrosia in these – which our comrades at this moment passed up steaming through the companion hatch, and which took its share with the strengthening sun in putting the joy of life into stiff joints and tired senses.

Scotland, Ireland, Cornwall – here the mental record of halcyon passages breaks off; for our friend is a headwind from the Lizard onward up-Channel, and it is only in wet and weary tussles against time to windward that one remembers him. But in a flash the memory makes a mighty easterly leap, and once more we are reeling over the steep blue Baltic waves from Sandhammer to Kiel, or 'dropping light on light' from Heligoland to the troubled Terschelling banks, steeling our hearts for once, perhaps, against the call of the sheltering Texel and the fleshpots of Ijmuiden; and so by the West Hinder and South Goodwin, all clear of the treacherous maze of the Flemish shoals – and Flemish watering-places – we rush into Dover, spent, triumphant, and withal absolutely unnoticed, after what surely, nevertheless, was an historic passage.

But the very word Dover sets the mind bounding westward

again. The particular boat, the particular companion, the particular joys, jokes, accidents, incidents of every sort, stamp a characteristic colour on each separate recollection. Every headland, bay, shoal and light has its own easterly significance, so to speak. Did we not ride out a blow that August in Dungeness West Road, and near the end of it scuttle gingerly into perilous Rye at the top of high water, close on the heels of a guiding smack? And that far-off youthful escapade, singlehanded in a half-decked lug-boat from the Hamble, every minute of it is fresh; the tremulous exultation as we spun smoothly out of the Needles Channel on the first of a roaring ebb and the crowd of novel and surprising experiences as the wind hardened and the waves rose and buoys that looked so fat and black on the chart proved to be invisible, and unidentifiable cliffs blended distractingly with one another in the hazy perspective. And then – the heart still thumps with the thought of it – that sudden stumble into a bedevilled maelstrom off St Alban's Head: breakers over uncharted rocks, our scared fancy pictured it. No longer were the rollers chasing superbly up in disciplined ordered ranks. It was savage warfare – a furious onset of dervish irregulars with weird heathen gestures, hissing cries and beetling crests, who gallop in from the rear, the flanks, and even – a dreadful portent – from the front, and in the midst of whom we stagger with frenzied leaps and dives. But then a strange thing happens. Almost before we can gather our wits to invent new tactics for this wild guerilla host, lo! it has swept unaccountably away to the rear and its hoarse tumult slowly dies away. What on earth can these rocks be, and what a miraculous escape! And as soon as circumstances and our stricken nerves permit we sternly scan the lying chart, only to find some queer wavy lines and something about a 'strong ripple' – an absurdly mortifying and inadequate phrase to describe such a tumultuous cauldron. But it is the way with charts, we afterwards discover, to minimize dangers, while the Admiralty Sailing Directions magnify them till your flesh creeps. In truth it is our first rough experience of a tiderace, that most formidable of all obstacles to the small coaster, especially if half-decked; and it is in chastened mood that we sail on in smoother water to contemplate the beauties of Worbarrow Bay, swoop for an instant into Lulworth's exquisite little rock-ringed cove, and so on to Weymouth.

From cape to cape westward, in pursuit of the westering sun, runs the train of thrilling memories:

Ich eile fort ihr ewiges Licht zu trinken,
Vor mir der Tag und hinter mir die Nacht,
Der Himmel über mir und unter mir die Wellen.

Portland, the Start, the Prawle, the Bolt, the Dodman – how intensely individual and appropriate those bluff titles are! And how grandly they guard those Devonshire or Cornish fiords – Dartmouth, Salcombe, Yealm River, Fowey, Falmouth, Helford – into whose peaceful bosom we may glide from out the masterful grip of our good northeaster! Last comes the grim snout of the Lizard, with the deadly protruding tongue of half-submerged rocks; and there we link up to the Irish end of the chain of recollections. 'Bitter east wind,' our acquaintance is still muttering. But we who in those few seconds have been a thousand fairy leagues on his wings know better than to assent to the feeble malediction.

And that is only one of the noble company of winds. If we were to begin about the west wind (to say nothing about the rest) whose works and ways are entirely different and arouse a correspondingly different set of associations, though in identical seas and coasts, our reverie might grow tedious. Soon, under Providence, many of us will be doing, not dreaming. 'There lies the port; the vessel puffs her sail; there gloom the dark broad seas.' Let us invoke fair winds and piously exorcise fogs and calms for all those who in this year of grace go down to the sea in small cruising ships.

varnish, paint, spotless decks & snowy sails. & were foppish absurdities not to be thought of. of a hateful past. "What can we do to-day" I asked.

"We must keep well inside the banks & be precious careful wherever there's a swell. It's coming in here you see in spite of the barrier of sand. But there's plenty we can do further back."

We retreated into warmth & breakfasted with gaiety & horrible discomfort; then smoked and talked till the roar of the breakers dwindled. At the first sign of hard sand & we got under way, under mizen and the head-sails only, and I learnt how to sail a reluctant anchor out of the ground. Pivoting round we scudded east before the wind, over the ground we had traversed the evening before, while an archipelago of new banks slowly began long dark backs above the surface fast-weakening waves. We trod delicately among and round them, leaving to, where space permitted, the latter to do our business. I began to see where the risks lay in this sort of navigation. Wherever the ocean swell penetrated or the wind blew fair down a long deep

A portion of the manuscript draft of The Riddle of the Sands
related to the log of the Vixen.

Wind W fresh. Grey day & thick haze.
Took the flood and beat in short tacks
north-westward along the booms. At last made out
Newerk Island through the haze. Held on
till the lighthouse & East beacon were in
one & then kept away W by S. Very thick
& booms ceased. Suspense - ended by a crash
on the sand. Futile kedging. Dried ourselves 1.15 pm.
ourselves on Kleine Watt sand having
just kept away 100 yards too soon. Long
walk on sands. Pendennis. Philosophy.
Blew hard in evening. Floated at 9 after
severe humping and groped with the lead
for the Channel. Picked up the weather
side of it & let go in 4 fathoms.

Wind W very strong. Thick haze & fog.
nasty sea when the banks covered. Great
job to get up anchor. Started 3 reefed about
11, high water, & groped from boom to
boom closehauled southwards. Soon
Channel turned west again & it was
a dead beat against foul tide. Anchored
about 2 under the Greune knecht said
in company with a Schooner; which we visited
& got water from in exchange for cigars.
We were here in a most desolate place
several miles from land and nothing seaward but the sands - view none.
Very bad night with a heavy sea at
high water and gunnel under rolling.
At midnight E was flung out & kedged.
Lockers burst open & floor paved with
honey, flour, broken glass & petroleum.
At 5.30 wind shifted to N & we swung